BACK TO THE
BATCAVE

CW00952694

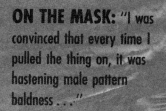

ON THE MASK: "I was convinced that every time I pulled the thing on, it was hastening male pattern baldness . . ."

ON JULIE NEWMAR: "Julie felt that Catwoman should be pure evil, teasing Batman rather than actually falling in love with him . . . She also caused curious stirrings in my utility belt."

ON THE SHOW: "We were farce. We were a lampoon. We were the movie serials of the 1930s and 1940s done against a fun-house background."

ON TIM BURTON'S *BATMAN:* "I'll admit I was angry and profoundly disappointed when I was not asked to reprise the role . . ."

BACK TO THE
BATCAVE

MY STORY...
ADAM WEST
with JEFF ROVIN

TITAN BOOKS

BACK TO THE BATCAVE
ISBN 1 85286 529 6

nt October 1994
10 9 8 7 6 5 4 3 2 1
Copyright © 1994 by Adam West. All rights reserved.
The right of Adam West and Jeff Rovin to be identified as
authors of this work has been asserted by them in accordance
with the Copyright, Designs and Patents Act 1988.

"Batman" is a trademark of DC comics.
The publishers would like to thank the following organisations
and individuals for their kind permission to reproduce the
photographs in this book: Jean Cummings: (ii), 21, 44, 68, 76,
83, 85, 89, 94, 99, 102, 106, 108, 111, 116, 119, 138, 143 (top
and bottom), 146, 152 (top and bottom), 157, 164, 166, 167,
177, 208; Yale Joel, *Life* magazine: 125, 170 copyright © 1966 by
Time Warner; MCA: 185, 190 copyright © by Universal City
Studios, Inc. Courtesy of MCA Publishing Rights, a division of
MCA Inc.; Adam West: 15, 18, 24, 128, 135, 162, 174, 178, 182,
194, 196.
Front cover photo: copyright © Twentieth Television, a division
of Twentieth Century Fox Film Corporation. All rights reserved.

British Library Cataloguing-in-Publication Data. A catalogue
record for this book is available from the British Library.
This book is sold subject to the condition that it shall not by
way of trade or otherwise, be lent, re-sold, hired out or otherwise
circulated without the publisher's prior consent in any form of
binding or cover other than that in which it is published and
without a similar condition including this condition being
imposed upon the subsequent purchaser.
Printed and bound in Great Britain by Cox and Wyman Ltd,
Reading, Berkshire.

To Marcelle, Jonelle, Hunter,
Moya, Jill, Nina, and Perrin

Thanks to Executive-Producer William P. Dozier,
Producer Howie Horwitz, Bill D'Angelo, Lorenzo
Semple, Jr., and Charles FitzSimons, who
put all the pieces together. And, of course,
there was Bob Kane.

" . . . to be handsomely consequent, one would perhaps rather not have appeared to celebrate any rites."

—Henry James

It is certainly not my intention to celebrate anything about myself within these pages. Bookshelves are heavy with autobiography. To add my two cents' worth of glowing comments on my life and times seems an unworthy exercise. This modest book is not the memoirs of an aging actor, nor written simply for the pleasure of the author. This book is for the many loyal Batfans who have asked for it. I want you to know that I do not spend my days and nights running around in a cape and cowl. However, I *have* heard that a few of you do. Don't be overly concerned. We know it's fun to be Batman. This offering should prove it.

—Adam West
Ketchum, Idaho
1994

Introduction

THERE'S A fifty-something crimefighter who's as hot and compelling today as on the day he was delivered onto paper by a young artist named Bob Kane. And it doesn't take a genius to figure out who that Caped Crusader might be.

For twenty-five years on the tube and on the screen I have helped Batman become a legend, a world-class pop culture icon as recognizable as Bond or The Beatles. It has brought me joy and heartache and frustration with many stops in between.

There's something about Batman that appeals to all ages. Regardless of how he's interpreted, from darkly gothic to carnival bright and fun, that appeal is not diminished. Batman is one of the best-known, most enduring heroes of the twentieth century. Without any Hollywood humility, I have accepted my role in catapulting Batman from comic books to satellite and to the big screen, and into the homes of half a billion people each day.

I have run into enthusiastic Batfans all over the world—on the sparkling waters off the coast of Greece, on plains in Spain, in jungles down South America way, in metropolitan Japan, in the scrub of Africa, and in frozen northern Norway. I am always surprised and amazed that people everywhere, of all ages, have heard of three American institutions: Mickey Mouse, John Wayne and Batman.

What accounts for the ongoing popularity of the Caped Crusader? Why does he continue to thrive and prosper while Superman, his stablemate at DC Comics, had to be killed off for a couple of months to get some attention?

I'm often asked what makes Batman so special, so enduring, but I can never give a simple answer. It's like *Hamlet*. When you're a teenager, you read the play and it's "Hey, I get it! Hamlet's having a few problems at home and they drive him crazy." Twenty years later you're not so sure and you can't sum it up so succinctly.

Just to say that Batman's flashy and exciting doesn't do it. That doesn't differentiate him from Superman or James Bond or Tarzan or Michael Jordan.

What does? We'll get into that a bit later. For now, it's enough to say that he's one of a kind, a character so multifaceted that he can be interpreted in dramatically different ways.

I played television's Batman from 1966 to 1968 in 120 half-hour episodes in all, and I also played him in a feature film released in 1966. For many, our interpretation remains the classic and definitive one. For others, it's a fondly remembered part of their youth. For still others, it's a plague and an eyesore. The show is still in syndication around the world, and even today there's rarely a magazine or newspaper article about comic books that doesn't open with a "Holy something-or-other!" playing on Robin's catchphrase, or a "Pow! Zap!" reminiscent of our fight-scene garniture.

This book is about the show, the phenomenon, the legacy, the stars, and the spectacular highs and difficult lows I've experienced as a result of being part of that particular slice of TV history. It's a story I've been asked to tell for many years, though until now I didn't feel the time was right.

What makes now the right time? I think the simple answer is perspective. The wine of experience and contemplation has properly aged. I've had over a quarter-century to digest the character from inside the mask and out, to reflect on the phenomenon, to see someone else play the part, to meet and talk to fans and critics at conventions, on college campuses, on TV talk shows, in the street.

I confess, too, that I've always felt some reluctance about undertaking this project because I find it embarrassing when some actors assume their lives are grand enough to write about at length. We aren't world leaders, captains of industry, or great discoverers. I'm not a Winston Churchill or J. Paul Getty or Thomas Edison. My work and life and childhood experiences did not affect world history in profoundly important ways.

Yet some of the things that have happened to me are strange and unique. They may help to illuminate certain aspects of our culture, of fame and misfortune. As for my childhood, I'll go into it only so far as it pertains to something in which I strongly believe: the power of a young imagination, its importance in shaping a life and, thus, the world itself. Calculus and chemistry and physics are vital in a modern world, but it is the dreamers who give the mathematicians and scientists and others of their kind direction. I hope in these pages to make my own small case on behalf of heroes and fantasy, comic books and movies, Batmen and Batgirls.

Reminisce with me as we join my modern-day Hamlet racing once more to the Batpoles and back to the Batcave!

Prologue

TWO SNOW-WHITE poodles yapped at my feet as my agent Lew Sherrell and I stepped into Bill Dozier's office on the 20th Century-Fox lot.

The offices I'd visited during my seven years in tinseltown had usually belonged to lower-echelon TV producers or casting directors, men and women cramped into wood-veneer cubicles or trailers, nervous and harried as they looked for cowboys to be shot by Marshal Dillon, innocent partygoers to be sprayed with champagne by Lucy, or even astronauts to be stranded on Mars. Recently, I'd played the latter—twice, no less—on *The Outer Limits* and in the feature film *Robinson Crusoe on Mars*.

As I entered Dozier's office, I remember thinking that the fiery red sets of Mars were just a little less ostentatious than this Hansel and Gretel–esque half-timbered, mauve-carpeted cottage, situated near the soundstages and editing rooms and run by three drop-dead gorgeous secretaries.

Dozier was the wunderkind producer of such hits as *Dennis the Menace, Hazel,* and *The Donna Reed Show,* and though his recent Charlie Chan pilot, *Number One Son,* had failed to sell as a series, ABC had given Dozier a new project. I'd been told he was under the gun on it, too: ABC wanted to see a pilot episode and, if they liked it, go right into production for a January debut. That was just three months away. The sets were already under construction and scripts had been written.

Looking at the fifty-seven-year-old Dozier, you wouldn't have thought he had a network breathing down his neck. Dressed Polo Lounge perfect in a pink sweater, white button-down shirt, and white trousers, he was calm and collected. He held a shiny gold leash in one hand, though he didn't bother to reign in the noisy little animals as we approached. Maybe, in a spin on Dorian Gray, he'd arranged for them to feel the pressure for him.

Dozier and his assistant, producer Charles FitzSimons—actress Maureen O'Hara's brother—were seated behind a desk the size of a small atoll, laughing at something they'd read in a script. They didn't acknowledge us, which didn't surprise me. If a producer regards actors as people, it's tougher to fire, underpay, or otherwise take advantage of them. Unless you're a major star, that's a fact of life in Hollywood and you learn to live with it.

As I stood there, looking at a wall of photographs of Dozier with various celebrities, politicians, and dignitaries, I found myself thinking again about the part I was here to meet Dozier for. It was a big move, possibly the role of a lifetime. But it was also a role that could brand me for a lifetime, and I started going over the pros and cons again.

When we were both eager young contract players at Warner Brothers, Roger Moore had said to me over lunch and cigars that life is like chess: you can sit and think and think some more and still get blindsided by a pawn. Or you can make what seems like a good move only to set in motion a disastrous new pattern. He was right. In Hollywood, you can never factor in all the variables, which is why I'd always made decisions instinctively.

But there was one thing young Roger hadn't factored into his philosophy that maybe he should have, which is that most actors rarely *have* choices. They take the work that's offered and are glad to have it. In my case, if Dozier asked me to do this role, I'd have to choose between the starring role in a modestly budgeted foreign film or the lead in a big-budget TV series. Movers and shakers all over the world see movies, which could lead to a big break, whereas for the most part only the public watches TV. On the other hand, the public writes letters, and when the public speaks the studios listen and TV can lead to movies.

A slight cough and Dozier looked up and ended my reverie. He rose slowly, and I felt a little uncomfortable as he studied me from toe to head, his expression impassive as he costumed me with his eyes picturing me in a blue-and-gray suit.

Charlie FitzSimons did the same, following Dozier's every move like a big shadow. Wearing an expensive dark suit and vest, he was easygoing but obviously the hard-nosed businessman, Yang to Dozier's creative Yin.

After another pass from head to toe, the lanky, six-foot-two Dozier extended his hand across the desk. I offered him mine. He had a firm dealmaker's handshake.

"Adam, it's a pleasure to meet you."

"Likewise," I said.

"We ran *Crusoe* last night. Very nice."

"Thanks," I said.

Dozier allowed himself a smile and I relaxed a little. Though I was supposed to go from here to a fitting and a screen test, I suspected he'd made up his mind about me in the few seconds it took to look me over. I'd heard that's about how long it had taken him to decide that he *didn't* want former movie Tarzan and L.A. Rams linebacker Mike Henry or Lyle Waggoner for the part. Why, I didn't find out until years later. My guess is that their features and physiques were too sculpted. (He *had* wanted to look at TV star Ty Hardin for the role, but Hardin was busy studying to be a preacher or something.)

He sat down again, reeling the dogs in like brook trout. They panted quietly and sat by his side. He didn't invite Lew and me to sit, which pretty much told us where we stood in the pecking order.

"I understand you've been doing a spaghetti western," Bill said, a little condescendingly, I thought.

Spaghetti westerns were made-in-Italy slices of Americana that were just becoming the rage in the States, with Clint Eastwood the biggest beneficiary.

"Yes, I just finished one," I told him, "*The Relentless Four.*"

"Sort of like *The Magnificent Seven?*" Charlie asked.

"Right."

"But without the budget for all seven," Dozier observed.

I laughed out loud. The man had wit.

Now the ever-vigilant Lew said, "He's been offered another film, a bigger one, that starts shooting next month."

"So you came back just for this?" Charlie asked.

"No," I said. "I flew in to spend some time with my two children." The truth.

I later learned that Dozier himself was a devoted husband and father. But after his family the thing that mattered to him most was being the first to succeed at something, whether it was finding a new star or creating a new kind of TV show. Being second or third held no appeal for him whatsoever.

"Have you ever read a Batman comic book?" he asked.

"Sure," I said.

When I was growing up on a farm in Walla Walla, Washington, I found a cache of comic books in an old bunkhouse, and Batman had made a big impression on my ten-year-old mind. He was so many exciting characters rolled into one: Sherlock Holmes, Zorro, even a bit of Dracula. And he was more believable than Superman, who came from another planet, or the Flash, who'd sucked up fumes from a chemical spill. Batman had made himself what he was, and each time I read one of the comics, I was so inspired I threw myself on the floor to do push-ups. I thought anyone could have that chest.

Dozier asked, "Can you read something now?"

"Sure," I said, and Charlie handed me the script they'd been laughing over.

I glanced at the purple cover, on which was printed *"Hey Diddle Riddle" by Lorenzo Semple, Jr.*

I experienced a *ping*. This was it—the Batman script Lew and I had heard so much about from the people at Fox. For weeks, we were told, it'd been the talk of the lot, and I couldn't wait to find out why. A brilliant mystery plot? Fresh insights into the Caped Crusader? Glib Nick and Nora Charles–type exchanges between Batman and his sidekick Robin?

"You can take it in here," Charlie said, showing Lew and me to an adjoining conference room.

"Enjoy," Dozier chuckled, watching me as we left.

"I hope so," I said, as Charlie shut the door.

Lew clapped a hand on my shoulder and immediately began to "sell" me on Dozier, lest I be put off by his manner. One of the reasons I'd left Hollywood was that I didn't like the polished ones who sent limousines for you one day and wouldn't take your calls the next.

"They're okay, once you get to know them," Lew said. "With Bill, the bullshit's all on the outside. Inside, he's a nice guy."

"I'm sure," I whispered. "And inside that, he's got some steel."

"True," Lew said. "You don't want to cross him."

I nodded and sat down at the long table to concentrate on the matter at hand. Lew sat next to me, took out a little notebook, and began writing. He wanted to remember everything that had been said. A one-time vaudeville dancer with years of experience in all facets of show business, Lew was warm, funny . . . and meticulous.

While he scribbled, I stared at the cover of the script.

My feelings were still definitely mixed. With this important meeting with Dozier, I knew that I might have to decide whether or not to put my movie career on hold to do another weekly series (I'd costarred with the late Robert Taylor in *The Detectives* three years before). And, more importantly, I'd have to decide whether or not I wanted to play Batman.

Although I loved the character, the conventional wisdom in Hollywood was that donning a costume was the equivalent of slipping into a career straitjacket. The good work George Reeves had done in films had been forgotten as soon as he became TV's Superman, and the only work that wonderful man Clayton Moore could get was personal appearances as the Lone Ranger. The farthest Johnny Weissmuller got from being the movies' Tarzan was playing Jungle Jim on TV—just another neighborhood in the same back-lot rain forest.

Screw it, I thought. Don't overanalyze. There were exceptions to every rule, and besides, I hadn't even *gotten* the part yet.

I opened the script, began reading, and almost at once started laughing.

Lew shot me a look of horror. "What's wrong?"

"Nothing," I said.

"It's *funny*?"

"Hilarious," I answered, without looking up. I didn't want to stop.

I knew writer Lorenzo Semple by reputation, a young Turk living in Spain who'd made his name by coming up with unexpected, brilliantly innovative twists on tired themes. And, as I read, it didn't take long for me to find out just what he'd brought to the party: a wild, unbridled sense of fun, humor, and adventure tied up in a neat bundle.

After a few minutes, I was on the floor.

In the script, Batman had just entered a restaurant, in full costume, and was telling the maître d' he preferred to sit at the bar instead of a table since "I shouldn't wish to attract attention."

What was funny wasn't only the concept of this man in a flashy cowl and cape honestly thinking he could be inconspicuous. What made the script and the character work was the scrupulously formal language that made you believe *he* believed it.

Lew was growing uneasy. "I thought this guy was a serious crime-fighter."

"He is," I said. "That's what's so entertaining."

"Oh," Lew said. He folded away his notebook and began reading over my shoulder.

I was excited by what I was reading, and when I wasn't laughing, I was shaking my head and murmuring, "Yeah, yeah, this is good. This is really good."

Lew groaned. "You've got to dance in this thing. Look."

"I know," I said. "I can *do* something with that." The word "Batusi" came to me. That may sound a little silly, but keep in mind that most of what I'd done over the past seven years was guest spots on *Maverick, Sugarfoot, 77 Sunset Strip,* and *Perry Mason,* where I was shot at, beat up, or put on trial. Not much creative leeway there. This irreverent, innovative script had opened the floodgates for me, and every scene gave me ideas.

"I like this, Lew," I said. "I like it a lot." I stopped reading for the first time and looked at him. "And you know I want to do comedy."

"I know," Lew said, "but you should take some time to think. We can go to the commissary and talk it over—"

I shook my head. The truth was, I wanted to *stop* thinking. The script was like nothing I'd ever read, and I didn't want to think about George Reeves or Clayton Moore or Johnny Weissmuller or anyone else. I just wanted to *do* it.

I said so to Lew, and as I resumed reading he rose and headed back to Dozier's office. Through the open door, I heard him say, "He likes it—"

"I thought he might," Charlie replied.

"—but we don't want to do a screen test."

I stopped reading. Lew was a small, very smooth and likable man.

He could play the power game, too, though I wondered if he was out of his league with Dozier.

"You've seen film on him," Lew went on. "If he's going to turn down the next western, I want to be able to tell them this afternoon."

Dozier, I later learned, was a man who played his instincts; he'd made it to the top because those instincts were usually correct.

"He had the part when I watched him walk into the conference room," Dozier replied, deftly declawing Lew's ultimatum. "Very graceful, but very masculine."

"Can he do the lines straight?" Charlie asked. "No funny business?"

"He can do anything," I shouted from the other side of the door. "Trust me."

Lew and Charlie laughed, and as hands were shaken they got busy arranging a screen test—not for me but for a wiry nineteen-year-old realtor named Sparky Gervis, whom Dozier knew and thought might work as Batman's sidekick, Robin.

Things would move quickly from this point forward, with costume fittings the next day and Sparky's screen test a few days after that. Rehearsals would begin two weeks later.

As Lew and I stood beside his car parked just outside the bungalow, he congratulated me and I thanked him not just for his help, but for his faith in me over the years. I asked if he thought I'd done the right thing.

"You wanted the part?"

"Yes—"

He shrugged. "Then you did the right thing. Besides, you'll be making TV history. This is going to be a big, visible show. I don't know very many actors who'd lose sleep over the fact that thirty or forty million people will know your name who didn't know it before."

I nodded. He was right about that. It was going to be a big production, and from what Dozier had said, it was going to be first rate, the most expensive hour in television history. And it would have the added prestige of being filmed in color, which fewer than half the network shows were at the time. Assuming ABC was enthusiastic about the pilot episode, *Batman* would also be heavily promoted, shown on two successive nights every week, with world-class guest stars.

Lew drove off, and as I climbed onto my motorcycle and gunned to the apartment I'd rented in Malibu, excitement replaced the lingering fears I had about the project. After years of guest spots and second-banana roles, of low-budget films and following the leads Clint Eastwood or Roger Moore had made, I was finally going to blaze a trail for others to follow. It was a nice feeling.

Would I have made the same decision had I known then what I know now, that the serious career I'd worked so hard to develop, that the quiet and happy private life I knew, would both slip like sand through my soon-to-be-blue-gloved fingers?

For the answer to that question and much more, stay tuned—same Bat-time, same Bat-channel.

1

I HAD MORE mundane philosophical matters on my mind some twenty years before, when I was twelve-year-old Billy West Anderson.

I lived with my mother, Audrey, and her husband, a neurosurgeon, in Seattle. I also have a stepmother, named Adele. She tells a story about how, one Saturday, my mother had dropped me and my nine-year-old brother, John, at the Roxy Theater in my old home town of Walla Walla, where we'd stayed all morning with friends, watching a Bill Boyd Hopalong Cassidy film and another western, with Bob Steele. Both actors were heroes of mine, and I was full of the shoot-'em-up West when Adele and my dad, Otto West Anderson, came to pick us up for a week-long stay on their farm some twenty miles outside of town. As the city turned to country and rolling hills, I sat in the backseat of the sedan, pretending to be riding a horse, chasing outlaws just as Hoppy had done. John, of course, was the outlaw: young brothers always are.

Adele remembers vividly that near the end of the drive, on a steep hillside just before we turned into our long gravel driveway, I turned to stare at a cloud of summer fallow dust that swirled skyward like a tornado. I watched as a horse and rider churned and slid over the brow toward us. The Morgan mare was plunging down the hill, and the rider was waving his big hat as if he hadn't seen us in ten years. He had the reins in his teeth, which gave him a dashing wide smile, and in his hands he held a rifle. At that moment I was back in my seat at the Roxy.

Scenes like that were not unusual to Adele and my dad, but they were to me. Adele says she never saw such a look of awe on a kid's face as the one I had as I watched the hand ride toward us. And when he reached the car and my dad stopped, she says she didn't know which was wider, my eyes or my mouth. I must have felt like I was the luckiest kid in the world, that I'd been driven right into a movie. When my folks were still married and I was living there, I'd never appreciated what a magical place the farm was. Now, two years later, books and movies and radio shows and comic books had stirred my imagination. What used to be just a farm with chores and more chores was the Bar 20 Ranch where Hoppy and his sidekick Red Connors (my brother again) got into all kinds of exciting adventures.

That kind of rich inner life is a vital tool for any actor, and Adele thinks that the endless skies and the room to roam on a ranch stimulated my active imagination. Though it makes me squirm like a child in church when we visit her in Walla Walla and she tells stories about how I hog-tied poor John or pretended chickens were a herd of stampeding buffalo, a young person is fortunate if he or she has someone close who senses how important an unfettered, unselfconscious imagination is and nurtures that. Hoppy may have been a hero to me, but Adele's enthusiastic encouragement was every bit as important. It continues to this day and I am grateful.

Sadly, my mother was a different story. The distance of years since her untimely death has given John and me the freedom to remember and even laugh at her misadventures and wayward romances. An alcoholic, she would probably be diagnosed as manic-depressive today and treated accordingly. But, unfortunately, that wasn't available to her in the 1940s and her demons got the best of her. It was a tragedy.

Quite beautiful, talented and headstrong, she was usually the center of attention. She sang and played the piano and was the leading lady in the local historical pageants. She was the queen of the famous Pendleton Roundup while the greatest of all the early Hollywood stuntmen, Yakima Canutt, was being toasted as the best all-around cowboy. She won a scholarship to study opera in Los Angeles, and after she married my father she uprooted him and an infant me from a wheat field, to live in the Hollywood Hills. My brother, John, was born there, but three years later it became clear that there was too much distraction and responsibility in her life for her ever to become a star. We returned to the Walla Walla Valley, and Mother was never able to overcome her frustrations and bitterness, or balance family life with career. In a moment of pique, she once told me that she blamed my birth for the fact that she hadn't become Joan Crawford. Perhaps she believed that, and to this day, when I think about her, I find myself coping with lingering feelings of guilt.

My mother was ill-matched with my father, something that became obvious to me when I was ten and walked home from school to find her in bed with a handsome local minister. (Too much communion wine?) My unsuspecting Gary Cooper–type father was far away on a ranch struggling to make a living. My mother was full of colorful surprises like that, little things that shocked a young man's psyche and gave me clues to the infinite and complex levels of human nature.

However, in her own way, my flamboyant mother was helpful in my development as an actor. I can't say whether I inherited a "genetic" need to perform, but her melodramatic style made a big impression on me. It got results from people, made them respond.

So did her parties. Every VIP who happened to wander through our hometown found his or her way to our doorstep, victims of my mother's considerable charm. Many were the nights that two young boys could be found in their pajamas, listening on the stairway as the likes of Nelson Eddy, James Stewart, General Jimmy Doolittle, Alan Ladd, and Lily Pons laughed and sang and got down at my mother's soirees.

Between those nights of eavesdropping and Saturday mornings at the old Roxy in Walla Walla, I knew there was a bigger and more exciting world than mine out there.

When I look back now, I realize that my mother's indiscretions and her weaknesses

At age one with my grandfather, Bill Speer, on his ranch

weren't evil, weren't intended to hurt my father. She was simply searching for happiness, attention, and drama in an unsatisfying life. Ironically, her legacy to me usually caused a stab of guilt whenever I got a
part: while celebrating my good fortune, I was always aware that any
success of mine was something my mother wanted but that her personal
demons would not allow her to have.

My father was a strong, kind, and decent man, and he was able to
tough out the relationship for fourteen years. Even when the crops
were bad, he said nothing about her spending hundreds of dollars
entertaining celebrities. Eventually, though, he could no longer take
the whispers of friends about what she was doing behind his back.
Though it was a blow to his pride, he felt it was best to divorce. It's
strange, too. Though my mother's aspirations were closer to my own,
I got the impression that she was angry about the prospect that I might
succeed where she had failed. My father, on the other hand, was always
supportive of me, even though he had seen what show business did to
my mother. Inside, I'm sure he'd have preferred me to stay on the
farm as John would do. But he never let on about that. Whatever I
wanted to do, he was behind me.

When my mother married Dr. Paul Flothow, she moved to Seattle
and a stone mansion. John and I went with them, sad to leave the farm
but excited to be in the big city. When I was fourteen, I was sent to a
school for boys in the suburbs, Lakeside School. It was tough and disci-
plined, and in making a man out of a boy it helped turn a dreamer into
a doer. After several unfortunate, rebellious false starts that landed me in
trouble (such as "borrowing" the school bus for dates), I found my foot-
ing and got a real head start on life. I learned the discipline to become a
very good athlete, was voted president of the student body, and made a
few lifelong friends. I remain grateful to the teachers who were challenged rather than daunted by my restlessness and high spirits.

Summers were spent working on ranches or in canneries to help
earn money for college, which I wanted to attend in my hometown. Walla
Walla has two famous institutions: Whitman College and the Washington
State Penitentiary. I managed to graduate from the former with a degree
in literature and psychology, though those who joined me for wild rides
on horseback or motorcycles said I belonged in the latter.

By this time I also had a young wife, whom I'd met and married in the last year of college. Billie Lou Yeager was four years my junior, a strikingly beautiful seventeen year old, and my grandparents gave us a tiny old house they owned in town. Billie Lou worked for Sears Roebuck while I managed to get a job as a deejay at a local radio station, intending to save up enough money to go to graduate school and study communications. By this time I was thinking seriously about becoming an actor, but I also wanted skills besides farming to fall back on. After a year I enrolled in Stanford and started post-graduate studies, doing a little radio, a little reporting, and a little writing. But I didn't get to spend much time there: after six weeks, someone from the McClatchy newspapers and radio conglomerate in Sacramento, California, heard me on the campus radio show and offered me a job.

I accepted, figuring I could always go back to school.

At McClatchy, I ended up producing, directing, and voicing radio shows. I also did my first stage acting: at the annual music circus, I appeared as the title spirit in *The Dybbuk*, based on the old Hebrew legend. It was a great story, full of intriguing mysticism, and playing a dead Yiddish scholar was a challenging stretch for a guy from Walla Walla. My reviews were good, and I guess I was hooked on performing from then on.

I was fired from McClatchy after a year for being too "innovative," especially during commercials (my irreverence can best be described as early, less crude Howard Stern), even though my inventiveness increased audience awareness of the sponsors. Having tasted the real world, I didn't want to go back to school; in fact, I decided I wanted to travel. The army draft board obliged. I had been accepted into Naval OCS, but I went for the army because it was only a twenty-four-month hitch, and after basic training I was assigned to the Signal Corps. I was part of a team that was starting a military TV station in San Luis Obispo, California. When we finished there, I was sent east, to Fort Monmouth, New Jersey, to do the same.

The work was fascinating. TV was just starting to heat up, and being involved with that new technology made me feel like Dr. Huer in the Buck Rogers strip. I had a radio background; now I was finding a place in television.

After my discharge, Billie Lou and I remained in the East, where I worked as a milkman. The only memorable experience I had making

At sixteen, with a buzzcut
by Jack of Walla Walla, Washington

my rounds was when a hurricane hit the Jersey shore. I felt that the milk and eggs should get through, and so, as Batman surely would have done if he'd become Milkman, I kept delivering the goods as the storm worsened. I was blown off several porches, and the strong winds finally tipped over my truck. What a mess of broken glass and spilled milk to clean up! I ended up having to hitch back to the factory. But the dairy was impressed and actually gave me a medal for milkmanship above and beyond the call of duty.

When we had enough money saved up (or so we thought), my wife and I went to Europe on a walking tour. It was a walking tour because we ran out of money early. We blew it fast on warm Italian hospitality on the Isle of Capri. But it was a grand adventure and some of my rough edges were polished away by the sophisticated, cultured people we met. After three months of trekking through Italy, Switzerland, Germany, and France, we returned to Walla Walla. We planned to stay on the farm for about six months while I went to work to replenish our empty coffers.

But things didn't quite work out that way: Robert Burns was right when he wrote that "the best laid schemes o' mice an' men gang aft a-gley." However, I must confess that I've always preferred the wisdom of Horace, who wrote, *Misce stultitiam consiliis brevem: Dulce est desipere in loco.*

Mix a little foolishness with your serious plans: It's lovely to be silly at the right moment.

2

THE SILLINESS that Horace spoke of came in the form of an unexpected letter from a childhood and college buddy, Carl Hebenstreit. While my wife and I were busy backpacking around Europe, Carl had gone to Hawaii and quickly become the top TV star there thanks to *The Kini Popo Show,* a variety and comedy series in which he shared the stage with the popular Peaches the chimp. They didn't do surveys back in those days in Hawaii, but Carl was always worried about who was the bigger draw.

Carl and I had worked together in local radio during college, and he was convinced that if I came to Hawaii I, too, could be a TV star. At the time, not many people who thought about acting went to Honolulu . . . except maybe Carl. Serious thespians headed for New York, Los Angeles, and London. That left the South Pacific wide open.

It made sense to me. Besides, Carl assured me that the scenery was spectacular and so were the women. I only told my wife about the scenery, and we left the following week.

We moved in with Carl for a few weeks, sleeping on a sofa bed in the living room of his apartment. I played assorted characters on Carl's show, did spots on the local CBS affiliate, acted in dinner theater, and drawing upon my literature background, wrote what I considered to be hot copy for an advertising agency. Not many admen came to Hawaii, either. After several months, Carl and I also started a business: we bought a used airplane, learned to fly, and hand-painted the old bird with what we thought was a compelling motif of yellow pineapples and green palm fronds. We planned to earn extra money by flying visitors around the island, and though I didn't have a commercial license, nobody bothered to ask in those balmy, more innocent times.

Unfortunately, harsh reality did set in early in my new career. I was a lousy husband once we hit the Islands. While I was busy acting and copywriting and flying and doing some race car driving for recreation, my wife was working for Standard Oil. I saw very little of her, and she got to know a handsome, older man who was a top executive there. He had plenty of free time and a nice sailboat; he also adored her and gave her the attention she needed.

I was upset with myself for having let things reach that point, but I also knew that there wasn't much I could have done about it. The "inner life" that had fired the imagination of twelve-year-old Billy Anderson was coming to life in Hawaii. Working creatively when the curtain came up or the cameras came on gave me a sense of purpose, and good feelings I hadn't found elsewhere. My wife understood that, at least, and in a bittersweet meeting we agreed to a quick, amicable divorce.

I wasn't alone for long, however. Just two months later I met a beautiful dancer who had come from Tahiti as a young girl. Her name was Ngatokoruaimatauaia Frisbie Dawson; I called her Nga. After a short courtship we were married. She became the mother of my oldest daughter, Jonelle, born in 1957, and my oldest son, Hunter, born in 1958.

I did my first film work back then as well, though both experiences were so bizarre that I have to wonder now if someone was trying to tell me something.

Late in 1956, casting people from United Artists came to Hawaii looking for an actor to play a radio operator in a film called *Voodoo Island*. Boris Karloff was the star, with Rhodes Reason as the leading man and Beverly Tyler as the leading lady. Karloff was playing a debunker of the supernatural who is brought to a tropical island by a resort owner to find out if those really are zombies roaming about, or simply guests who weren't getting a good night's sleep. Something along those lines.

Most of the film was being shot in Los Angeles, but the cast was coming over for two days of location shooting in the jungles of Kauai where, more recently, *Jurassic Park* was filmed. The casting people were looking for someone who was not just photogenic, but also stupid

In Hawaii

enough to crawl around in some of the lushest, wettest, hottest, buggiest jungle on earth.

I got the part. I was thrilled, not only because it was to be my first motion picture, but because I would get to meet Boris Karloff, whose three Frankenstein films had scared the pants off me as a kid and whose work in *The Body Snatchers* remains some of the best and most underrated screen acting of the 1940s.

Two mornings later, a prop guy and I were flown over to Kauai in a plane that looked and rode as if it were left over from *Wings*. (Someone had actually managed to underbid Carl and me on the charter; so much for having "connections.") The prop man brought me and a vintage World War II radio into the jungle, where he left me and flew back to Honolulu.

The crew was supposed to have followed, but after an hour I began to wonder if maybe the plane had gone down. I shooed away insects and watched my costume slowly mildew for about two hours, then decided to try the radio. I cranked it up, but it didn't work, of course, so I just sat there as morning became afternoon and the skies went from blue to dark blue to blue-black. Before long, I was picking out constellations between the big, drooping fronds overhead.

As the night dragged on, I wondered if maybe the prop person had forgotten where in the jungle I was. But I wasn't about to go crawling through spiders and land crabs to find the beach in the darkness, so I curled up and went to sleep, prepared to suffer for my art.

I was up with the sun the next morning, and after picking a few bananas, I made my way to the shore and waited.

No crew, no plane. Dutifully, I returned to my post and ate more bananas.

And more bananas. It was two full days before the crew showed up. The director, Reginald Le Borg, had been preoccupied with Mr. Karloff, and the prop guy thought the second unit director had gone to get me, and vice versa. When the crew finally showed up, the prop man apologized profusely, glad to find me alive and Le Borg was thrilled with my stubble-faced, "weathered" look. I offered them bananas. We shot the scenes and went back to Honolulu. Naturally, I never did get to meet Mr. Karloff, who had come and gone while I was going native. For days thereafter I had to listen to Carl and my wife and everyone else on the island telling me how gracious and soft-spoken and wonderful Karloff had been. Even Peaches had gotten to meet him.

My second film was equally inauspicious. It was called *Ghost of the China Sea*, about the Japanese invasion of the Philippines, and it starred Jon Hall of *Hurricane* fame.

The director, Fred F. Sears, didn't want actors but three scuba divers, and I went to the audition. Only three of us showed up; I got the part, a two-week gig. I'd never dived before, but I felt that if I watched the other two guys, I'd be okay. How tough could it be, after all? I knew how to swim, I knew how to breathe.

The scene was being shot in gorgeous Haunauna Bay, and called for us to jump off a boat, stay under while the stars talked among themselves on deck, then come up when they were finished and climb aboard. Our stern Boston-born director didn't tell us *how* we'd know he was finished, and he was such a gruff soul that none of us wanted to ask. We figured they'd fire a gun or shine a light or shout with a bullhorn to let us know when to surface. There had to be some kind of standard operating procedure for things like this, and we'd know it when we saw it.

As we suited up, I watched what the other two divers were doing and did the same thing. Piece of cake. Unfortunately, we were jumping off the boat together, so I didn't get to see how that was done. At "action," I leapt, and when I hit the water, the heavy iron tank rode up my back and cracked me in the skull. Dazed, I half-swam, half-sunk to the bottom. On the way down, I lost sight of the other two divers but my eye caught a chunk of coral; afraid that I might bob up and ruin the scene, I wrapped my arms around it to stay down. Floating there professionally like a strand of seaweed, I promptly passed out.

I have no idea how much time elapsed, but the next thing I knew I was breaking the surface of the water. Instantly alert, like Pee-wee Herman saying, "I meant to do that," I looked around and made for the boat. The other two divers were about twenty yards ahead of me, already there, with the director and his camera on the bow. They reached over the side and pulled me up.

The director came directly toward me. I was braced for a dressing-down, but instead he grabbed my shoulders and cried, "Wonderful!

As host of the *Kini Popo Show*

You were the only one who knew what he was doing! You didn't come up too soon!''

I thanked him, my head throbbed, and flashes of red stained my vision. As I walked off, I concentrated on not falling to my knees and spoiling my moment of triumph.

3

MOST DAYS, if I had no television show to do with Kini Popo and his pal Peaches, no live commercials for Piggly Wiggly Market, Primo Beer, or Thrifty Florist, I'd head out to the Honolulu International Airport to greet incoming tourists. Grouped with well-browned native Hawaiians who were doing the same thing, I would sort of stand out like a white missionary as I murmured, "Aloha. Alooooha. Welcome to my beautiful island." Then I would drop slightly wilted day-old plumeria leis from—where else?—Thrifty Florist around pink, mainland necks. As I did so, I was able to present my card:

Kamaaina Tours
Oahu from the air
Safe . . . Fun . . . Reasonable . . . Private
See more quicker

Our names and phone number were there as well (though some joker once called and asked for Seymour Quicker), and as gentle trade winds feather-dusted away mainland inhibitions we would actually get calls to fly people around. As I usually had less to do than Carl, I ended up doing most of the flying.

One morning, my leis fell around the necks of Jack Wilens and his wife, and they called that afternoon to arrange a tour. It was a flight that would change my life.

The air was calm as we went up the next morning, updrafts lifting us high over the Pali cliffs as we banked toward the windward surfline. The Wilenses were enjoying the ride, and as our conversation got friendlier, I told them that I was an aspiring actor working in local TV and playing the lead in the Hawaiian Community Theatre production of *Picnic*. Not that competition for the part had been fierce.

Jack listened with interest: as it turned out, he was a movie producer who was here to use some of *his* profits to open Hawaii's first car wash. (Anything to spoil the virgin beauty of the islands.)

But what really got my attention was when Jack mentioned that a friend of his, an agent named Lew Sherrell, had just arrived with his wife and that he'd introduce me.

"Perhaps," Jack said, "we'll make an evening of your play."

Well sure, I thought. He and his wife and the Sherrells are in Hawaii and they're going to come see Bill Anderson and Mavis Tefaafana doing William Inge. But sure enough, two nights later, their last in Hawaii, the Wilenses and the Sherrells were in the audience. They came backstage after the performance.

They were effusive with their praise, and before Lew left, he asked me to send pictures to his office in Hollywood. He seemed sincere and I thanked him; even if nothing came of it, I appreciated his interest.

I went back to my routine, and a week later, much to my surprise and delight, Lew was on the other end of a bad phone connection from Hollywood.

His voice crackled about work of some kind.

"*What* kind of work?" I asked.

"*Westerns*," he yelled. "For TV. They're doing a lot of them, and you look like you could be a cowboy."

"I grew up in a saddle," I told him. "What do I have to do? I'll ride like the wind right over."

"Can you send me some photos?"

"No problem," I said. "You'll have them in a few days, special delivery."

I was elated as I hung up the phone, though I wasn't quite sure I was going to be able to deliver the photos. After living in Hawaii for five years, I knew that western-type clothes would be difficult to find: very few people wore heavy cowhide or buckskin to the beach, and local cowboys (*paniolos*) wore aloha shirts. But I went to the wardrobe department at the studio, dug up something passable, and borrowed a horse that had been eating kohala berries and had an unsightly case of mange. Trigger he wasn't, but with clever camera angles I came up with shots that were kind of heroic, and off they went to Hollywood.

I heard nothing for several weeks. Meanwhile, Carl decided to ditch show business and move to remote Rarotonga in the Cook Islands. Talk about a career change! He said that Hawaii was becoming too civilized, and though I was sorry to see my friend go, he did leave me *The Kini Popo Show*, and the chimp. I wrote to Lew Sherrell and told him he could tell Hollywood casting agents that I was a bona fide TV star . . . at least on Oahu.

And so I waited, excited for a while, then nervous, then disappointed, and finally resigned to the fact that I'd never hear from Lew again. I understood well my mother's frustration.

But there were nice memories from this period, too. I was excited when nineteen-year-old Natalie Wood came to town to promote the Hawaiian opening of her film *The Searchers*. In any walk of life, there are people you meet who make an instant and lasting impression— Natalie was one of those: warm, intelligent, and charming.

My TV station sent me to emcee the Hawaiian premiere, and as I escorted Natalie to the microphone in front of the theater, several fans asked for my autograph. Mine, not hers. I couldn't have paid for better PR.

"How do they know you?" Natalie asked, apparently impressed.

"I have a TV show," I said with a casual, it's-no-big-deal shrug.

"What kind?"

"Morning," I said evasively. My necktie suddenly felt very tight. "It's a variety show, sort of . . . "

"Is it all your own?"

"Not really. I share it with a very talented performer named Peaches."

"A native?"

"No," I said. "A transplant, like me."

Trying to change the subject, I fervently hoped that she didn't turn on the TV the next morning and see Peaches and me in hula skirts, strumming ukuleles and singing "Mala, Mala, Mala" to a puppet octopus. Or Peaches (a male) doing obscene things under my desk.

After Natalie's appearance at the theater, we went back to her hotel, to a suite that was larger than my house and my CBS office combined. She introduced me to her mother and her voluptuous sister

Lana, who were chaperoning her. When we finally had a moment alone, I asked Natalie if she would have dinner with me; she said she'd be happy to.

I felt inspired as I contemplated an evening with Natalie Wood.

"As long as I'm back by midnight," she added.

"Of course," I said.

The thought of Natalie as Cinderella made the fairy-tale image complete. And I was going to be Prince Charming, I thought, as I drove home to change into something less restrictive and more tropical.

Later, at Don the Beachcomber, singer Don Ho had just finished his first set. I felt pretty important sitting at a romantic table for two with someone as beautiful and famous as Natalie. My friend Don knew it, and he crooned a couple of love songs our way.

Natalie smiled. I was falling in love over a mai tai with a little blue paper umbrella up my nose.

Unfortunately, as we talked, I realized that I was alone in fantasizing about our future. Natalie was going on about former loves James Dean and Elvis Presley, and her new flame, Raymond Burr. Yes, she had a crush on Perry Mason himself. The actor who fought Godzilla out of court and so many other villains in.

The rest of the evening was a little spoiled as I tried not to picture the two of them together. (Not Godzilla. Raymond.) However, I resolved to get to Hollywood, play a movie or TV hero, and see Natalie again on equal terms. It was a shallow motivation, I know, but I needed something to jump-start things.

Midnight curfew arrived, and as I said good night to Natalie, her mother, and Lana at their hotel door, I told them to keep an eye peeled, since I planned to be in Hollywood one day soon. They smiled politely and withdrew quickly, though Lana's green-eyed gaze caught and held my own for a long moment. As it happened, I would be seeing more of her in the future.

Two weeks later I was the guest of honor in the Banyon Court of the old Moana Hotel at Waikiki for a rowdy farewell lunch. Mine. Lew had called a few days after my date with Natalie and said that MGM wanted to see me for a screen test. So it was aloha to the islands, to my airplane, and to Peaches. I loved Hawaii, and I had made many friends there, most of whom didn't think I would ever leave such idyllic beauty and the perks of local fame. But the truth was, I couldn't do what I wanted to do there.

I hated to leave my family, but I promised them and myself I would send for them soon.

Before going, I threw a lei on the sea and hoped it wouldn't drift back until my dreams came true.

4

"LOCK THE gates! Call security! Don't let this guy off the lot!"
I was in the office suite of Bill Orr and Hugh Benson, VPs at Warner Brothers and the heads of television. Benson was yelling into the phone, his blond mustache twitching and his blue eyes examining me.

I had just finished reading a scene I'd already done several times that day for producers under Orr's command, lower-echelon types who occupied correspondingly lower floors in the tan stucco producers' building at the studio in Burbank. The character I'd just read was a sniveling cavalry deserter and would-be rapist. I must have been pretty convincing, because Benson became very excited.

"Get Eddie Foy in here! Get a contract ready! This kid doesn't leave the lot! He's ours!"

Hugh Benson was yelling like he'd just discovered sex. Was he nuts? Was I that good?

I began to entertain thoughts of thespian genius. Then a flash of reality kicked in. If Benson got this agitated over a cowboy type who could ride a horse and maybe speak his lines with some honesty and emotion, what did he do when a Brando or Olivier walked in the door? Who was he kidding?

Casting director Eddie Foy, Jr., a scion of the famed vaudeville family, sprinted into the room. He stood between Benson and me, and while they huddled, my agent took me aside.

"These guys want you," he said. "You're the luckiest guy in the world."

Lew had a charming way of making me feel as if I never deserved anything. Despite my suspicions about Benson, I allowed myself a moment of satisfaction. Then I asked, "So what does it mean?"

"They'll offer a seven-year contract," Lew said, "and if you've got what it takes, they'll make a star out of you." He winked. "Take it, you'll love it." Not profound, but probably good advice.

As good as I felt, I was also uneasy. I'd read for MGM a few days before, and they'd liked me, too, albeit with just a smile and a handshake and not the P. T. Barnum hyperbole. They wanted me to take a screen test that very afternoon, and we'd stopped off here at Warners not expecting much. I felt that I was morally obliged to go ahead with the test, or at least give them some kind of right of refusal.

I boiled all that down to, "What about MGM?"

Lew looked at me. "What about them?"

"They expect me. They've been nice to me."

"Nice?" My agent looked pained. "They'd lend you out for a buck more than they signed you for."

"Wouldn't Warners?"

"Sure," Lew said. He came closer, his arm in a black silk coat sleeve around my shoulder; his diamond pinky ring seeming to grow larger. "But you know the saying, kid: a bird in the hand . . . "

Benson and Orr left and went into a side room. Foy motioned to Lew, and with a pat on his back, they followed the other two in. As Foy closed the door, he flashed me a big smile.

I was alone, and as I sat there in the office decorated with framed movie posters, I bought into the whole ball game. Completely. I could see my name and likeness on one of the posters; I could imagine a fine screenplay, something like *Notorious* or *His Girl Friday,* with me helping to bring it to life.

And, of course, there would be an Oscar waiting.

I told myself that everything I'd heard since I walked in the door, about how great I was, how Warners had to have me, was pure Hollywood flummery. But this *was* the studio where Errol Flynn and James Cagney, Humphrey Bogart and Bugs Bunny had fought and loved their way into the hearts of millions. Benson's superlatives aside, these guys had promised to put me on a launching pad. With the right conditions, I could be fired into the stratosphere.

Three years before, in 1956, Warners had branched out into TV production in a big way. Again, this was the era of the western, and starting with *Cheyenne* the studio was making a major commitment to them. That probably factored into Benson's enthusiasm for me.

The thing was, I had no burning desire to be a TV star. I know that could sound arrogant today, but then TV was considered a less prestigious medium. The picture tube isn't a towering movie screen where dreams are big and important, and where people go out of their way to see you. You're in their homes. If the phone rings, you get turned down. If the dog needs walking, you get turned off.

On the other hand, TV was beginning to launch some extraordinary film careers, for the likes of Charlton Heston, Jack Lemmon, and George C. Scott, so I told myself I was being stupid. And even if I didn't become a Scott or Flynn, I was way ahead of where I'd been when I had Peaches in my lap.

The doubts evaporated. I was beginning to feel as if I'd just caught a long bomb for a touchdown.

Lew emerged triumphant, a price agreed upon: a whopping $250 dollars a week. Less the agent's commission. Although I felt uncomfortable with the low figure, Lew said that it was more than the other actors on the lot had gotten to start. At least I understood now why Benson was so effusive in his praise: it was free. Also, it kept the price down. It was hard to refuse a man who had just given you a rave review.

Not that any of that mattered. What was important was that I was in. I had a studio. I also had a new name: Adam West. There already was a "Bronco" Billy Anderson (he was the first movie cowboy) and, besides, Benson and Foy thought that my middle name would make a more memorable surname, especially since westerns were all the rage. As for Adam, I just liked how it looked with West. The name stuck to me quickly, though my family and good friends continued to call me Bill (and still do.)

Benson called an assistant, a lovely young woman, to show me around, and I walked a little taller as I met some of my fellow contract players—Roger Moore, Efrem Zimbalist, Jr., Bob Conrad, Jim Garner, and Connie Stevens.

Roger had just come over from England, where he had starred in a short-lived adventure series, *Ivanhoe*. As soon as he signed with Warners, they put him in another short-lived adventure series, called *The Alaskans*. After that, he put in a season as Beauregard Maverick on

Maverick. Roger was a lot of fun, a little more jaded than I (he *was* a year older) but with a droll sense of humor and a fondness for bad jokes and barbershop philosophy.

I didn't get to know Efrem that well. He was a quiet and sophisticated man, genuinely nice and about ten years my senior. Also, he had a hit series, his first, *77 Sunset Strip,* which kept him pretty busy. (Ironically, as I write this, he's providing the voice for Alfred on Fox's animated *Batman* series. Is it a small world, or is Gotham just a big town?)

Bob Conrad was several years my junior and busy with his show, *Hawaiian Eye.* He had a raucous sense of humor and the girls loved him; he had guys hanging around him just to catch the runoff.

Jim Garner was a real pleasure. His *Maverick* was a smash, but success hadn't gone to his head. He was hardworking, generous with fellow actors (unless they were too rough with the stunt crew, with whom he was very *simpático*), and affable with fans. The only thing that got him really riled was when the studio tried to take advantage of him or any of his coworkers. If the executives pushed too hard, Jim was always right in their faces, pushing back. Fame never mattered to him as much as dignity.

I would have loved to get to know Connie Stevens better, but the former Concetta Rosalie Ann Ingolia was tight with Eddie Fisher. Besides, Connie was kept busy being *Hawaiian Eye*'s goofy photographer Cricket Blake and working in the recording studio, singing with Edd "Kookie" Byrnes (on "Kookie, Kookie, Lend Me Your Comb") and other stars before going solo.

But I liked my colleagues, and discovered how important it was to be able to fraternize with fellow actors, writers, and directors. When you sign as a studio contract player, you come when you're needed. Some weeks I worked every day; a few weeks I didn't work at all. But I was there most of the time, talking to other actors, learning what they'd done and hoped to do, listening to old-timers, and getting the kind of education you don't get in schools. There were organized actors workshops, which I never missed, and when other actors weren't working, we'd meet at the studio, sit under the warm sun, and explore Shakespeare and Shaw and Tennessee Williams. It was like a college campus we were being paid to attend.

I also had to earn my paycheck.

The first project I did after being signed by Warner Brothers was an episode of *Colt 45*. Its star was the late Wayde Preston, who played tall, gunslinging cowboy Christopher Colt. I was that sniveling cavalry deserter and would-be rapist whose threats and apologies had won me my contract here. It was a choice part, a dramatic beginning for me, and I was going to make it count. But it wasn't easy.

Little did I know that our director, Lee "Roll'm" Sholem, the speediest director on the lot, would take such a personal interest in the new kid.

"West," he said, "when I yell 'Cut!' I don't care where you are or what you're doing, you freeze. Got it?"

I said sure. I was eager to do well and just as eager to please.

We were filming out of sequence and about to shoot the climactic fight where the hero knocks me into a lake. I was going to do the four-foot fall myself; no problem for a guy fresh from the Hawaiian surf.

"Roll'm" had me knocked into the lake eight times: each time I was in mid-fall, he'd yell cut. He'd give me hell in front of everybody because I didn't stop when he said to, then send me struggling back up the muddy bank. He'd wait impatiently while I poured the water from my boots, and watch as I got the stuffing knocked out of me some more.

This, as it turned out, was my hazing. When I found out that was why "Roll'm" had given me a rough time, I had a good laugh. He later told me that one of the reasons he'd felt frustrated directing the *Superman* show with George Reeves was that they used an ensemble cast, and victims were few and far between. Wasn't it nice I could make him happy.

During my first year at Warner Brothers, I worked almost every day and guest-starred in most of the series the studio was producing: *Hawaiian Eye, Maverick, 77 Sunset Strip, Sugarfoot*, and others. In 1959, I made an hour-long TV pilot of my own, *The Frontier World of Doc Holliday*, inspired by the success of *Gunfight at the O.K. Corral* two years before. Actually, I thought it carried the vogue of the realistic adult western too far. Holliday was a dentist and a drunk who suffered from tuberculosis, and though it didn't happen this way in history, our show opened with a nice dramatic hook: Holliday being told by a doctor that he had six months to live. The way Holliday saw it, since he was going to die anyway, he might as well ride around doing good, killing anyone who tried to stop him. They had me drinking a lot, and I came up with this miserable, consumptive cough for the character. We used to joke that if I kissed my horse on this show, he'd keel over dead.

The series was supposed to be given a big send-off as an episode of *Cheyenne*, and I was promoted to Madison Avenue as a "traditional western star, tall and good-looking, suggesting great strength and good breeding." Obviously they hadn't bothered to look at the show. ABC concluded that the series would be too grim and off-putting to any sponsor (except one who was selling cough medicine), and they decided not to run with it.

I don't know if anyone's done a study of pilots, but I believe that *The Frontier World of Doc Holliday* marked the beginning of my career as the most piloted actor in history: thirteen to date, with three more that actually made it onto the air as series. I know Richard Crenna's done a lot, and Marty Landau,. and Lassie did a few . . . but I still think that I hold the record.

Despite my disappointment at not getting a series, the numerous TV roles I did were good experience. They allowed me to play a variety of characters and forced me to learn to work quickly. In and out of a character's head in a few days, tops. I've seldom had the luxury of developing a character without time pressure.

My disappointment was short-lived: that same year I got my first film, *The Young Philadelphians*, in which Paul Newman and Barbara Rush played an ambitious lawyer and his high-society girlfriend. Though we're contemporaries, I played Paul's rotten stepfather in a flashback.

Paul's work on the film was an inspiration to me. He was very intense and professional, and he was generous with whomever he was playing opposite. His commitment helped make us all look good, and I was surprised to learn from one of the costars that he wasn't happy with the script or the film. In fact, he wasn't happy with Warner Brothers, period. At first I was taken aback to hear that this rocket-hot star who was making prestigious films was disgruntled. Then I learned that his salary was around $25,000 a film, even when the studio loaned him out for three times that (banking the difference). Considering the success of pictures like *Somebody Up There Likes Me*, *The Long, Hot Summer*, and *Cat on a Hot Tin Roof*, I couldn't really blame him for being upset.

And just a few months after *The Young Philadelphians* opened, Paul coughed up a half-million dollars to buy out the remaining three years of his contract. It proved to be a good investment: he got nearly a quarter-million dollars for his next film, *Sweet Bird of Youth,* and never looked back.

I was still relatively happy to be getting my $250 a week, but I have to admit that Paul's example made a big impression on me. I began to wonder how I'd do on my own.

It didn't take me long to find out.

WHEN THE contract with Warners came along, I moved my young family from Hawaii to a cottage in Hollywood, on Fountain Avenue. It was a great little place, and a terrific location. We had film people as neighbors, mostly writers, and it was an exciting, creative time.

A fine character actor lived next door, Regis Toomey, who was sixty-odd years old and a veteran of such classics as *Meet John Doe, Spellbound, Show Boat,* and *Guys and Dolls.* Our families often had dinner together, and he was both helpful and encouraging. I'd tell him what I'd studied in the workshops, and he'd tell me what would and wouldn't work in the "reel" world. He also told me which directors to watch out for, what they liked to see, and whom never to cross.

One thing Regis reminded me of over and over again was that this was a fickle business, especially where leading men were concerned. You could be hot one day, ice the next. You could be cold one day, and suddenly your look is "in" and you're on top of the world.

"It's also cruel," he would tell me, shaking his head. "The studios are loyal as long as you enhance their hand. When they don't need you, you're discarded."

I wondered if Regis had been tapping my agent's phone. Not long after *The Frontier World of Doc Holliday* failed to sell, my contract was not renewed. Warner Brothers provided a lot of programming for ABC, and when the studio swung and missed, creative heads rolled. In this case, I took the fall for Holliday. They figured I'd made a bad impression on the network and they'd never want to see me in anything again. (ABC, of course, is where *Batman* ended up.)

I was given one day's notice. I was dismayed: I realized that I loved the constant flow of work and wondered if I could be as prodigious as a free-lancer. And I liked the steady check, small as it was. I was also concerned about being dormant for too long. Would I get rusty and fearful? My agent was confident I could cut it on my own, but you never know.

Free-lancing turned out to be quite an adventure. My agent and I had decided that my résumé was full enough of run-of-the-mill adventures and melodramas and that I should hold out for some light comedy or solid drama. Unfortunately, at that time the industry was hit with a long, drawn-out writers strike, which made work scarce. I wasn't able to turn down anything that would enable me to support my family. I did episodic TV at various studios, I did bit parts in movies, and I did commercials, including one for Kellogg's that won an award at the Irish Film Festival in Cork. I also did some regional theater to keep my acting muscles in shape. But that paid very little and I didn't get to do as much of it as I'd have liked.

I also went to a lot of parties, my agent having convinced me that that was the way for a free-lancer to become known by directors, casting agents, and stars. I've always disliked large show-biz parties, because everyone who's there has come either to impress or be feted. In a land of acting, this is where some of the best and worst and most important performances are given.

However, there are always people who don't play the game, and one in particular stands out in my memory: Gary Cooper. I only met him once, at a party thrown by a producer in the Hollywood Hills, but no one before or since has impressed me as much as he did.

Of course he stood tall and had charisma and was a Star. You knew that just from watching him on the screen. What you didn't know was that he was also a fine gentleman.

We both happened to be standing nearly shoulder to shoulder at one point, talking to no one, when he turned to me and offered his hand.

"Hi. Gary Cooper."

I felt honored. I shook his hand and smiled.

"Adam West. It's a pleasure to meet you, Mr. Cooper."

"You're not a native," he said and smiled.

"How can you tell?"

"You look like you'd rather be sitting on a hilltop somewhere, taking in the scenery."

I laughed and we talked about our backgrounds. I was surprised to learn that he didn't grow up on a ranch but was the son of a state supreme court judge, had been educated in England, and had come to Los Angeles to be a political cartoonist. We talked for about a half hour, about horses, about cartoonist Thomas Nast, and about politics, without ever once mentioning movies, and he seemed very happy about that. When he died just over a year later, at the age of sixty, I felt as if I'd lost a patron saint. Certainly Hollywood had lost one of its class acts.

I saw Natalie again at another party. I wasn't exactly the conquering hero I'd vowed to be, but she seemed happy to see me—once I reminded her who I was. I asked how Raymond was.

"Things have cooled," she said.

I couldn't resist: "Burrrrrr," I said, shivering.

She looked at me strangely, then went to get a drink.

6

I N 1962 I played the role of the good-guy cavalry officer in *Geronimo,* with Chuck Connors as the Native American warrior, blue eyes and all. We shot the film in Mexico, something that's always cause for celebration by the locals because it puts money in the local economy. They respond with fiestas for the cast and crew, and they really went to town the night we wrapped up production.

There was one absolutely gorgeous young lady at that party, with the sweetest face and smoothest skin I've ever seen, and I started dancing with her early in the evening. Around about the fourth dance, one couple took to the floor of the outdoor café and came whirling in our direction. I was only vaguely aware of them, dazzled as I was by my partner's big brown eyes, until I felt a sharp pain in my arm. I looked to my left, saw the male half of the new couple glaring at me, then saw blood on the sleeve of my jacket.

The guy had stabbed me. Talk about cutting in.

My dancing partner was unaware that anything had happened, and I wasn't sure how badly I was hurt. Rather than make a stand and have every man in the village try to get himself a piece of gringo, I moved away with my partner, dancing and bleeding, until I was near the exit. Excusing myself, I walked through the gate to the street. A quick backward glance and I saw my attacker and three other men leave their partners and push through the crowded floor in my direction.

It was like a scene from an Alfred Hitchcock film. What do you do in a case like this?

There were no cast members or crewmen nearby, and even if there had been, I didn't know if they'd be sober enough or stupid enough to help. All I knew was that if I stuck around, I'd end up like a piñata the day after Christmas.

Running along the dark street, the underside of my left arm wet with blood, I felt like Bernardo in *West Side Story*. I turned a corner and looked for a place to hide. I had my choice of a darkened door-way or a tortilla wagon full of steaming corn tortillas. I

As the young detective sidekick, Steve Nelson, in *The Detectives*, starring the late Robert Taylor

ran for the latter. I didn't know where the owner was, nor did I care as I shut the lid and held my breath.

You can't hear much with a layer of tortillas over your ears, and I lay there for several minutes, catching my breath, hoping the bad guys would go away. Suddenly the lid flew open and a young woman looked in: it was Maria, one of the makeup ladies from the film.

I'd expected a take-out order or a machete.

"Señor West," she said with some passion, "are you all right?"

I told her what had happened.

"Oh, that was Pedro," she said, "and you were dancing with his property. He owns the local brothel."

With an eye on the future, I told her I was sorry and asked if she would relay my regrets to Pedro. She said that he wouldn't listen, and I should come with her. I didn't need a second invitation.

She helped me climb from the tortilla wagon, and I followed her to her small room down the street. I showered, she dressed my wound, and once again I discovered that the kindness of strangers is interna-tional. It wasn't an altogether unpleasant night, and the next day I was due at the airport for the flight back to L.A. It was an interesting end to my heroic pursuit of Geronimo, and preferable to what the dour Pedro had in mind.

Geronimo was not a great film, but the producers of the TV series *The Detectives* were impressed enough with my performance to make me a costar on the Robert Taylor series. The show had been on for two seasons and was expanding to an hour, in color, and I was hired to play plainclothes detective Sgt. Steve Nelson.

Taylor was fifty at the time, with a long movie career behind him. The former Spangler Arlington Brugh was a fine if formal gentleman who didn't socialize much with his fellow actors. Though he was utterly professional, I got the feeling that he didn't enjoy the show much. His own MGM movie contract had not been renewed, and with nothing else in the offing, he'd turned to TV to pay the bills. There's nothing wrong with that, of course, though he seemed to resent having gone from costarring with Jean Harlow and Joan Crawford and Katharine Hepburn to uttering weekly variations of "Hold it right there!" and "Put your hands up!" It's unfortunate how, with just a few different blips along the way, a leading man like Gary Cooper can continue to get top-drawer movies until the end, while someone like Robert Taylor doesn't.

Still, I learned a lot about acting from Robert Taylor, and about acting for the close-up camera in particular. I also learned more about the silences. He taught me how not saying or showing things gives the viewer's imagination a chance to fill in the emotional painting. We did thirty segments before we were canceled.

The roles kept coming, a few good, most middling, some terrible. In 1963 I supported Sandra Dee and Peter Fonda in *Tammy and the Doctor* and had a small role as Captain Blekeley in *Soldier in the Rain,* starring Steve McQueen and Jackie Gleason. My name didn't make the posters of either film. I was also the star of a not-bad little film called *Mara of the Wilderness,* in which I raise a little girl who spent her early years growing up in the wilds.

My best role during this period was on a show that has since become a cult favorite, *The Outer Limits.* I starred with Rudy Solari in an episode called "The Invisible Enemy," which we shot during the fall of 1964. It was about astronauts stranded on Mars with dragons living under the sandy surface, trying to consume us. Considering how little time and money we had to make the show, veteran science fiction director Byron Haskin (*War of the Worlds*) created a nice, *Jaws*-like tension that still plays very well.

I moved up, sort of, in a 1964 film which I also think holds up well today: the science fiction adventure *Robinson Crusoe on Mars*. This time I was killed in a crash-landing on Mars in the very first reel, though I did get to come back as the walking dead in Crusoe's nightmare later in the film. (Critics who have called my Batman work deadpan obviously never saw me in that film. Trust me: it isn't easy playing a zombie who has to convey feelings.) I was fourth-billed this time, behind Paul Mantee (Robinson), Vic Lundin (Friday), and Mona the monkey. In fairness to Mona, she did manage to live through the entire film.

That film was followed by more pilots, including *Johnny Cinderella, Rio,* and one that may well be the worst hour of TV in history: *Alexander the Great,* an epic dramatization of the Battle of Issus between the Greeks and the Persians in 333 B.C. I costarred as the wine-, women-, and song-loving Cleander to Bill Shatner's more upright Alexander, and the show was so bad that it sat on a shelf until January 1968, when the two of us were sufficiently well known to guarantee some kind of audience. The script was so thin that we had little to do other than ride our gorgeous Arabian stallions at the head of an army, pop a lot of grapes, and watch heavily made-up belly dancers at what were supposed to be orgies in our command tent. Joseph Cotten costarred as Antigonus, Simon Oakland was Attalos, and John Cassavetes was Karonos. During the nine endless weeks in a desert outside of Saint George, Utah, the wonderfully free-spirited John was also my drinking buddy in the one-bar motel; even then, he was cursing about the "vandals/sharks/cannibals" (it changed from day to day) "who run things in Hollywood," and was busy making plans to shoot affecting low-budget movies his own way, which of course he did.

Things got a notch better in 1965, when I starred with the Three Stooges in *The Outlaws Is Coming*. I played Kenneth Cabot, a straitlaced Boston newspaper editor and conservationist who heads out west with his printers (guess who?) to help save the buffalo. We end up being shot at by every gunslinger in the west, though, fortunately, Annie Oakley (the stunning Nancy Kovack) is there to help us. Though Moe and

Larry were both in their late sixties, Moe in particular had the energy, enthusiasm, and creative passion of a man one-third his age. He was a real take-charge guy, bursting with ideas . . . and humor. The day we finished, he announced to the cast and crew that the wrap party would be at his house that night. And what was on the menu? Buffalo barbecue. Joe DeRita, who was the third Stooge at the time, was in his mid-fifties and the kid of the bunch. He was the sweetest, gentlest man I've ever met, though he insisted that he wasn't really docile, it was just all those hits on the head he'd taken during his career. . . . That's why I was delighted to be asked to speak on the day Curly, Larry and Moe were awarded their star on the Hollywood Walk of Fame. There was a large, enthusiastic crowd and a lot of press hosted by a *Batman* alumnus, the talented Gary Owens. They seemed to love my remarks, which only attests to the continued popularity of our dear departed Stooges.

That same year I played a villain on *The Big Valley* and got to work with one of the great ladies of American film, Barbara Stanwyck. Ms. Stanwyck was lively, professional, and no-nonsense. In fact, never before or since have I seen a star's personality so completely define the personality of the set. There were smiles but no horsing around (except for the horses), and nobody showed up late. I remember in particular my death scene on the long stairway at the Barkley home: she was so totally involved and supportive that it brought out the best in me. Unlike Robert Taylor, she never gave me the feeling that television was merely a stepchild to movies. Everything Ms. Stanwyck did mattered to her. And, I might add, even late in her career she was one of the most attractive women I've ever met. She had a warm laugh and a wonderful, zestful manner.

7

A S MY career was picking up steam, my marriage was losing it. I was away too much on locations and—déjà vu—my wife had met someone who gave her the attention and love she needed and deserved. She, Jonelle, and Hunter remained in a house in Tarzana I had bought for them, and I moved into a beach apartment at Malibu. On my own again, my life became consumed with work. One frequently looks back and realizes that there were more important things in life. But it was difficult to balance auditions with Little League games and socializing with movers-and-shakers with ballet school recitals. It doesn't matter which one would rather do; it's always agonizing for a divorced father trying to deal with the demands of ambition in a tough profession.

At least I spent any free time I had with my children, and I was in touch with them every day. In fact—isn't it always the way?—I ended up spending more concentrated time with them now than when I was married. We remain very close to this day.

I have a nostalgic fondness for the six years I lived in the Malibu apartment, in an old Mediterranean-style mansion on the beach. I had about one-fourth of the house, and it opened onto the ocean, where I took daily swims with my German shepherd Stormy. My landlord, Sy Salkowitz, was a writer, and it was his job to collect rent for the owner of the building, actress June Havoc, the sister of Gypsy Rose Lee. June had been smart: while she was earning money, she put it into real estate, buying buildings and even an entire town, Cannon Crossing, in Connecticut. When the parts dried up, the rentals were still rolling in.

In those days, Malibu was uncrowded and a lot of fun. It wasn't tacky, a house on every square foot of beachfront; it didn't reek of new money, just mystique, a sense of fun and freedom and youth. Lee Marvin lived on one side of me, and the clothing designer Jean Louis lived on the other. Lee and I had some rollicking good times together, though I managed to cause Jean Louis some heartache. Or rather, Stormy did. My male shepherd was a big animal, well over two feet high at the shoulder, but he was actually the sweetest dog I ever owned. I had taught him to bodysurf along with me, and he enjoyed digging in the sand, both of which caused him to grow exceptionally strong.

Madame Jean Louis owned two small male pugs, and they were truly pugnacious and aggressive little dogs. One afternoon, my big sweetheart of a dog washed in on a wave before me, exciting the two pugs so much that they broke loose from the patio where they were tied. As my shepherd shook the salt water from his coat, the two tough, furry rockets blindsided him. He went down and the sand flew. I shouted to him as I hurried toward the shore, but it was no use: he made quick work of the two pugs, and by the time I arrived, he was already burying them in the sand. I turned and swam slowly toward Japan.

I was a social outcast for many weeks, though privately, Sy and Lee approved. The pugs were noisy little things, and quiet reigned until Madame Louis got two new ones. She also got stronger leashes.

Things got a little slow in Hollywood. *Alexander the Great* had been defeated, *The Outer Limits* was gone, and poor *Robinson Crusoe on Mars* was getting mostly kiddie matinee bookings. I did a few commercials to pay the rent, including several James Bond parodies for Nestle; these were fun, and more important than I knew at the time.

Taking stock of things, I realized I'd done some good work of late, though not in the kind of studio-driven attention-getting vehicles on which careers are built. In Hollywood, it's important to be part of a commercial success. Otherwise, it's doubly difficult. I hadn't had a hit, even a small one, and that was discouraging.

The so-called spaghetti westerns were starting to boil in Italy and Spain, and I decided to go to Rome to try and wrangle an audition for a film Lew had heard about and knew I'd be right for. I checked into a small *pensione* near the Parco Borghese, in quarters that required me to walk up six flights of marble stairs to my small room with a bed. But that didn't discourage me: I was in love with *la dolce vita* and determined to make it as an overseas cowboy.

Through Lew, I found an agent who arranged a meeting for me with the director, and within a month I found myself starring in *Los Quattros Implacables*. We shot the film in Italy and in Spain, and it was a lot of fun. I spoke my lines in English, the rest of the cast members spoke in Italian or Spanish, and it was all fixed in the dubbing. In fact, acting that way isn't as difficult as you might think: these films rely a lot on the posturing of the actors, and it's easier to react to that than to some of the English dialogue I've had to speak.

The one event from that time that really stands out in my memory occurred when we were shooting the last scene. The director had scheduled it for last because it involved dynamite: I suppose they were thinking that if they blew me up, they could still finish the film. As it turned out, the explosion went off just fine. In fact, the director got a far more dramatic shot than he'd bargained for. I was riding along a dry riverbed, toward the cave the special effects crew had rigged to blow up. When the dynamite went off, a leathery black cloud swept over me as thousands of bats hurtled out of their home. As the cameras captured the swarm, with me in the foreground, I reared my horse to a stop and watched as the creatures moved swiftly this way and that, scattering frantically into the daylight.

It was to be the last shot I did before playing the role of Batman. The symbolism was chilling and strange. All Bruce Wayne had was one bat flying in through a window. I had a caveful.

Doing this movie was an exotic experience in many ways. There was one memorable night in Madrid when I went to an extremely popular hangout where the stars came to listen to hot new bands. I chanced to meet actor Keefe Brasselle, who had become a producer and was in Spain scouting for locations.

As we were sitting there having a few drinks, who should take the stage to thunderous applause but a drop-dead blonde Keefe said was Doris Day. I hadn't heard she was in town, but naturally I trusted the word of a man who'd insisted on buying the drinks, and I assumed she was probably here filming a sweet romance.

Doris began singing and I fell in lust. She was in fine voice, poised and beautiful and wearing a clinging dress, her silver-blond hair shimmering in the light. I thought the screen didn't do her justice; I couldn't take my eyes off her.

52   ADAM WEST

And she couldn't take hers off me. Every song was meant for me. Every emotional moment was breathlessly caressed by her voice and sent my way. I was the luckiest man in old Madrid.

When her set was finished, I asked Doris to join me for a drink, and smiling like a real buddy, Keefe delicately excused himself. There was very little talk, just a lot of eye contact, and after we'd drained our glasses Doris and I went back to my suite at the Plaza Towers.

We had a few more drinks. The flickering lights of the city behind us delicately brushed her skin with a soft pink glow. Then we kissed. Her mouth was hungry. Her breathing became tiny explosions of desire. She suggested we go to the bedroom. She murmured, "It's never happened like this. Our passion will have no boundaries, no limits . . . "

I didn't need a second invitation. She went in ahead of me. Her dress fell to the floor. She slipped into bed and I followed. This enchanting delicate nymph was mine. My busy hands roamed from her arm to her back to her waist—and then to a shocking reality.

I had passionately caressed a cold, hard plastic cup. I leapt out of bed swearing.

"What's wrong?" she cooed.

"Who the hell *are* you?" I was shaking.

"I thought you knew, you rogue." She seemed hurt and surprised. She told me who she was. Or he did. Or both.

My Doris was a hermaphrodite who taught scuba diving as a man by day and went out as a woman by night. She said she sang at that nightclub regularly and that Keefe knew who she was; she thought he'd told me.

I said he hadn't, and after pouring myself a drink, sitting down, and trying to get over my embarrassment, I confess I became curious about this strange person. We talked for most of the night, and I heard a fascinating life story. I occasionally wonder what happened to Doris. I have a bittersweet vision of him still singing in that cellar by night, older in body but still young in spirit, still searching for an affair "with no boundaries, no limits."

Los Quattros Implacables was a hit overseas and did all right in the U.S. as *The Relentless Four*. As a result, I was offered several other foreign films of the same genre.

I felt good about that. The Italians treated me with respect, the fans in Europe had a reputation for being loyal, the pictures had good production values (even if the scripts were on the thin side), and the money was good. I was inclined to accept. Other actors were going abroad: not just Clint, but the likes of Nick Adams and Russ Tamblyn, who went to Japan to appear in science fiction films, and Jeffrey Hunter and Lee Van Cleef, who were also doing spaghetti westerns. The drawback, of course, was that once you left Hollywood it was tough to return. European commercial films don't count for much here. And actors who do them can lose status at home.

But that was Hollywood's problem, not mine. I enjoyed getting out in the morning, working with people I liked, and seeing my work on the big screen.

Before I had made a definite commitment, though, I felt I needed to return to California and spend time with my kids. They always had a cleansing effect on my soul: their love was pure, and I needed that. We all do, I think. Children don't ask us to be anything but what we are, and their honesty and affection would help me make decisions best for all of us.

I hadn't been home for more than a few days when my agent told me that it was a good thing I'd come back. Some people at 20th Century-Fox were interested in talking to me about an unusual new project for TV. They had seen my Nestle commercials and thought I might be someone who could play the title role in *Batman*.

My initial reaction was lukewarm. As a child, I'd loved the comic books, but I felt that playing Batman would be a dumb move for someone who aspired to a career as a serious actor, and that an athlete would be better suited for the part, someone with buns of steel.

Lew argued that I should check it out. "This could be an opportunity for you." He reminded me of a picture he'd once seen, *Jason and the Argonauts,* in which a non-body-builder actor named Nigel Green had made the best screen Hercules ever.

I agreed to think about it.

After I hung up, I began to chew on those images from my childhood. I remembered the bat flying in Bruce Wayne's window, giving him the idea for his new identity, and the Joker shooting at Batman, who ran boldly toward him, taunting him at the last second about the bulletproof vest he was wearing.

I began to feel some interest. How many people get the chance to play a hero that is a part of our cultural heritage, that influenced two generations of American readers?

I went out and bought a bunch of the comic books and read them. Batman had changed from the two-fisted vampiric figure I remembered. He was now a combination of James Bond and acrobat Karl Wallenda, but I was intrigued. How would I play a character who has two lives, one of them staid and conservative, the other colorful and violent? How would the whole comic book medium translate to live action on film, using up-to-date film techniques and special effects?

I began to cook with the idea of creating a Batman. I managed to be optimistic. I told myself this could be even more exciting than spaghetti westerns or working with a chimp in a hula skirt.

I called Lew back and said okay: let's talk to the folks at Fox.

8

FOR DOZIER, deciding who would play Batman was relatively easy. Getting Batman on television wasn't.

Early in 1965, Harve Bennett (who would later produce several *Star Trek* films) was in charge of West Coast Development for ABC. The 7:30 time slot was when most network affiliates began airing prime-time programming, but it's also a time when kids control the dial. Then, as now, someone who could create a show that children and adults would all enjoy might have a gold mine.

Harve thought a comic strip character would be a good bet to capture a broad demographic; after all, that's what they did in the funny pages. He told New York–based Edgar Scherick, Director of Programming, that they should do *Dick Tracy,* and Scherick agreed. But the price was too high, and in what may have been a peremptory strike, deeper-pocketed NBC got *Dick Tracy,* and then did nothing with it.

Harve, Edgar, and their staffs were understandably disappointed. Then one of Scherick's coworkers, Yale Udoff, suggested they go after a favorite of his, *Batman.* Scherick thought that was a little *too* far-out, but Doug Cramer, who was the director of development and a fancier of pop art, disagreed. He thought *Batman* was a great idea. Scherick came around, network boss Thomas Moore got behind it, and ABC obtained the rights from DC Comics, which was called National Periodical Publications at the time.

The ABC team decided to do *Batman* as a twice-weekly series and approached 20th Century-Fox to produce it. That made sense: Fox was already producing the twice-weekly *Peyton Place* for the network and had shown they could make those kinds of maddening deadlines. They also had experience with big shows, like *Voyage to the Bottom of the Sea.* Fox's head of TV, William Self, who had cut his teeth as a producer on *The Twilight Zone,* was one of the forces responsible for running that tight ship, and he met with the network in New York in spring of 1965. Self dropped the project in the lap of Fox producer Dozier, who had never read a comic book in his life and was horrified. Then he was intrigued. He told me once that his first thought was to hire his friend mystery novelist Eric Ambler to write the show, but Ambler wasn't interested. (I suspect, though, that he would have done an interesting *Batman.* Have a look at the novels featuring his sleuth Dr. Jan Czissar of the Prague Police. Czissar goes to London to work with Scotland Yard, and while he may be in an alien environment, he puts his fingerprints all over the London force.)

Dozier had worked with writer Lorenzo Semple, Jr., on his ill-fated *Charlie Chan* pilot, and that summer, after reluctantly giving up on Ambler, he went to Spain to get Semple to write *Batman.* Dozier doesn't remember at what point he came up with the idea to do the show as a lampoon comedy, but he once said it grew out of his embarrassment from being seen on airplanes with the comic books in his briefcase. I never understood the loathing he had for the medium (but not for comic strips or pulp fiction). He never explained it to me. Maybe he didn't like people thinking he enjoyed looking at what he considered kid stuff.

In any case, Lorenzo ran with Dozier's vision and put his own spin on it. Meanwhile, back in Hollywood, Dozier and FitzSimons began working out the technical aspects of the show. What kind of fabrics photographed best? Should the Batcave be big and bright or small and claustrophobic? Should the Batmobile be sporty or tanklike? They also had to worry about lighting: most people still had black-and-white sets, and what looked great in color might look terrible in black and white. The tilted-angle shots were also a problem because the cameras we were using were big and clumsy, and special rigs had to be built to accommodate them.

I came on the scene after most of these decisions had already been made. But there was still room for input, and I had a lot to say in those early days. I really never had the time to get into story ideas and casting, but Dozier always listened when I had thoughts about my own character.

Over the years, I've read articles written by pundits and heard from viewers who assumed that when I got the part of Batman, I was fitted for the suit and went out there and winged it.

It's a comic book character, right? Just read the word balloons and collect your paycheck.

No. The same kind of preparation and concentration that goes into any role was essential in playing Batman. If you don't have a point of view, if you haven't developed a character, if you lack an attitude, you can't go back and do the role the same way day after day. There'll be no consistency. Whether you're playing Captain Bligh or Captain America, you won't be able to pick up a scene where you left off. And Batman required an emotional honesty.

Almost every actor I've known does some kind of research before starting a role. Though it was tight between the time I got the part in late September and the time when shooting was to begin, on October 20, I wanted to try and figure out what kind of man we were dealing with here. Obviously, Bruce Wayne was scarred as a child seeing a thug, Joe Chill (not the Joker), kill his parents during a robbery attempt. But what do you *do* with that? The origin wasn't going to be shown in the series, perhaps not even alluded to. Besides, the show was going to be villain-driven and action/comedy-heavy. There wouldn't be time or a situation to use Bruce Wayne's massive trauma in the characterization. You couldn't stop the action and have Batman say, "I never had a puppy when I was a child."

I took a look at the first episode of *Superman*, in which George Reeves lost one set of parents and then his adoptive father. By the time he got to Metropolis, he was a well-adjusted Clark Kent, eager to please as a reporter, determined to do right as Superman, and sparring confidently with Lois Lane.

In other words, George pretty much ignored his suffering, though he was an excellent actor with a remarkably compassionate face. He did a great job registering the pain of his loss in one early scene.

Still, even though I couldn't use the childhood trauma, I needed some kind of characterization. I flipped through the comic books but didn't find much (as it turned out, I wasn't looking at them the right way) so I screened chapters of the two movie serials: *Batman*, made in 1943 and starring Lewis Wilson, and *Batman and Robin*, made in 1949 and starring Robert Lowery. Unfortunately, both films were cut from the rock 'em–sock 'em serial cloth and weren't much help. Messrs. Wilson and Lowery played the part pretty much the same steely way most serial heroes were played.

I decided to read novels that scraped around inside the heads of characters who maintained dual identities, such as *The Scarlet Pimpernel* and *Scaramouche*. I was a bit alarmed when I found the villain of the latter piece, the Marquis de la Tour D'Azyr, more interesting than the hero, due to his clever repartee and icy cruelness. I began to realize that whatever I did on the show, the villains were invariably going to be more interesting.

I poked through *Don Quixote* to see what Cervantes had to say about the differences between the mad hero and his sane alter ego, Alonso Quijano. The common thread in all of these stories was that the heroes were in some way liberated by the costume or uniform, like an actor wearing makeup. That was something: even though Batman was the serious crimefighter, he could be played looser, physically and emotionally, than Bruce Wayne.

The only nonfiction book I had time to read was the marvelous *The Great Comic Book Heroes,* in which author Jules Feiffer psychoanalyzed the appeal of the hero and figured he would have a pretty healthy ego: Batman naturally assumed that he could dish out more pain than someone else could give him. A touch of arrogance. That was nice. I could play it with a touch of smugness, a bit tongue-in-cheek. (Feiffer also made one important point that I passed along to our executive producer: artist Bob Kane drew the strip in an extremely cinematic fashion. Weird angles, bird's-eye views, iris shots, forced perspective. It turns out that that had also occurred to Bill Dozier—I don't think he'd read Feiffer's book—and it was the approach he'd instructed his set designers, lighting people, and director of photography to take.)

And, of course, I talked at length to Bob Kane, a charming man who had first come up with the idea for Batman when he was thirteen. He sold it five years later, in 1939, a year after Superman single-handedly created the superhero comic book genre. Kane told me what his influences were: Douglas Fairbanks's 1920 film *The Mark of Zorro;* the 1930 film *The Bat Whispers,* in which Chester Morris played a detective and a bat-masked killer; the pulp magazine hero the Shadow, who skulked around in a cloak and slouch hat; and Leonardo da Vinci's drawings of a batlike flying machine.

I looked at the movies, read a few *Shadow*s, and came away with very little—other than respect for the teenager who'd been clever enough to synthesize a whole that was greater than the sum of these parts.

So where was I? Not where I wanted to be. I had some good ideas, but as yet no really solid point of view.

In my radio days, I'd read somewhere that composer Frederic Chopin used to write a musical passage, work on it over and over, change notes here and there—and after hours, sometimes days, of struggle, invariably put the music back the way he'd written it in the first place.

In a sense, I realized I had to do the same. I decided to go back to Batman as he had first been written and presented to the public, the Batman of the comic books. Only this time, I didn't look for what made Batman tick. I looked for what made the entire strip work, not just in the art but in the scripts.

I read the comic books carefully: old ones from the 1940s, and new ones. I made a list of traits or themes that recurred, and ended up with six of them:

1. Batman freely, and without hesitation, risks his life for the underdog. It really doesn't matter whether that comes from a need to punish every criminal as if he were Joe Chill, the desire to prevent someone else from suffering a loss like his, or both. *He's always there in the line of fire.*

2. His adventures, especially the early ones, are set in the urban jungle, often among the downtrodden, which gives many of the tales a Dickensian flavor. That means you've got to reach kids and adults with the same performance.

3. Billy Batson needs the mystical word "Shazam!" to become Captain Marvel (which didn't work for the rest of us); Peter Parker had to be bitten by a radioactive spider to become Spider-Man; and if you weren't an Amazon from Paradise Island, you couldn't become Wonder Woman. But Batman is as plausible as a superhero can be, and in the world of the comic strip that would carry certain responsibilities. Batman would know that there are kids out there doing their push-ups and studying chemistry, who think they can grow up to be like him. So

he is always on his best behavior. You can be sure that the hurt kid in him doesn't ever want to disappoint other kids.

4. Clothes help to make the man, and Batman's costume helps make him a hit with readers. Cold, stony blue and gray, lots of sharp, dangerous lines (pointy ears, ribbed cape, scalloped gloves, knife-edged cowl), and a dynamic symbol on his chest. Most superheroes wear garish reds and blues and yellows, and strike Mr. Universe poses. That's not Batman. He's a creature of the night, at home in the shadows, a bit of the vampire in him. Crooks see Plastic Man or Aquaman, they've got to wonder if the circus is in town. Crooks see Batman, they quake in their boots. I had to make Batman believe he was frightening and give him a touch of mystery. And, at the same time, he had to be funny.

5. Like Sherlock Holmes or Simon Templar, Batman's a detective. He's got a good mind. He's always thinking and analyzing, maybe at the expense of his emotional health.

6. He's blessed (or cursed) with the most memorable rogues' gallery this side of Dick Tracy. The Joker, the Riddler, Catwoman, and the Penguin are nearly as well known as Batman himself, and even the second-stringers are fun. There's always someone flamboyant for him to play off. As a result, he has to be low-key. There has to be a balance.

All of these points were important to me. Together with Feiffer's observations and the idea of the costume as a liberating factor, they formed the basis of my characterization—which, fortunately, dovetailed perfectly with the pilot script Lorenzo Semple, Jr., had created. I really felt that I had something to bring to the party. In fact, one of the most important contributions I made was a result of this research.

Bill Dozier and I had some early discussions about how the character should be played, and the only real disagreement we had was over Batman's speech pattern. Lorenzo had sent a memo to Bill from Spain, stating that Batman's delivery should be staccato, wooden, and straight-ahead, like Sgt. Joe Friday in *Dragnet.* I strongly disagreed. I felt that Batman would be wooden enough in his suit, virtually expressionless behind the mask. I told Bill that Batman should muse and connect his ideas and sentences fluidly, similar to the way Basil Rathbone did as Sherlock Holmes, only a bit less tightly wound. That would put Robin in the position of being a juvenile Dr. Watson, which might be fun. Unlike Lorenzo, I also felt Batman should get excited when he hit upon a truth or deciphered a clue, as the adrenaline started to flow. That would help to fire up viewers, too.

Bill listened, thought for a moment, then gave me the okay to try it my way when we did the screen test for our prospective Robin. He agreed that that was probably the way to go.

I had my Batman and was anxious to begin, to buff the rough edges. However, "anxious" quickly gave way to "itchy" and—how's this for poetic justice?—being partly blind as a bat. It hadn't occurred to me that the costume would bring more than looseness to the characterization. It also caused me more discomfort than any of the cliffhanger traps I faced.

The shiny, blue-black cowl was sewn around a plastic bowl-type cap that had no give. I was convinced that every time I pulled the thing on, it was hastening male pattern baldness. Our wardrobe master, Jan Kemp, was able to stretch it a little, but there was a limit to what could be done: it would have been awkward for me to snap my head back in a fight scene, for example, and have the cowl shift on me, leaving one Bat-ear over my forehead, the other in back.

The cowl was separate from the cape and had to be worked onto my head, snapped under the chin, and then adjusted so I could see— sort of. I couldn't see up or down and lost my peripheral vision totally. I had to compensate by either turning to face whoever was talking, or not looking at them at all. Once we started shooting, I tended to do more of the latter, since it added to the feel of aloofness I wanted to project. The cowl also hid my eyebrows, so I ended up making expressive gestures with my hands: playing with my glove to suggest impatience, jabbing with a finger to underscore a point, rubbing my chin in thought, or toying with the phone cord when I was getting bad news over the Batphone. I probably would have indulged in a lot of those gestures anyway, though, since you'd be surprised how often, during conversation, people put their hands behind their backs or in their pockets, things I wasn't able to do in the Batsuit.

The rest of the costume was also no day at the beach. The gray tights were dry and itchy, and the blue satin shorts were worse. I'm not bragging here, but they were very smartly snug in the crotch. And it was sometimes embarrassing in front of the crew or visitors. It was like spending all day, every day in a wet Speedo. I hated those shiny blue shorts.

The cape was also a problem. I never kept track, but a common cause of retakes, besides flubbed lines or moves, was Burt's or my cape getting snagged on objects, stepped on, or caught in doors. I was strangled by the cape so often, in fact, that I literally had to fight the urge to shy like a nervous horse whenever someone new came near, not watching where they were walking.

The utility belt wasn't a problem unless I bent over suddenly, in which case I got a buckle in the gut or a Batarang in the side. And, sorry to disillusion any of you, but unless I had to take something from one of the compartments in a shot, the belt was empty. The strange thing was, I felt a little naked and incomplete then, as when I used to play cowboys as a kid: if the holster was empty, the illusion just wasn't complete.

Discomfort aside, one of the most memorable days of my career was when I put on the complete suit for the first time and walked onto the set. I admit feeling a little self-conscious when I took my first steps from the wardrobe department to the nearby soundstage. But I've also got to admit that I probably didn't feel quite as weird as some of the vegetable people and aliens I saw coming and going from the *Voyage to the Bottom of the Sea* or *Lost in Space* sets.

Still, there were all these macho technicians lugging plywood and fake trees and equipment around, and you assume they're thinking, He's getting a bigger paycheck, but he's got to wear tights for it. You figure they're going to laugh or try to cut you down to size in some way.

But that wasn't the case. Sure, there was some ribbing, a couple of "You lookin' for the belfry?" and "Bat Day at Black Rock" and "Hi, sailor" jokes. But nothing calculated to make me feel like a freak. In fact, a young messenger who was biking around the lot braked hard when he saw me, looked me up and down, and shouted, "Far out, man!" I said nothing but instinctively tipped my cowl to him. At that moment, I was not Adam West. I was Batman.

As a matter of fact, I realized it was good that people stared. People *would* stare at Batman. And he'd have to get used to it. Just the act of walking to the soundstage helped me bring the character into focus. And I was always amused by the fact that Batman believed no one could recognize him or identify his voice. His serious delusions made him funny in a goofy way.

9

THE FIRST time I went to the soundstage in full regalia was a day they were screen testing me with a prospective Robin, just to make sure the chemistry was right.

Bob Kane had introduced Robin nearly a year after the first Batman adventure was published. Kane felt, correctly, that kids would relate to a "junior Batman" in the strip; it was every young boy's fantasy, after all, to live in a mansion and fight alongside Batman. And if you look at those early Robin adventures in the comic books, you'll see that a change came over Batman then. He started making jokes with his young ward and became humanized. Thanks to the bright colors of Robin's costume (patterned, like his name, after Robin Hood, not after the bird), the strip also became less grim. Some Batfans think that was a bad development; I think it gave the strip depth and, thus, greater longevity.

The casting of Robin was obviously very important to us, since he had to have the build and energy of a fifteen year old, but with adult sensibilities and wit to sell the character. He also had to be fully grown: if we lasted for more than one season, it wouldn't do to have a Robin getting taller than Batman. Dozier was very concerned about that.

The young man with whom I was being tested that day was nineteen-year-old Bert "Sparky" Gervis, Jr., who had begun his show business career touring the country in his dad's *Rhapsody on Ice* show. He was two years old at the time and was billed as "The World's Youngest Professional Ice Skater." He later told me two conflicting stories about how he got his nickname: the first was that it came from the way sparks flew off his ice skate blades whenever he made one of his dramatic leaps, and the second that it was given him when he landed on the frayed end of an electrical cable during a show. I've always believed the latter: Sparky always seemed to have bad karma on the set where electricity, fire, and explosives were concerned.

After graduating from high school, he'd worked in summer stock (with Rob Reiner, as I recall), studied acting at UCLA and at the University of California at Santa Barbara, gone on auditions (without any luck), and supported himself by selling real estate, with only marginally more success than he'd had in acting: in the year or so he'd been doing it, he'd only managed to sell two houses.

"Yeah," he used to say, "but that was all I needed!"

True enough. One of the houses he sold was to Fox producer Saul David, whom Sparky, in his forward but ingratiating Eddie Haskell way, implored to help him get work as an extra. David told him they were looking for someone to play Robin on *Batman* and he'd see about getting him an audition.

But Sparky couldn't wait. He went over to the studio late one afternoon, stopped at the gate, and asked the guard if he could see whoever was casting the show.

The guard called FitzSimons. Charlie had already seen dozens of young actors, without success, and figured he had nothing to lose: he told the guard to send Sparky over. As soon as the young hopeful walked into his office, Charlie knew they had their Robin.

Sparky got more than the part, though. A few weeks later he also got a new name, which was suggested by Charlie: Burt Ward. Ward was his mother's maiden name, and Dozier liked the fact that Dick Grayson was Bruce Wayne's ward. Sparky also thought the spelling "Burt" was a little more rugged than "Bert," à la Burt Lancaster, as opposed to Bert Parks.

So there I was, waiting for a young man who was still named Sparky Gervis. While the small camera crew got ready, I took my first look at the enormous Batcave set.

About ten days before, the studio had begun feeling that after an initial burst of enthusiasm, ABC was suddenly getting cold feet, reluctant to go ahead with the show because it was so different, not a straight-ahead detective show. Since Dozier was married to his and

Lorenzo's concept, and Fox had signed me and felt confident that Burt would be Robin, they decided that the test should be as elaborate as possible in order to convince the network that *Batman* was something worth sinking a lot of money into, not to mention giving two nights of valuable prime time.

We were shooting the test in a jury-rigged Batcave, a U-shaped cyclorama that had been a cavern in an Irwin Allen project (originally built for his feature-length *The Lost World,* I think, then later recycled for *Voyage to the Bottom of the Sea*). The real one was being built nearby, and I walked over. "Elaborate" doesn't do justice to what our great art director, Jack Senter, had done to create the illusion of a functioning Batcave. The cave itself was about ninety feet long and eighty feet high, polyurethane built on a wire frame and sculpted into rocklike formations. There was no ceiling, just lights and catwalks overhead. The foreground was filled in with rocks.

Sets rarely look real in the unflattering light of day, and the nearly completed Batcave was no exception. While the big studio doors were open and the lights were off, it looked to me like walls of crumpled gray wrapping paper hung from a wooden frame. No substance, no real sex appeal. But a few minutes later, when the doors were shut and the colored lights were switched on, it was like that wonderful scene in *Mary Poppins* where Dick Van Dyke, Julie Andrews, and the two children jump into the chalk drawing. I stood in awe, feeling like part of a comic book panel, my own reality overwhelmed by the spectacle of the drawings made real, the crags shining devilish and gaudy everywhere I turned. And no sooner had I taken in this sight than the props were turned on.

The comic book had come wonderfully alive, and I couldn't help but feel like Batman as I turned and looked at all the crimefighting apparatus, the lights flashing brightly, the gantry-like atomic pile towering above me, the bright gold Batpoles disappearing into the darkness of catwalks sixty feet overhead.

People have asked me why, to this day, I'm so protective of Batman. The answer is simple: that moment sparked a love affair with the magic that Batman can create, the excitement and joy he brings to people. Now, when the set came to life and I looked down and saw Batman's gloved hands, not mine, I came close to believing in the existence of Batman myself. In the years that followed this would happen the moment I pulled on the cowl.

But *what* an experience this first time was! Alone and undisturbed for nearly a minute, I reveled in the power and isolation and beauty of the character. It's the kind of experience that never leaves you, and creates a very special bond with a character. (Charlton Heston says he had that same experience when, playing Moses, in full makeup and costume, he walked barefoot on the slopes of Sinai. He's never quite shaken it either, though it may have been easier for him to make a living playing Deliverers than it has been for me playing comic book heroes.)

In another area of the soundstage was an impressive set for our first episode, the Republic of Moldavia pavilion at the Gotham City World's Fair. The centerpiece was a bejeweled mastodon standing under a silk umbrella behind a large pink-and-white cake. In the story,

the Moldavian prime minister was to carve the cake and it would explode, sticky pieces flying everywhere; from one of the pieces, a parachute would open and drift down with a riddle from the Riddler. ("Riddle me this, Batman: What do an orange and a bell have in common?") Dressed with extras, I knew it would make for a spectacular scene.

The unfinished Batmobile was there as well, finally having shown up after breaking down several times on the freeway. Even with its dashboard not quite finished, some of the paint still needing to be applied, and the Gotham City tags not yet in place, the Batmobile was a thing of beauty. I ran my hand along its sleek tail fin.

I was really starting to get into this. There had never been sets like this for TV, and I didn't see how it could fail. Neither did Dozier, who had told me that if ABC and Fox liked the test, they were going to spend an unprecedented one million dollars promoting the show. In every way, creatively and in terms of marketing, this was going to be a mold-breaker.

I cracked up at a prop that caught my eye, with its label "Film Developing Tank. Super Fine Batgrain." The show was going to work, all right. Absolutely no stone had been left unturned by everyone from Dozier to the prop people.

I went back to the faux Batcave, where the cameras were set up. I was practicing throwing the Batarang when Sparky arrived with our director, *Hogan's Heroes* veteran Robert Butler. This may seem strange for someone in a Batsuit to say, but it was an odd sight. All that was missing was the Yellow Brick Road. There was Butler, nearly seven feet tall and topped with a head of wild red hair, leading this wiry, five-foot-eight, red, green, and yellow bird of a young man in a thin black mask. Holding the bird's hand was another "bird," Burt's wife Bonnie, an early flower child with long, dark hair. She had an endearing sweetness and was constantly on the set in the first few weeks, supporting him in any way she could. (Her father was Mort Lindsey, the orchestra leader for Merv Griffin, whose talk show was based in New York. That was probably why Merv's was the first such show we did after *Batman* hit it big.)

I walked over. Butler introduced us, and Burt and I walked over to the Batcave set. We made small talk, and when Robert settled into his chair we rehearsed the scene.

We had only a minimal crew for Burt's screen test with me, but that didn't matter. It was what was in front of the camera that was important.

The sequence we were doing was from the second episode, featuring the Penguin. Batman and Robin were slowly turning and examining one of the villain's umbrellas on a lathe while punching computer buttons.

We rehearsed the scene once, making sure we both had the lines and timing right. Butler had decided that he didn't want much rehearsal because (a) there wouldn't be much time to rehearse once the show went into production, and (b) he wanted to see how Burt's instincts worked.

The director called for action. I started turning the lathe. Robin stood there with his mouth open, eyes narrow.

"Wow, this green color could stand for money, Batman."

"Yes. I still think the clue is in the colors, Robin."

"*Holy rainbows!* They're so pretty. The colors in this umbrella are just like a beautiful dawn."

"Beautiful dawn . . . wait a minute! Great Scot! Dawn Robbins, the beautiful movie star! She's on location here in Gotham City for *Funboy* Magazine."

"Holy popcorn, Batman!"

As Burt said that last line, he slammed his fist into his palm with punishing enthusiasm. As he did, I knew Batman had a Robin. The chemistry was right, Burt had nailed the character, and his Robin would be able to show all the youthful exuberance my Batman wouldn't be able to.

Butler also filmed Burt doing some action. Burt was a Tae Kwon Do black belt who, I later learned, once lived in the same building as Bruce Lee and says they frequently sparred (though I can't help but think that Bruce was holding back: he was an amazing one-man-army).

Burt broke some planks and a brick for Butler. We could see he was well coordinated. Then we shot him in his civilian identity of Dick Grayson. Our director was happy when we finished. After Dozier and

FitzSimons had a look at the test, Burt had the part.

Just as importantly, we produced a five-minute test reel that ABC loved, and on the strength of it they ordered thirteen weeks of the show, two nights a week.

We were committed.

10

THE SHOOTING of the first episode, "Hey Diddle Riddle," is very vivid in my mind, like a first love or a first car. In many ways, it was also one of my most surreal experiences.

One of Director Butler's most important contributions was his sensitive staging of the show. He liked to have Burt and me moving, even in dialogue scenes, which gave the show and the characters a sense of urgency. We were really in synch with this. If you watch the first scene in Commissioner Gordon's office, as we discuss the Riddler's modus operandi, you'll see us pacing a lot, the restless crimefighters eager to cut to the chase. However, Butler and I didn't see eye to eye on everything: in one scene, for example, when Burt and I were in the library, I took it upon myself to drop some fuller's earth inside an old tome so that when I closed it, a fine film of dust rose up to catch the light. Butler thought that was too extreme and had us do it over again, without the dust. I usually deferred to him. His comedic taste was wonderful. And that first show set a real tone for the series.

We shot at four studio locations during the run of the series: at the Fox studio in Century City; at Warners' Burbank Studios, usually for exteriors; at the Fox lot on Western Avenue; and at the Culver City Studios.

On day one, we were working outside in a corner of the Fox Century City lot, which was in the process of being sold, piecemeal, to pay for the red ink spilled by *Cleopatra* three years before. We were filming near one result of the sell-off, the nearly completed Century Plaza Hotel. I wasn't needed in the first shot, but I wanted to be there just the same. I had the costume on, except for the cape and cowl, and I sat in my chair to watch the special effects crew set fire to the Riddler's overturned car.

I was comfortable. Confident. Content. And about to be reminded about the suddenness with which life can change.

The small explosives in the car were rigged, by wire, to a control panel off-camera. I watched, feeling like a kid at a circus, as Frank Gorshin, our Riddler, scampered away with Molly. When they were safely out of range, the charges were detonated and the car started to burn.

It was all very nice, very impressive, until the car exploded.

Smoke filled the air and rubber shrapnel spun toward me. My military training kicked in, and I literally hit the dirt, covering my head with my arms. We later learned that the air in the tires had become superheated, faster than the effects people had expected, and had blown up. The rubber had also slammed into a pair of the giant arc lamps we used to erase shadows cast by sunlight on outdoor shots, causing them to explode as well.

But it got worse. Still lying on the ground, I looked up and peered through the nightmare of bustle, smoke, and confusion. Burning shards of rubber had also blown toward the hotel, and my sharp crime-fighter's eyes discerned that the thirty stories of burlap that had been hung to cure the cement walls were on fire, flames racing toward the top. Sirens sounded in the distance, and crewmen were already rushing hoses to the wall that separated the movie lot from the hotel.

This was shaping up as an exciting first day. We took a break as the crew moved indoors, Director Butler joking nervously that we would be safer there.

If he only knew.

We had a great, and I mean truly legendary, special effects man working on our show. His name was L. B. Abbott, and he'd begun his career in 1926, when Fox was the William Fox Company. He worked his way up from assistant cameraman to special effects designer and, during his long career, created spectacular work in films like *Tora! Tora! Tora!, Fantastic Voyage, Doctor Dolittle,* and *The Poseidon Adventure* (winning Oscars for the last three).

The problem with *Batman,* especially in these early days, before we went on, was that time and time again, ABC or Fox or both became gravely anxious about our pop art approach. As the airdate neared, more people than not were convinced that we were going to fail, big-time. The Fox and ABC top brass, who had been so confident when it was all conference room, became more and more unhinged as the big bills started rolling in and the reality sunk in that the network was anchoring two nights on our success. If we failed, we could very well drag down whatever shows were on after us.

ABC got really nervous when they learned that Dozier, Semple, and Butler had cooked up this idea to superimpose sound effects cards over the fight scenes. The idea first occurred to FitzSimons when we over-spent on sets and had to cut back on the number of scenes we were shooting. While looking at the explosive POWs and AIIEEEEEs in the comic books, he realized that by dropping those in, he could eliminate three or four transition shots in each fight.

It was a brilliant stroke, but ABC felt we'd gone round the bend, that no one would think that was amusing. But as Dozier put it to ABC in one anxious meeting, they were the number three network: all they stood to lose was their mediocrity. Whatever reservations I had about Dozier, he had the guts to go after what he wanted.

(I should mention that National Periodicals, publishers of the *Batman* comics, weren't too hopeful either. They'd been trying to sell a straight *Batman* action show just a year before, and had gone so far as to shoot photos of former football star and movie Tarzan Mike Henry in the role to try and interest prospective sponsors. That was the con-cept ABC had optioned, only to have Dozier and Semple tweak it. After the show was a hit, of course, ABC executives claimed to have been behind us one hundred percent.)

Naturally, everyone, Dozier included, was nervous when the first episode was tested among a cross-section of viewers. These were people who had been recruited from supermarkets and department stores, and they were broken into four groups: men, women, under-thirties, and over-thirties. That was as sophisticated as demographic studies got back then.

Each group of one hundred or so was brought into a screening room where every viewer sat behind a dial. The dial had five settings: one, two, zero, minus-one, and minus-two, and the dials were hooked up to a relatively sophisticated $300,000 computer. The viewers were

told to adjust the dial constantly as they watched, and the results were channeled to a control booth in the back of the room. This would tell the producers what worked and what didn't.

First, the group was shown a "control film": a cartoon, *Mr. Magoo Goes Skiing*. It scored what it usually did, in the middle-sixties, which meant that the group was indeed a valid cross-section of viewers.

The average pilot also usually scored in the middle-sixties; *Batman* came in in the upper-forties, the worst score in the history of pilot testing. Someone in the booth suggested that the only reason it didn't test lower was that the dials didn't go any lower.

I wasn't there, but I heard later that Dozier was convinced the dials were broken. They weren't. Ed Scherick said they weren't, but added that he didn't give a hoot what the audience had said. He knew the show was good and that America would get it.

ABC wasn't so sure. The network told Dozier and FitzSimons to put a laughtrack on the show. Against their better judgment, they did. The show was retested and the results were the same. A third test, with moronic narration ("Hiss the villains and cheer the heroes!"), also failed.

The show went back to the way Dozier had first done it, but as a result of all the boardroom panic there were many small adjustments as well as a number of heavy-duty changes. Most of these involved Mr. Abbott and the adding of huge new special effects gags that would look great in promos. Unfortunately, many of these would get dropped in Abbott's lap the morning of the day they were being shot. He was really wonderful about coming up with things, and coming up with them fast, but some of the challenges gave him a really rough go.

In one sequence, I was supposed to enter the Riddler's subway hideout to rescue Robin. For scenes like that, a crew would usually build a breakaway set, a section that can be pulled apart with wires and smoke but no real explosion. The sound effects would be added later.

In this case, a real set had already been built when it was decided that Batman should blast his way in. There was no time to rebuild the set; we'd already shot our Batcave scenes and there was nothing else to shoot. Rather than lose a half a day, Abbott's effects team said they could rig a small charge to blow down the wall. Butler said do it. After all, they'd done a masterful job blowing up the Riddler's car. A subway wall made out of plaster and two-by-fours couldn't be much trouble.

Well, Abbott wasn't there for the explosion (these "floor effects" weren't his direct responsibility, and besides, he was also working on Irwin Allen's *Voyage to the Bottom of the Sea* and *Lost in Space* at the time), and one of his assistants figured a "small charge" was a stick of dynamite. (Burt says he remembers three sticks of dynamite being used, but I'm pretty sure that would have brought down the soundstage, not just the set. If you've ever been a Navy SEAL or an old-time miner, you know that one stick can go a long way toward bringing down a mountainside.)

Burt, me, and the director didn't know what was going on behind the wall. On most shows, you do run-throughs of dialogue when you get the script. But the actual blocking of a scene, exactly where everyone's supposed to move and stand, has to wait until you're on the set. That's what we were doing now.

It only took the effects crew about twenty minutes to rig the charge, after which we finished rehearsing and went to do the scene. Burt lay down on a table near the wall; I was offstage. When the crew was clear of the set, Butler called for action. The effects man pressed his button.

The roar was deafening. If I hadn't had the cowl on, my ears would still be ringing. Wood and pieces of plaster went flying all over, mostly in Burt's direction, and smoke filled the air. Holding my breath, I rushed through the opening in the wall. Off-camera, I could see people coughing and waving their arms in big, broad sweeps.

As soon as Butler yelled "Cut," Burt was on his feet and complaining, and justifiably so, though I'm not sure anyone could hear him. I *know* no one could see him, as dust from the explosion filled the soundstage. It was a half hour before the air was clear enough for us to move on to the next scene; I was glad it involved dialogue, not an explosion. Later, Abbott came over to assure Burt and me that it would never happen again.

He meant well, but things always seem to come in threes. And once again, it was Burt in the hot seat.

The scene involved the Riddler trying to steal the Batmobile. Robin is lying comatose inside, having been shot by a drugged dart. The Riddler presses a button that Batman has mislabeled to confound criminals. So instead of starting the car, he sets off rockets which come flying from the three launchers that rise from the back.

Again, this was the kind of expensive, time-consuming shot you only want to do once. Butler called "Action," and as Burt lay there, sparks from the prop fireworks exploded from the launchers, flashing and pinwheeling, shooting every which way. Several of them flew in Burt's direction, and though a few embers landed on his back and sizzled through cape and flesh, Burt didn't budge. Not then, anyway.

When Butler yelled, "Cut," Burt was on his feet again, shouting at the special effects crew and holding his singed arm, which was peppered with first-degree burns. He was complaining louder than before, and while he was being hurried to first aid, one of the Brooklyn-born crew members cracked a "Boint" Wonder joke. I was glad Burt hadn't heard; our feisty bird might have gone for the man's throat.

Effects people are great, and some of them are geniuses. I really don't blame them for these mishaps, because the unexpected is part of every profession, from movies to medicine. Actors and directors tend to get a little blasé about explosives and gunfire, but as the accidental death of Brandon Lee reminded us, most painfully, these things can be dangerous. And when you do as many of them in as short a time as we did on that first episode, you're really pushing your luck.

The first days of *Batman* shooting were difficult in other ways as well. Not only were the actors getting to know one another in front of the camera, but some of our key personnel behind the camera just didn't get what we were doing. It took time for some of them to grasp our bigger-than-life posturing and the kind of deadpan humor we were striving for.

For instance, in the first episode, Jill St. John is the Riddler's moll and a part-time go-go dancer. When she tumbles into the atomic pile in the Batcave and is burned to a crisp, Batman leans over the edge in close-up and says, "What a way to go—go," as a tear slips from under his mask. After the take, the camera operator whispered to our director that I'd made a mistake, that I'd added an extra "go."

Butler asked me about it, and I said it just came out. I argued that it fit, and he thought about it, snickered, and agreed. I also thought about taking off my cowl and holding it over my heart in a show of respect for the dead, but it took too long in rehearsals.

Later, when we did the discotheque scene, the drugged Batman slid onto the dance floor and did the Batusi with Jill St. John. As Semple had written the scene, the Batusi was a nondescript dance that simply enabled Batman to move among the revelers. I felt it should be a little more than that, and I worked it out on my own, made it a singular moment of madness inspired by the ongoing debate in the media about whether drug use was mind-expanding or debilitating. I wasn't trying to make a social statement: I just felt it would be funny and abstract to have Batman slightly out of his well-trained mind, losing control as a result of the drug.

Virtually everyone in the crew laughed when I finished the scene, but there was some front-office type who nervously jangled the change in his pocket and said he thought it was ridiculous.

"He's drugged," I yelled, as I Batusied in his direction. "What do you do when *you're* drugged?"

I didn't find out, because he turned and left. He never came back, either, and to this day I wonder what he and others like him thought when the Batusi became a national dance craze.

11

THE FIRST show was especially pleasurable because it was all new, challenging, and full of promise.

It was also full of birdseed.

On our show, we were fortunate to have a brilliant director of photography, Howard Schwartz. A great, great innovator with color and angles, Howard was as important to the success of our show as was Dozier, Lorenzo, or any of the stars. But he had a habit that drove me insane. He was constantly chewing on bird seeds of some kind. He'd pop these things all day long and spit out the shells wherever he happened to be—all over the set, outside the soundstage, in the parking lot, in the men's room, you name it. There was never a risk of misplacing Howard: all you had to do was follow the trail. The nutrients in those seeds must have been enormously beneficial, however, because as the day got old, Howie got quicker and louder and could spit faster than he had in the morning.

Since I couldn't see downward in the cowl I became positively paranoid about the shells, and imagined the little, wet hulls landing on my blue boots or somewhere more private. It was terribly irritating for many of us, but we loved the guy, and I, for one, did not want to be the one to deprive him of such a healthful habit. Besides, as Alan Napier, who played Bruce Wayne's butler Alfred, pointed out, he could have been drinking vodka instead, though the avant-gardists really would have loved *those* camera angles.

On the first show, we had as wonderful a cast as you could ask for, and two of my favorite guest stars: Frank Gorshin and, of course, Jill.

At age thirty, Frank Gorshin was already the top impressionist in the country, a huge draw on the nightclub circuit and on TV. He'd had a short movie career, doing teen roles in the late 1950s and early 1960s in movies like *Ring of Fire* and *Invasion of the Saucer Men,* but it was as a mimic that he made a name for himself. Unlike other impressionists, who did short takes on a lot of celebrities, Frank would do entire scenes, such as Richard Burton from *Camelot,* or lengthy, hilarious dialogues between Burt Lancaster and Kirk Douglas, the two stars for which he was best known.

Frank and I became very good friends. He's a gregarious man with a great wit and terrific sense of humor, and more energy than even Moe Howard. We were especially fortunate to have him as our first villain, not only because he was so good in the part but because he helped me shape my Batman. In these days of everyone second-guessing us about our approach, *my* only concern was whether my performance was entertaining enough.

Frank helped me answer that question. I experimented a lot in run-throughs, when we were working out the blocking, and even during takes. If I broke him up, if he literally fell on the floor with that high-pitched laugh of his, I knew I was on the right track. He was a good barometer as to what was working in that fun house of ours. He was also a phenomenal actor to play off. When he was in the scene and in character, his concentration was a great inspiration. It was easy to believe he truly was the demented Edward Nigma.

Frank's maniacal laugh certainly helped us all believe he was the Riddler, and it proved to be one of the character's most memorable features. He told me his inspiration for the laugh was the 1947 movie *Kiss of Death,* in which Richard Widmark, as the demented Tommy Udo, pushes a wheelchairbound old woman down the stairs. Richard (he *hates* being called Dick) cackled madly when he did that, and Frank drew on that laughter and Widmark's wild expression for the Riddler. Like me, Frank didn't just waltz in and wing the character: he gave it a great deal of thought. In fact, during a break in the initial read-through of the first show, we were talking about our respective characters and he made an extremely astute observation about the Riddler. He said the Riddler was clearly a brilliant man who could have been anything he chose, be it a scientist, a writer, a politician, or whatever. But he elected to become a supervillain, so he had to love what he was

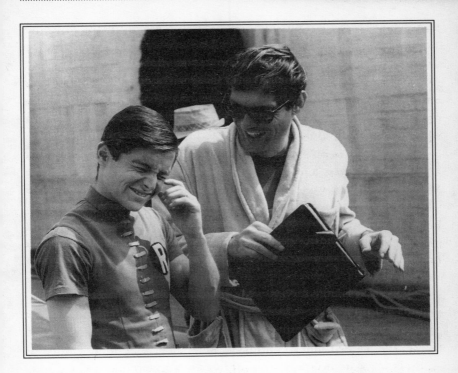

doing and certainly would feel passionately about his crimes . . . and about Batman. Frank put all of his formidable talent into that passion and intensity, which is what made his laughs and rages and hates so believable, and helped make the Riddler so memorable.

But Frank is also quite colorful himself. He may be one of the most impatient men on the planet, and I often felt he could, if he tried, turn one of his cigarettes to ash in one long, unbroken drag. Once he had that energy of his throttled up and ready to go, he didn't appreciate delays. And if he flubbed a line or missed a cue or failed to grab a prop *just so,* he'd get furious with himself and storm around the set asking, "Why? Why? *Why?*"

Off-camera, he was still a high-energy dynamo, always an adventure to be with. We closed a few bars together, which was always good for a laugh because people were surprised to see Batman and the Riddler together. If not for our celebrity, in fact, we might have been asked to leave some of the establishments we visited; we were a high-decibel duo.

Frank and I also share the same off-the-wall sense of humor. Once, we walked into a party where clothing was unwelcome. However, after Frank and I got comfortable amid the sea of legs and breasts, I felt a little silly so I began to do Batman. Somewhere across the room, Frank became the Riddler, and it was so ridiculous in that setting that we couldn't stop laughing: we had the distinction of being thrown out of our first and only Hollywood orgy.

Frank lives in the Northeast these days, and I don't see him often. That's too bad. He's in my thoughts a great deal as a friend, and in my heart because he was our first Batman villain. We owed much of the success of the series to his contribution.

Frank did four shows with us that first season, none the second, one the third, and costarred in our *Batman* film. John Astin, a fine actor, filled his green tights the second season and brought a kind of Gilbert and Sullivan flair to the part. Although there was some problem with money that may have kept Frank away for that season—villains were paid a standard $2,500, however often they appeared and however popular they proved to be—I really think it was a question of identification that caused him to step back. Remember that, unlike other villains, Frank wore no special makeup. He was grateful not to have to sit in the makeup room for hours like the others. We wanted his insane demeanor as a young hoodlum prodigy. Frank felt that his career would suffer because he was so well known throughout the country as the Riddler; that was a trap I'd get to know very well.

Still, he came back for the third season, because you can't beat reaching forty million people in one night to remind them you're out there. Besides, he already *was* the Riddler where America was concerned, and if you can't beat 'em . . .

Jill St. John only did the first show, playing the Riddler's moll Molly, and her job was to infiltrate the Batcave by masquerading as Robin, after having fooled me by donning a latex life-mask.

Oh, sure. That'd do it.

Jill had just turned twenty-six, a former child star who had grown up just perfectly. I had never met her before, and I found her, as her former beau Frank Sinatra had, to be sexy, attractive, and exceptionally intelligent. I wanted to get to know her better, but we ended up being

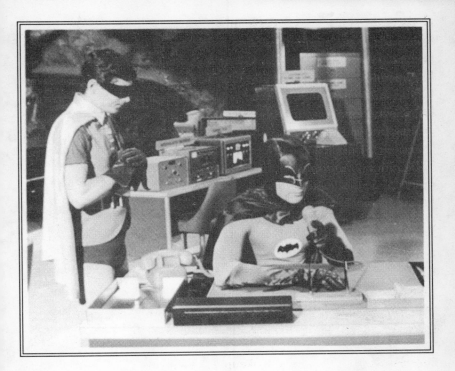

ships passing in the night . . . literally. After she did the show, I saw her socially just once, when the studio arranged for me to escort her to the Golden Globes. After the ceremony, we went back to her home where, despite my considerable charm and repeated innuendo, I came away with a good-night kiss only.

Still, it's always fun when our paths cross on the slopes or at various events, and I'm glad she's found happiness with Robert Wagner.

12

*B*ATMAN WAS scheduled to air just two months after we began shooting the first episode. Each two-segment episode took from ten days to two weeks to shoot, with weekends off, but it was still a tough schedule. The first episode took us twenty-one days to shoot, and as soon as that was was done, we rushed right into episode two, featuring Burgess Meredith as the Penguin. We got that one down to eighteen days. After that we began episode three, featuring Cesar Romero as the Joker, by which time we were getting them done in two weeks and under.

Those weeks are a blur of activity in my memory, but one night stands out vividly: the night of Wednesday, January 12, 1966.

We'd wrapped early, courtesy of our producer, Howie Horwitz, so we could all go home and watch the debut of our show. We'd seen it at a special screening at the studio, and we'd heard that the extravagant premiere party at a hot New York night spot, Harlow's, had been a smashing success, attended by the likes of Andy Warhol, Roy Lichtenstein, Roddy McDowall, and five hundred of the Manhattan elite, who got to see both parts of the first adventure.

The omens were good and the reviews were generally great, though some of the critics thought we were too straight for a comedy and too silly for an adventure. But what really mattered was what the viewers thought, and ABC had beaten the drums loudly and relentlessly for weeks so that people would know we were coming. We figured they'd probably watch just to be able to discuss the show at school or work the next day. But that wouldn't necessarily mean they'd like it.

Adding to my jumpiness was the fact that *Batman* had tested so badly with the sample audience that had been wired to adjust the dials to record their reactions. During the show, not one audience member had moved. They just sat there, frozen, because they didn't know what to make of what they were watching. It was too different, and they had no reference points. I hoped that a national TV audience, primed and prepared by several weeks of advertising, would look at things differently.

You're always on a griddle when you're waiting to hear if you've gotten a part of if a pilot has sold. That kind of tension creates a roller coaster ride of emotions. But waiting for a show to debut or a movie to open is a worse form of torture. Your name, your face, and your words, all of the choices you made, are on the chopping block. Months of struggle and dedication could be gone with a flick of a dial or the publication of next morning's newspapers. Years of work, of building your career and your reputation, could be dead at dawn.

Conversely, a real treasure could fall in your lap. In one day, one night, you might establish a position that could lead to a fine career, or at least to your becoming the flavor of the month. It's all very heady and frightening. In my case, everything I'd been working toward was riding on this one roll of the dice. Thinking about the work I had for tomorrow helped me stay calm, though I was aware that if the show bombed, going in and doing that work would not be a very pleasant experience. We'd probably appreciate special effects using too much explosive.

So I was in a hurry to get to my beach apartment and watch the show alone, to try to stay relaxed. Somehow, I felt that through my television set I'd mysteriously be wired to the feelings and emotions of everyone else watching. Then I'd call my children in Tarzana and they would quickly and honestly set me straight, let me know what the rest of the country was thinking.

I decided to stop at the Colony Market in Malibu and pick up a steak for dinner. As I headed for the checkout counter in these pre-VCR days, I heard two people telling the clerks,

"C'mon, get us outta here!"

"Yeah, hurry! *Batman*'s on tonight!"

One of the clerks said that she was getting off early to watch it, too. Everybody was laughing and excited.

I quietly paid and hurried out. My mood had swung from cautious

to positive about the show. I told myself they were going to love it because they could have fun with it. It was going to work.

As I climbed onto my old Triumph motorcycle and headed into the darkness down Pacific Coast Highway, I sensed my anonymity drifting away like the fog.

13

THE SHOW was a huge success. I could not have imagined just how big *Batman* was going to be.

The Saturday morning after the show premiered, I drove to Big Bear with my kids for some skiing. In my ski clothes and goggles, my wool cap pulled down low to protect me from the cold, I got out of the car in a tiny place named Fawnskin. As I crossed the road to the general store, I heard people behind me yelling excitedly, "Batman! Batman!"

They had to have known me just from my walk, since my face was barely visible; I was stunned. I turned and waved at the group of young skiers, and they ran over. As I paid for sodas and cheeseburgers, they began telling me how much they loved the show. And they weren't just responding to the fact that I was a "celebrity": it was *who* I played.

I would find this phenomenon repeated over and over through the years, and to this day. Fans never simply want to shake my hand or get an autograph. They want to talk about what *Batman* meant to them, how it made them feel secure and happy in a time of chaos and war. Don Adams has people ask him to sign their shoes, and Bob Denver will always get a "Yo, Gilligan!" from fans. But from the very start, *Batman* touched the child in viewers, and that has always made for a very special bond with the people I meet. As I said before, for better or worse, richer or poorer, I'm married to the cape.

In any case, I was fascinated by this group's effusiveness and sincerity, and gratified that, creatively, we'd hit the nail squarely on the head. I also learned something important as the weekend progressed: unless I wanted to be recognized, I had to walk fast and keep my head down. I had to avoid eye contact and not talk too much. That may sound affected, but after being recognized at the inn, on the slopes, and even by someone passing my car, I realized it was the only way I could give my time to my children. (I was never one for wigs and fake beards. Not only would I have had to spend much too much time in front of the mirror, but I didn't want to be stopped by some security guard or police officer and have to explain what I was doing in a long white beard or my wife's size four dress. Better to be mobbed than to be led from a bank in women's clothes and handcuffs, I always say.)

The other actors, the writers, Dozier, and the rest of the staff were also thrilled and surprised by the hysteria *Batman* caused. But the question that concerned us all was, would it hold?

Yes, indeed. In fact, Batmania grew the second week as the Penguin proved as big a draw as the Riddler. Everyone was talking or writing about us, wanting an interview, trying to understand and explain the appeal, raving about the innovative camerawork—tilted angles for the bad guys—or the lavish sets or Neal Hefti's catchy jazz score. Old pals would call to congratulate me and also to ask, "Are those horns or voices saying 'Batman' during your theme song?" (They were horns.) Sales of the comic book quintupled and potential licensees who had failed to tie in with us earlier were running to DC or Fox with pens drawn, checkbooks open, wanting to do gum cards or soundtrack albums or model kits. We even ended up with some Emmy nominations, one for Frank, another for Best Editing, and a third for Best Comedy.

We joked around the set that ABC stood for A Big Cashbox, as the demand from advertisers was so strong that the network truncated the opening credits so they could fit in an extra commercial. Regulators grumbled, but the network was also A Bit Cocky and got away with it. I was glad they were making so much money, though it would have been nice if they had passed a little along to the rest of us.

I was constantly dealing with overload. As the weeks passed, and more and more people became aware of the show, it became difficult for me to go anywhere in public. Even when I called Information on the phone, operators recognized my voice and wanted to ask me questions about the Batmobile, the Joker, the Batcave. I quickly realized an interesting thing about TV actors: unlike movie stars, who appear larger than life on the screen and tend to intimidate people, TV stars come into peoples' homes. As a result, they're treated like family members.

And this was in the days before bodyguards, when a fan could approach an actor without fear of getting a fist in his or her Brownie Starflash. (I don't like that trend: we're well paid, and our fans and the press deserve a smile and a photograph.)

I dutifully signed every magazine photograph, napkin, and brown paper bag that was thrust in my direction (except during meals). I also signed countless items of apparel and parts of women's anatomies when I felt reckless. To this day I'm still surprised and a little disconcerted when I'm asked to sign a lady's bosom, though I usually go ahead and do it. It's a bit of a challenge to write one's name on a quivering breast without using the other hand to steady it. And it's even more difficult with a husband or boyfriend looking on.

And, yes, quite often, women would also come up and ask for more than an autograph. Sometimes they were demure, which I found appealing, and other times they were more aggressive, which I found daunting. There was one assertive and enthusiastic female who was waiting in a stall in the men's room when I entered.

"Here?" I deadpanned. "You'll have an audience."

Without missing a beat, she shot back, "Maybe they'll throw money!"

I laughed and walked away; I tried to keep things in perspective concerning the difference between my appeal and the character's. But I must confess I wasn't above using whatever I had at my disposal when the situation was irresistibly inviting.

The industry took note of us, too, and we were asked to every party, every opening, every awards ceremony, every talk show. Concerned about being overshadowed by my alter ego, I agreed to go to any event or show where I could be Adam West, which is how I found myself singing with Dean Martin, Bing Crosby, and others on TV. That was one of the reasons I cut several records around this time, an album of songs released domestically and another for the Target label in England, where it went to number one. Unfortunately, it had somewhat of an opposite effect on my career here: without even listening to them, people assumed I was "camping" it, that the records were a joke. I'll admit that Sinatra I wasn't. But because Leonard Nimoy and Robert Horton and Jerry Lewis and so many other non-singers were also cutting albums, some of them god-awful, my efforts were also dismissed

The Bruce Wayne study set, complete with batpoles

out-of-hand. Today, if you find the platters at all, they're in the novelty bins of old record shops.

Still, it was Batman the public wanted, and it was the Caped Crusader that ended up on the cover of *TV Guide, Life, Screen Stories,* and countless other magazines.

The *Life* shoot was actually one of the less pleasant experiences I had. Mask or no mask, I was flattered to be on a cover that was typically graced by the likes of John F. Kennedy, George S. Patton, and Elizabeth Taylor. But it was also, literally, a pain to do, as well as personally upsetting because they weren't going to use Burt (which hurt him, and I don't blame him) and because Bill Dozier used it to ace me.

For the photo shoot, I had to jump from the top of the Batcave Atomic Pile in full costume. I ended up doing it eighteen times, landing on a stack of mattresses twelve feet below. Never mind that I felt utterly undignified, leaping around like a kid in a playground, but during an early jump I twisted an ankle, and it was agony going back up over and over until the photographer got the shot he wanted. I always felt the cover caption, "BATMAN Makes a Mighty Leap Into National Popularity" should have had a subheading, ". . . As BATMAN actor limps to work the next day."

It was heady stuff, tempered by the realization that it could end as quickly as it had begun. As it happened, Dozier very unnecessarily made that point to me early in March, the day the *Life* issue reached his office. I hadn't seen it yet, and he phoned my agent, very sweetly, and asked us both to come in for a "little chat." We did, and it was little indeed. As we walked in, Dozier said, "I want to show you something wonderful." He threw the *Life* magazine on his desk, cover up. I limped over, picked it up, and smiled; Lew looked over my shoulder.

"Nice," I said, the throbbing in my ankle momentarily forgotten.

"Yes," Dozier agreed, "but don't get any big ideas. Remember, there have been thirteen Tarzans."

I looked at him. He was serious, though he was astute enough to temper his warning with a little smile. Following my lead, Lew backed out of his office, mock-bowing. But I never forgot what he said, because it reminded me that in Hollywood you can like someone, work closely with them, have fun with them, and go to their house for dinner, but that doesn't make them your friend. If the ratings drop, if the ship starts to sink, it's every Batman for himself.

Fortunately, I was so busy I didn't have time to dwell on these darker issues, any more than I had time to savor our success or all the attention we were getting. I was just a cork on the storm-tossed sea.

In those first few weeks, the most amazing thing that happened was that stars *I* admired were coming up and asking for my autograph for their kids and friends. One day, we were filming outside on the Fox lot, around a giant umbrella the Penguin had left in the street. Between takes, I went over to greet a crowd of children who'd been watching the filming. The first two I greeted were standing next to a small, thin, blond-haired man in a seersucker jacket and a white shirt: it took me a long moment before I realized it was Steve McQueen. He introduced himself, said he had a day off from shooting *The Sand Pebbles* and had brought his kids to meet Batman. It was a strange feeling: just three years before I'd been sitting in a movie theater watching him elude the Nazis in *The Great Escape*. Now here he was, smiling like a kid as he shook my hand and called me Batman. And I admit getting a small ego boost by the fact that none of the other kids gave the movie star a second glance. Their eyes were on me.

Clint Eastwood also paid a visit to the set, and we later became friends. At the time, he and I shared publicity agents, Ruth and Paul Marsh, and they brought him over. It was an odd meeting. I was in full costume, in character and reflective as I waited to go into a shot. So our "conversation" consisted of Ruth and Paul doing most of the talking, like interpreters, while the two of us stood there and nodded. Clint had just returned from Europe where he'd been making his spaghetti westerns, the first of which, the three-year-old *A Fistful of Dollars,* was finally going to open in the U.S. The "buzz" on the film was terrific. We all felt that Clint was on the verge of major stardom, though none of us, including the self-effacing Clint, could have imagined just how major it would be.

(Thanks to the success of his films and *Batman,* my *Relentless Four* got a few bookings. But the reviewers were unkind: they wondered where Robin was and commented on how they wanted me in a Batmobile not on a horse. As I read the reviews, I felt a chill up and down my spine; I wanted to be Jimmy Stewart in *It's a Wonderful Life,* to see what the reviews would have said if Batman had never lived . . .)

Breathtaking Kim Novak also came by one day, and told me she wanted to do a role on the show. Though it wouldn't come to pass, I asked her to lunch. When we broke, I pulled on a bathrobe, which was easier than climbing in and out of the costume, climbed into her Jaguar, and she drove us to a nearby restaurant, an intimate place that allowed me to eat there any way I showed up. She also brought in two large dogs, who sat dutifully by her side during our meal.

Our booth was dark and romantic, and as we talked I slipped my arm around her shoulders. There was a nip on my wrist, and it wasn't Kim. One of the dogs had climbed up and given me a little proprietary warning. It must have made an amusing picture to the other customers: Kim Novak, two snarling dogs and me in a bathrobe enjoying lunch.

The biggest thrill of all was when Jose Ferrer brought his and Rosie Clooney's kids to visit. Jose was such a great actor and such a fine and gracious human being that I was quite star-struck the morning they stopped by, and very inhibited. It's like having to sculpt with Michelangelo looking over your chisel. However, I was struck with an inspiration, and as soon as we broke for lunch I asked Bill Dozier to try and come up with a spot for Ferrer on the show. I suggested a criminal called the Bloodhound, with a Cyrano-sized sniffer. Bill said he'd think about it, though nothing ever came of it; Bill liked to come up with ideas himself.

14

SPENT MY time off alone with my children and their friends at my apartment, though it was often necessary to ignore the ringing phone and chiming doorbell and knocks on the beachside windows as fans found out where I lived and came calling, or agents called suggesting lunch, or reporters got through wanting stories.

All of that was new to me, not so much a bother as just plain fascinating. I was still the same person I'd been a few weeks before, but now everyone wanted to meet me. I was lucky, too. Our show was light and it was loved, and people were friendly and funny and full of good-will when they met me. Stars of more somber or rough-and-tumble shows, like Efrem on *The F.B.I.* or David Hedison on *Voyage to the Bottom of the Sea,* got different kinds of reactions, people with questions about stakeouts or oceanography or criticisms about inaccuracies in govern-ment or marine procedures.

Not us. There were no veterans of the Gotham City Police Force tuning in. People were happy just to see us and thank us and smile at us. Once, when we were shooting in a park, I stepped out of my trailer in costume and walked over to the barricade that had been set up to keep people back—about five hundred of them, in fact. There was an old woman in the front, and as I stood there shaking hands and signing the autograph books of those around her, she extended a trembling hand, touched my cape, then slowly withdrew the hand and looked at it as though she'd touched the Shroud of Turin. I wanted to say some-thing to her but decided against it, not wishing to spoil what had ob-viously been a moving experience.

As the show's renown spread, the crowds increased; one day, we showed up at Rancho Park and found over three thousand fans waiting.

We hadn't sufficient personnel for crowd control at that level, and after Burt and I waved to the fans and thanked them for their support, we were forced to leave. There were cries of disappointment, but no rowdiness or rioting. Most of the time, our fans were well behaved. Or maybe it was just the times. But Batmania continued.

The fans were so pleasant, in fact, that one Halloween, feeling a little goofy from overwork and sleep deprivation, I went out in the Batsuit for some experimental trick-or-treating in Beverly Hills and Culver City. Residents of La La Land may be used to spotting stars, but not superheroes. They couldn't believe the real Batman was at their doors. Some of them tried to be cool and smiled politely, but most of them lost it, laughing and calling other family members to the door. One woman fainted.

But the show had its drawbacks as well. The hours were long. That costume got more uncomfortable and restrictive as it rubbed parts of me raw. And, on a personal level, there were disappointments, too—especially the money, which wasn't what it should have been.

By the last season I would be making $4,500 a week, over $75,000 a year. That was double what I had started at. Not much by today's standards (stars of hit shows make more than my yearly fee each week), and even by then, our guest villains made more. Burt was making even less than I. We also had a standard, take-it-or-leave-it employment contract which paid us for a total of six reruns of each episode, and we burned that off in our first two years of syndication.

Burt and I were also hurt on the licensing. We got nothing when the likeness of the comic book Batman was used, which was fair enough, but we only received a pittance on toys, games, bubble gum cards, and publications that used our photos. I once sued for an accounting but settled out of court . . . for a fraction, I'm convinced, of what I was due. (In retrospect, I realize that I should have gone right out and endorsed color TVs, since the show accounted for a huge increase in sales.)

Yet the things that bothered me the most (and still do) had nothing to do with money or pressure. They had to do with the perception of the show.

I loathed the word "camp." It demeaned our efforts by suggesting that what we were working hard to achieve was so easy or corny or bad

that anyone could do it. We just made it look that way. Critics and pop culture historians say we defined camp, but that was really just a convenient shorthand for them. Dozier only used the term in public, as a press-pleasing shorthand, and never in any directives or memos from his office. He didn't like the connotation either.

So that I could make my anti-camp case with reporters who "camped" out on us, I read Susan Sontag's 1964 essay on camp and also looked up the etymology of the word. I found out that camp was short for "camp brothel," a place where gay men met and "flaunted" their sexuality. In art, "camp" had come to describe something so pretentious or ostentatious that it was amusing or pseudo-sophisticated.

We weren't that. We were farce. We were a lampoon. We were the movie serials of the 1930s and 1940s done against a fun-house background. Instead of G-Man Rex Bennett stuck in a runaway airplane or Zorro cornered in a burning warehouse, Batman and Robin were trapped inside a giant hourglass or lashed to a perforation machine to be turned into player piano rolls.

Bizarre? You bet. If you expect people to come back on Thursday night, you've got to give them an unusual cliffhanger that demands an unusual escape. But unusual isn't camp.

Pop art? Sure. This was the age of Warhol and Lichtenstein. These artists and others had elevated to "art" status objects or subjects that were formerly considered artless or undistinguished. The big ZAPs and POWs during our fight scenes were pop art. So were the overstated voiceovers ("Tune in tomorrow . . . same Bat-time, same Bat-channel . . . "). But while camp can be pop art, the reverse isn't automatically true. And I'm still not sure what "avant-camp" is, which was something the *New York Times* came up with.

As if the camp label weren't rankling enough, there was and still is a belief—especially among a small cult of comic book fans—that we somehow ruined the character by "making fun" of him. The comic book purists have always been a vocal bunch, and I'd like to address their charges . . . or, at least, put them in context.

At the time we did our show, the comic books themselves, the magazines that I and Dozier and others had gone to the newsstand and bought, were sillier than anything we ever created. Batman was battling foes that ranged from the Creature from the *Green* Lagoon to the other-dimensional Bat-Mite to the Bat-Ape, a gorilla in a Batman suit. In one of the comic books I read, the evil Clayface flew away from a crime by molding himself into Pegasus: a winged horse with a suitcase in its mouth!

Batman himself was turned into a giant, a merman, the Zebra Batman, the Invisible Batman, and Rip Van Batman. He met an alien version of himself and was even mummified. His utility belt was equipped with a Magnet Batarang, a Flash Bulb Batarang, a Seeing-Eye Batarang, a Police Whistle Batarang, and he once built and used Batarang X, capable of carrying a passenger. He had a Flying Bat-Cave, a Whirly-Bat, and a Frog Man Batsuit complete with pointy ears.

In addition to Robin, he was helped in his crimefighting escapades by Batwoman, a midget Batboy, Batwoman's niece, Bat-Girl, a different Batgirl, and Ace, the Bat-Hound. Yes, a German shepherd who donned a Bat-mask and narrated his own adventures. Maybe I should have made room for my Wonderdog Stormy on the series.

In another comic book, published shortly after we debuted, Batman teamed up with Jerry Lewis, a.k.a. Ratman.

And *our show* was silly?

Mind you, the publishers had a very good reason for coming up with the stories they did. As comic books faced increasing competition from TV throughout the 1950s, and then from color TV in the 1960s, it was necessary for them to get more and more outlandish. And the newly formed watchdog group, the Comics Code Authority, made it impossible for writers to create stories with teeth. No more gun-toting, neck-breaking Batman as in the 1940s.

The point is, not only didn't we start the trend toward the "silly," but we were far from its most flagrant practitioners.

Perhaps more importantly, the time was wrong for a sinister, film noir Batman. When ABC TV president Thomas Moore first sat down with VPs Edgar Scherick and Douglas Cramer in January of 1965 to talk about a Batman show—before Dozier was brought aboard—they wanted something along the lines of *The Man from U.N.C.L.E.*, something to appeal to kids and to the adults the advertisers wanted to reach. A *fun* Batman. That's why they approached a sitcom producer like Dozier in the first place, even if he did take ABC to places they'd never expected to go.

But they were right in their initial thinking. There was a lot of tension in the world, and TV news—which had come of age just over two years before that, covering President Kennedy's assassination—was, for the first time, feeding satellite-relayed violence into the nation's homes. Every night there was vivid footage of the growing war in Southeast Asia, civil rights unrest, and a heated space race with the Soviets. (Viewers complained mightily, in fact, on March 17, 1966, when ABC dared to cut into our show on the East Coast with news that astronauts Neil Armstrong and David Scott were in danger aboard their Gemini 8 spacecraft. I've always been embarrassed rather than flattered by how many thousands of viewers called to complain.)

Rock and roll music was getting angrier and more "relevant" all the time, and when we premiered in January of 1966 serious dramas like *Combat* and *The Fugitive* were on the way out. The airwaves were dominated by the likes of *Gomer Pyle U.S.M.C.*, *The Lucy Show*, *The Andy Griffith Show*, *The Beverly Hillbillies*, *Green Acres*, and *Get Smart*. To have done a grim Bat-and-robbers show would have been wrong for the time.

Look what happened to the played-straight *Green Hornet*, which debuted in September of '66: it was gone by July (too bad; it was a fine show).

Moreover, to those fans who complain that we were obviously making fun of Batman because I didn't have a Mr. Olympia build like the guy in the comic books, and my costume had softer lines than those in the early stories, I must report that these were conscious choices made by Dozier, myself, and the costume designer, because we felt that a real-life Batman would be supple and trim, but more like James Bond than like Steve Reeves's Hercules. (Ron Ely felt that way when he became TV's Tarzan later the same year, and no one complained.) If we'd thought that approach was wrong, I'd have pumped up the way Christopher Reeve did a decade later for Superman, or—since time was tight—I'd have worn a partially padded suit the way George Reeves had for his Superman. But neither of those seemed the right way to go, though even *Newsweek* missed the point. They called me a "flabby travesty of muscle beach," to which I replied: "After reading your story I raced the Batmobile to my friendly neighborhood physician who assured me that I have not an ounce of 'flab' and offered to provide a notarized statement to that effect. Granted, I am not Superman. But neither is Batman."

(That was the truth. The problem was, the waistband of the tights was designed to be stop-your-breathing tight, to keep them wrinkle-free as I moved. Anything covered with skin cells was going to spill over, especially after lunch. The *Newsweek* article was typical of the media seeing "camp"—an out-of-shape Batman—where there really wasn't any.)

As for the design of the costume, as Michael Keaton would discover, a big, leathery cape makes fighting and running extremely clumsy and awkward, and we didn't have the luxury of a motion picture shooting schedule for retakes. My oft-criticized short Bat-ears were "clipped" in order to give us bigger closeups on TV; anyway, that's how they were being drawn in the comic book at the time. (Besides, it isn't the size of your ears, it's how you use 'em!)

We didn't ruin Batman. To the contrary. We rescued the Caped Crusader from the one foe he couldn't overcome: dismal sales. According to Bob Kane, in 1965 the *Batman* comic book was on the verge of being canceled after over a quarter century, and he said he was already looking into other ways of making a living. Had a "serious" *Batman* debuted and flopped, it would have taken the comic book with it. Our show saved the title and made it possible for a new generation to get to know the character. We kept the franchise of Batman alive for generations to come. About the only ones who won't admit it are Warner Bros. and D.C. Comics. They have made a point of giving no regard to our contribution. It doesn't make any sense to me, but I'm glad most of the world feels otherwise. One of my most prized mementoes of those days is a gift Bob gave me in June 1966, a beautiful drawing of the Caped Crusader, with this inscription: "To my buddy, Adam, who breathed life into my pen and ink creation—Wishing you continued and growing success always."

15

OTHER ACTORS have said that they avoid TV because the pace doesn't give them a chance to do their best work, and to some degree that's true. You don't have a lot of time to rehearse, to think, to create a character.

Fortunately, I pretty much knew who Batman and Bruce Wayne were before the cameras turned. And the speed with which we worked had one creative dividend: it helped to keep our show fresh and immediate. I've always felt that one reason shows like ours or *Star Trek* or *The Monkees* hold up today is the combination of good dialogue and a sense of spontaneity. The latter wasn't acting: it was real.

People are always surprised when I tell them that I don't remember a lot of what happened on specific episodes, and that there was rarely time to chat with the extraordinary guest stars we had on the show. But it's true. The schedule was murder.

I had a small clapboard cottage on the lot Fox owned in Culver City, which was where we ended up doing most of our shooting (not because we nearly burned down the Century Plaza Hotel, but because the soundstages were more accommodating). The cottage consisted of a bedroom and a small sitting room. It was located near our two adjoining soundstages, and I usually stayed there during the season. (Director Blake Edwards has it as of this writing: how many edifices can boast of having housed two cartoon characters, Batman *and* the Pink Panther?)

The typical Batday began with the alarm going off at six-thirty. If I wasn't alone, I'd excuse myself, shower, and be dressed in the tights, tunic, blue shorts, and boots by the time my lighting stand-in, Bill Dyer, arrived with breakfast. (Bill later became George Peppard's stand-in on

The A-Team, and remains a friend.) I would slip into a yellow terrycloth robe to keep from getting jam on my tunic or tights. To help me get into the Batmood, I'd had our wardrobe master stitch a Bat symbol on the pocket of the robe. As I ate my eggs and toast and had a look at the script, I felt every inch Bruce Wayne, master of the manor.

(The blue blazer I sometimes wore as Bruce Wayne also had a design on the pocket—the Wayne family crest. It was a lovely, very official-looking thing done in gold thread with a Latin inscription. People assumed it was something we'd lifted from a book of heraldry, and were always taken aback when I told them, truthfully, that the translation of the Latin was "Art, Nonsense, and Money.")

I had a stereo in the cottage, and Bill would turn it on when he arrived. We always played blues or jazz, usually Oscar Peterson or Charlie Parker, to get our energy levels up and put us in a creative mood. Classical music was too solemn and rock wasn't quite Batman hip. Jazz and blues went down just fine to get me in the starting blocks.

By seven-thirty, the makeup assistant would arrive. I'd wanted this

cottage in particular because it had a big antique barber's chair, and while the makeup was applied I could sit comfortably and run through my lines. The makeup usually took just a few minutes to apply. Bruce Hutchinson, my makeup man, knew I wanted minimal attention because I wanted Batman and Bruce to appear real since they were actually far from that. In those earlier days, makeup tended to fill in the pores, creating a smooth, evenly toned surface that always looked plastic.

Around eight, one of the wardrobe assistants would come over to check the costume. Usually it was Lee Harmon, who has since gone on to become Barbra Streisand's makeup artist. Lee would help me finish dressing, and he'd check the cape and the cowl and utility belt, making sure none of them was stained or torn. I think NASA could have taken a few pointers from our efficiency.

When I was pronounced A-OK, Bill would go outside and rev up the little electric cart we used to drive from the cottage to the set: on each side of the black cart, of course, was a golden bat symbol. I wasn't being lazy by using the cart: it helped me get from air conditioning to air conditioning faster, preventing unphotogenic stains on my costume . . . more on which in a moment.

When we arrived at the set, I was welcomed by one of the most important men on the Bat-team: Milton Stark, my dialogue coach, a well-traveled, articulate gentlemen with the soul of a poet and the curiosity of a scientist. I felt enriched just being around him. Milton's job was to keep everything organized for me. I know that sounds pampered, but we were often working on three and sometimes four shows at once, and, of course, I was in almost every scene of every show we did, either as Batman or as Bruce Wayne. It was difficult keeping everything straight. Again, doing *Batman* was not simply a matter of going in and speaking the lines. The character's relationship with Catwoman, or Riddler, or Alfred, or Robin—all required a complex creative process.

Sometimes Milton and I would go over dialogue I had to do later that day, or he would have fresh changes the writer or director had made in the lines. Many times we'd review dialogue from the next week's script, lines which he felt might not work or had some comedic or dramatic potential I should be aware of before we went into rehearsals. Now and then we'd go over a scene or two from a script that wasn't even finished, something I would be shooting ahead of time to accommodate the schedule of a guest star who was making a cameo. In those instances, Milton would have found out what the story was about and would fill me in.

Many times, Milton and I would also go over scenes I'd already done but had to dub. Most filmgoers and TV viewers don't realize how much dialogue is added to a film or TV show after it's shot. The recording may have to be redone because there was extraneous noise on it, such as wind or cars, or technical problems, or an actor may have flubbed a line. Sometimes the actor has to go and "loop" the lines because he or she wasn't even there when the scene was shot. When the camera is on another actor, a script girl or guy may read your lines so you can leave to get ready for the next scene. That always made me uneasy: I liked to be there to feed lines to other actors, as it helped to make the scene more real for them. But on *Batman* the schedule often didn't cooperate. (I'm disappointed, however, at how many actors, some of them very successful, prefer to lounge in their trailers instead of being there to feed lines to fellow actors. There's no excuse for that.)

If I had to do dubbing over a lunch break or in the evening, Milton would hop into the car with me for the ride from Culver City to Fox, where our shows were edited, scored, and finished up. It always amazed me how just a week or so after I'd finished an episode, I could forget it completely. I didn't want the clutter in my brain.

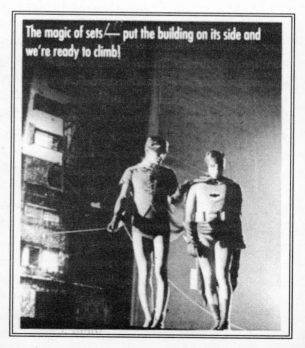

The magic of sets ⟵ put the building on its side and we're ready to climb!

Milton knew all of the scripts we had done or were working on, inside and out. He carried around a small stack of them, earmarked and indexed, and he could give me a line in context whenever I needed it. If I were blocking out a fight scene, I might step back for a moment and motion to Milton. He'd run over, give me the lines for the next dialogue scene, and I'd float them on the top of my head as I leapt back into the fight. It's surprising how much one can memorize that way. I also had a second dressing room, a small one built on wheels, and it was never more than thirty feet from where I was shooting. Whenever I had a minute (often it was literally no more than that), Milton and I would retire and go over the script. Those were helpful "quickies," as the crew called them.

Even with Milton's assistance, though, it was difficult to get through a lot of the pseudo-scientific dialogue they contrived for the Batcave. In order to speed things up, I suggested they get me a teleprompter for those scenes.

Dozier was against it. He didn't want to spend the money for some-one to run it, and he thought I'd soon be wanting it for every scene. I assured him that wouldn't be the case, but he wasn't buying. Annoyed, I came up with an admittedly childish way of convincing him: whenever I had a problem with a line like "Let's run it through the Interdigital Batsorter and Hyperspectrographic Analyzer, Robin," I'd drop a prop, something small that bought me ten or twenty seconds to nail the line so it would fall trippingly from the tongue. After a couple of days of this, I got my teleprompter. (Lest you feel that I was abusing my power, keep in mind that Dozier was making five or six times what Burt and I earned. He also gave the narrator—himself—a hefty raise the second season.) And later, everyone could see how much time was saved.

The teleprompter proved to be great for me. It also helped to make nonsense dialogue more exciting: since there were no emotional pegs for us to use, the teleprompters allowed us to give the lines a more spontaneous and interesting reading.

Lunches were usually spent working, if not on the show then on the phone, with reporters, or with Dozier or my agent or whoever needed to talk to me. In the early days, Milton and Dyer and I would leave the lot together for a quick bite, just to clear our heads. Unfor-tunately, sometimes we cleared them a little too completely and were late getting back to the set: after I was docked a few thousand bucks, I decided that was much too expensive for lunch and we stuck to sandwiches from the commissary.

Sometimes it was also necessary to do a little flesh-pressing on the soundstage. So many friends and relatives of the cast and crew wanted to visit that set that Dozier had come up with the idea of setting up grandstands on the soundstages. Empty seats were filled by selling tickets to the general public! I don't know who ended up with the money (it wasn't me and Burt), but in the early days of the show I always spent at least a half hour a day signing autographs and posing for pictures. I didn't mind, of course, because it was great for the kids in the audience and their affection was sincere. But it did slow us down considerably, and eventually ushers had to be posted to limit access by the guests.

If my kids were visiting, I tried to devote my lunchtime to them. Nga brought them over whenever they weren't in school, my relationship with her having settled into a nice, warm friendship. She was genuinely happy for me, which speaks well for her.

After we wrapped actual shooting for the day, which was usually around seven, the cast would assemble for rehearsals, or else I'd do the dubbing or work with Burt and the stunt crew on action bits. I'd get back to the cottage sometime between nine at night and midnight and, with or without Milton, I'd review the next day's lines. Usually I would have the company of a lovely assistant.

That was my life for three years. I missed not being able to get in more physical activity in the outdoors during the week. I liked to climb and bicycle and ski, and there was no time even for evening walks. I made up for it on weekends, though. Jonelle, Hunter, and I would go hiking or surfing or horseback riding or play volleyball. That was not only good for the body but for the soul: I'd come back to work on Monday whipped, cleansed, and ready to hit the Batpoles.

However, one Monday, I remember waking up wiped out and feverish. I went to the studio, could barely move, and was taken to the hospital with the flu.

Did that stop the Batcrew from working? Not at all. They put my stunt double, Hubie Kerns, in the Batsuit, shot from behind and from

a distance, and did nearly three days of shooting without me. Didn't miss a minute. When I came back, I shot the close-ups then went to the recording studio, where my voice was dubbed over Hubie's. I was amazed. Sixty percent of a *Batman* episode had been done without me, and no one from Dozier to Burt let me forget it. As Howie Horwitz put it, "Tell your agent not to be too tough negotiating your next contract. Between Hubie and all the tape we have of your voice, we could probably do the season without you."

Howie loved to keep me on edge with exaggeration. Fighting the Joker and the Riddler was easy compared to tackling movie magic and the threats of producers.

16

BURT WAS great to work with. He was really into the show, into being a superhero, terrific at taking direction, and his boyish enthusiasm as Robin really gave me something to play off of. He brought out the paternal wiser adult in my character.

Naturally, we had our spats; that happens in any relationship, especially in a high-pressure situation like *Batman*. The biggest and silliest one had to do with our accommodations on the lot. Burt didn't have a cottage, which rankled him, as it would any teenager. He also was making less than I was, but experience (not to mention a tough agent) has its privileges. And it was his first real credit.

Burt had a dressing room on the soundstage, and he'd closet himself there to study his lines, play chess (he's a sharp player), or entertain a lady friend. When we were all ready and waiting, he'd erupt with the flair of youth, punching his gloved fists together, raring to go, ready to be chastised by Bruce, cautioned by Batman, or beaten or blown up by a villain.

Sometimes, though, toward the end of the first season, he kept us waiting. I suspected that he was being petulant, so I'd retire to my dressing cubicle on the soundstage and work there until he was ready. Then I'd emerge.

Well, it didn't take long for this to evolve (or devolve) into a matter of protocol worthy of the United Nations. Burt didn't want to come out first and, as a matter of pride, neither did I. I liked Burt, and we were on the same team, but if I gave in on this, I was afraid he'd start throwing his weight around in the scenes themselves. Better to stop it now, I thought. So what used to be Burt's delays of three, four, or five minutes became, with my participation, schedule-destroying delays of a quarter hour or more. I felt terrible about it, but by that time I couldn't back down without losing face.

After a week or so of this, Dozier or Horwitz decreed that our dressing rooms were to be placed facing each other. When they were ready for us on the set, an assistant director would stand between the rooms like a referee at a fight and call us to the set. The doors would open together, Burt and I would look at each other, and we'd step out together. After a few days of *that* silliness, we agreed to end the feud and come out when we were ready.

It was all very silly, but it's like a company car or a corner office with a view, one of those trophies you want on your shelf because it indicates status and means respect.

Sometimes Burt's enthusiasm got him into trouble with the cast or crew. Writer Stanley Ralph Ross tells the story about how Burt came to him after the first or second script he'd written and complained that his part was too small. Stanley's one of the most easygoing writers I've ever worked with (he's also a minister, who officiated at Burt's most recent marriage ceremony), and he was happy to give Burt what he asked for. The next script he wrote had Burt in most every scene, which meant long hours on the set and in those uncomfortable tights. Burt complained again, this time about having too much to do. Stanley's solution: in the very next script, he had Burt kidnapped in the first scene and not rescued until virtually the last.

Burt wised up. He went to Stanley after that, apologized for having complained at all, and promised never to do it again. Everyone needs an experience like that, like my dunkings at the hand of ''Roll'm'' Sholem, as a reminder that actors serve themselves and the project best when they do what Spencer Tracy advised: learn the lines, show up, and don't bump into the furniture or the other actors.

In the first few weeks I became a sort of big brother to Burt where acting and studio politics were involved; in other matters, Burt was very definitely his own man. During the run of the show, Burt's wife Bonnie stopped coming to the set, which may have been a mistake: Vince Edwards's stunning ex-wife Cathy was cast in one episode, and she wasted no time in giving Burt a heavy-duty dose of dazzle. Once she entered his life, Burt's stays in the dressing room grew longer and his marriage came to an end. I can't really blame Burt for his wandering eye: fame was new to him, temptation was everywhere, and Burt had a high energy level and strong curiosity. He could also get in and out of his tights faster than I could, which was a distinct advantage. Cathy became Burt's second wife, though it didn't work out; as of this writing, Burt is happily married to a financier's daughter named Tracy. They have a daughter and live in a California beach town, where Burt pursues his various business projects, which include producing childrens' videos. Nowadays we only see each other at infrequent cast reunions.

Because of the grueling schedule, there wasn't time for Burt and me to "lose it" for very long if something struck us funny. This was more of a problem for me than for Burt. For one thing, his funny bone wasn't as close to the surface as mine and he could tough it through most situations, not laughing until the take was through. For another, I had most of the ultra-straight (and hence silly) dialogue. Once in a while, it would take us a quarter of an hour to get through a take twenty seconds in length, but there were two times when we had to scrap a scene altogether and move on to something else.

In one episode, the Catwoman had left us clues in the form of three golden cat statuettes. As we contemplated the figurines, I was pacing and Burt was sitting beside them on the table. During the take, Burt picked one up and held it up to his face. And I responded with the scripted dialogue: "Drop that golden pussy, Robin! It could be radioactive."

One of the crew members tittered, which was all it took. I broke up, and then Burt started laughing. It took us seven or eight times after that to get through it. We could hardly make it to that line, and the editor absolutely needed it to cut into the episode. We finally got it, with a great deal of pain. I would pinch my leg to keep a straight face, and I had tears from the effort.

Another time, Batman and Robin had planted a listening device in a drawer in the Penguin's lair. As I reached in to retrieve the bug, I saw that the prop people had replaced our Batbug with a cockroach the size of a prune. No one who has lived in Hawaii can stay afraid of bugs for very long, and this one didn't intimidate me. I picked it up and continued the scene as the bug microphone crawled along my glove and up my arm.

Madge Blake, our Aunt Harriet, was standing off to the side and

With Yvonne Craig

was the first to get grossed out. Others began to stifle laughs as the bug went across my chest and down the Bat symbol. Then the off-camera hilarity really started. But the cockroach wasn't the problem. After the real (or rather, unreal) bug was brought in, I tried to do the scene again and started laughing. And then everybody else laughed. We gave up on it after twenty minutes and came back to it later in the day.

A lot of stories like these fall into the "you had to be there" category. It's important to understand, though, that because of the pressure we were under, it didn't take James Thurber to set us off. Just a bug or a radioactive pussy was enough of a safety valve to get us going.

Usually, though, there wasn't time for these kinds of shenanigans, and the cast was utterly professional. In that respect, the show was lucky (and Dozier's casting people were smart) to have brought in actors who were not only good, but whose stature gave weight to the fluff. This was especially true with the casting of veteran Alan Napier as Bruce's butler and confidant Alfred. Like Alec Guinness in *Star Wars* or Marlon Brando in *Superman,* he was an anchor for the fanciful goings-on.

Alan was a courtly man who stood six-foot-five, a real sweetheart with an arch sense of humor that fit *Batman* perfectly. He was sixty-three when he came to our show, a veteran of classic films like *The Song of Bernadette, The Uninvited,* and *Julius Caesar,* and I was sorry (once again!) that I didn't have more time to socialize with him or with his lovely daughter, who came to the set from time to time. I'd often walk by and overhear him talking about "the good old days" with crew members or guest stars, and I would have loved to stop and listen to some of those stories.

I was so fond of Alan, in fact, that two of the most painful memories I have of my years as Batman (and after) involve him.

One was an episode where Alfred was forced to don the Batsuit, get into the Batmobile, and rush to our rescue. Alan has worn some unusual period costumes in his career, but never anything like the Batsuit. He felt self-conscious and a bit ridiculous. He had voiced his misgivings during the rehearsal, felt that we were pushing the absurd a little too far (I agree), but the writer, director, and Dozier thought it would be a nice way to show just how devoted Alfred was.

Though I ached for Alan and offered to intercede on his behalf, he wouldn't let me. He acted the scenes, pushing through like a member of Tennyson's Light Brigade, bringing what elegance and dignity he could to the material. Afterward, he told Dozier never again to debase Alfred, or him, like that.

Worse than this, however, was the reunion show we did on Fox's *The Late Show* in 1988, with comedian Ross Shafer hosting after Joan Rivers's departure. I've never cared for reunion shows; some fans enjoy them, but I find them bittersweet and shallow, like *This is Your Life* without the fun of the old schoolteachers and former secretaries.

This particular show was the worst of them. Alan had recently suffered a stroke. He was unable to leave his wheelchair and spoke with the greatest difficulty. When he did speak, he couldn't help slurring his words, and viewers who didn't know differently would have thought he was drunk. He had agreed to come on with Julie Newmar, Frank Gorshin, Yvonne Craig (Batgirl), Burt, and me, and I agreed that he should be there, of course. But absolutely no consideration was given to his condition, and I sat there, fuming, as he was asked questions that required lengthy answers, or as the camera would catch this wonderful human being gazing blankly into space. Naturally it was unintentional. But it was also insensitive and shameful. That show was a sad end to his distinguished career; he died shortly after the taping.

Madge Blake was a lovely Aunt Harriet, a character who was created in the comic book just to give Bruce and Dick a reason to be secretive about their dual identities. Otherwise, they could have lounged around in their Batsuits, which would have undercut the drama somewhat. Besides, for reasons we'll get to in a moment, Bill Dozier felt we needed to have a female at Wayne Manor.

Madge was sixty-six at the time, a veteran of films like *Singin' in the Rain* and series like *The Real McCoys* and *The Joey Bishop Show,* and she was a delightful, endearing, slightly dithery woman. She wrote poetry between setups, very heartfelt verse about the difficult times in which we lived and how we all needed to slow down; I was usually too busy to read much of it.

Madge was very much at ease speaking the words she wrote, reading them as fluidly and movingly as a Glenn Close or a Glenda Jackson. She was that good. But whenever the camera was rolling, Madge always paused, stammered, and groped, her voice fluttering. Usually, it's the other way around, the camera bringing out the best in people. Not

Madge. I don't know why this was, but I found it valuable in terms of the character, as it brought out something protective and even a little playful in Bruce.

I hosted at the Hollywood Palace three times and introduced The Supremes, Ray Charles, George Carlin, and many others.

Several of our directors were impatient with Madge, and her parts were cut down whenever they did our show. However, one of them was downright hostile his first day on the set, and that was one of the few times I had to throw my weight around. He didn't like the way she was tripping over her words and told her to learn the speech or he'd give it to Alfred. When he was finished, I glanced across the set and told him that Aunt Harriet *would* be somewhat halting in her speech, terribly concerned about the comfort of those in her charge, Dick and Bruce. Moreover, I told him that her age and sweetness provided an important balance to the intensity and insanity of the rest of the characters. I concluded my little speech by telling him to shut up and let her speak her lines in her own way, without pressure. If not, I told him, I'd give his job to Alfred.

He shut up and let Madge act. The next day, I found a lovely home-baked cake in my cottage on the lot. I don't think it was from the director.

Dear Madge died a year after our series went off the air. Though I didn't go to her funeral (that would have made it a media circus: "Bruce Wayne Bids Aunt Harriet Farewell!") I sent flowers, and even as I did that I realized I had never met her family. Not once, in three years. When I say there was no time to socialize, I mean there was *no* time to socialize.

Dozier himself did the narration for all of our shows, not only because he did a great, very urgent Walter Winchell impression that complemented what we were doing, but because he liked being in the spotlight. He also got paid extra for it. Ego and money were also the reason he played the maître d' in our first episode; as Mel Brooks once put it, "It's *good* to be the king."

The only actor it took some time for me to get in tune with was Neil Hamilton, our Commissioner Gordon. Neil was a veteran character actor who had appeared in classic melodramas like *The Cat Creeps* and *The Mysterious Dr. Fu Manchu,* had been a terrific Digby in the silent *Beau Geste,* and had costarred in one of my favorite movie serials, *King of the Texas Rangers,* playing a Nazi tangling with former football superstar Slingin' Sammy Baugh.

Neil was sixty-seven when we started, an old crony of Dozier's, and as he did all of his roles, he took our show very, very, *very* seriously. He hated having people fuss over him; he didn't even like wearing makeup, and would only take some powder to tone down the bright highlights on his forehead, nose, and cheeks. He never brought his family to the set, he rarely smiled, and he studied his script intently between setups. He usually knew the lines of everyone else in all of his scenes. And he got genuinely pissed off at me during the rehearsals of several early episodes because I laughed while reading the script for the first time. This was straight drama to him, and when you see him saying a line like "If ever we needed the Caped Crusader, it is now," he genuinely means it. More than once he threatened to leave if I didn't take the work seriously; when I told him I was, he didn't believe me. Or that this was comedy.

You couldn't fault Neil for his professionalism, and God bless him, he was never late, never screwed up, and his professional cool was a steadying influence when the rest of us felt like screaming from the deadlines and pressures. Out of deference to him, I would always endeavor to swallow or cover my laughs during the run-throughs, and tried desperately never to break up in any of our scenes together. If I did, I pretended to cough so he wouldn't think I was laughing.

Neil also didn't quite click with the big, earthy actor who played

Chief O'Hara, Stafford Repp. Staff was in his middle forties, a veteran of shows like *The Thin Man* and *The New Phil Silvers Show*. He had a great sense of humor, was also as professional as could be, loved the show, and was as thrilled as a kid to be a part of it. But he laid on the Irish a little thicker than Neil felt he should, and the more annoyance that showed in Neil's face, the more his mouth tightened, the more Staff slathered it on. He didn't do it to be mean: he did it to put an added kick in their scenes together, and in a failed effort to bring Neil into the group.

Staff was also smart enough to invest his earnings in a series of car washes, which I understand did quite well for him. Sadly, he died of a heart attack in November 1974. He was fifty-six.

17

CONSIDERING THE size of the show, the complexity of the fights and staging, and the intricacy of the special effects, problems like those that plagued the first episode were surprisingly rare. The crew was just so resourceful that nothing fazed them. I remember us staging one shot in the Batcave that was so big and complex we hadn't left room for the cameras! Since there wasn't time to restage it, our cameraman, a sharp pro named Ralph Woolsey, moved the camera *outside* the soundstage, threw up these huge tarpaulins all over to keep out the sunlight, and gave us one helluva shot.

Incredibly, we did have a glitch during the first show that no one caught until it was too late to do anything about it: when Burt and I slid down the Batpoles in the study, I was on the left side and Burt was on the right. When we emerged in the Batcave, we were on opposite sides. (I came down on the right so I could run to the driver's side of the Batmobile.) We re-shot it with our names on the poles, which some critics (of course!) saw as more evidence of "camp," while others just wondered about it (the same people who wondered, "How do they change while they're sliding down?")

I've also been asked why the switch that opened the concealed Batpole panel was hidden inside a bust of Shakespeare. There was no hidden significance (e.g., that the Bard might also have been a man of two identities, Francis Bacon or Edward de Vere). It was simply a bit of studied whimsy on the part of the production designer. It did work, though not in the way viewers were led to believe. When I pushed the button, it turned on a light behind the sliding bookshelf, the signal for the crew to pull it open.

The Batpoles were fun. Whenever we did the shot where we slid down from the library, I tried to slide around and around to present the audience with my face instead of my butt . . . and also because, frankly, I had fun doing it that way. And it looked more "dynamic" for the duo.

When we slid through the holes in the floor of the Wayne Manor library, we landed on old mattresses fifteen feet below. Naturally, crew members would use those mattresses for other things, and our landings began to kick up some unpleasant odors as the weeks passed. If you've ever used an outhouse, think about slipping through the seat and you'll have an idea what it was like to hit the mattresses. Once, I even landed on an empty wine bottle with a *Midnight Express* label. Not even the good stuff. But you learn not to complain about the crew too much, because they always get the last word, like the time they painted the Batpoles and "forgot" to tell us. Or the many times they'd "miss" their cues and forget to pull the doors open as we ran to the Batpoles.

The second part of the slide, into the Batcave, was filmed just a few times and reused from episode to episode. It was the more dangerous of the two, since we were up on catwalks and sliding down to the hard studio floor. I didn't do many fancy turns in those shots. I just held on and hoped I made it all the way down.

Another set we often used was the side of the building which Batman and Robin ascended in the wall-climbing scenes. We ended up using this a great deal because it was the only way we could accommodate all the celebrities who wanted to appear on the show. As our characters made their way up the wall, some famous face, like Jerry Lewis, George Raft, Sammy Davis, Jr., Edward G. Robinson, and Van Williams and Bruce Lee (as the Green Hornet and Kato), would pop out of windows to say hello.

This set was redressed each week so it looked like a different building, though the design and basic drill were always the same. The wall was built on a six-degree angle to keep us from falling over when we assumed our crouched Batrope-climbing positions. Nylon fishing lines were attached to our capes to hold them straight behind us (as gravity would do if we were climbing), and with the camera tilted on its side, Burt and I would "struggle" up the wall, usually pausing to have a close encounter with a celebrity. The celebrities actually had it tougher than we did, since they'd have to slide under the set, open the window "up,"

and awkwardly push themselves through so they looked as if they were leaning out.

No, as the weeks wore on the biggest problem wasn't the sets, props, and special effects. As I'd feared, it was the damn costumes.

It didn't take long for me to figure out how to not get choked by the cape. I got it out of the way by shifting my shoulders in a heroic manner as I turned to look at people. That would cause the cape to swing behind me—safely and, I thought, rather dramatically. But the cape presented other problems. It was made of a fine, light silk, and if it weren't hanging straight behind me when I threw a punch, it would cling to my arm and get in the way or tear. Sometimes it would snag on my utility belt and hang in an unbecoming fashion, necessitating a retake, and once it caught fire when as a Batador I was battling flames on a wall. That incident, at least, taught me how to get out of the cape *really* fast.

The boots were hot but bearable, but the cowl was a constant source of frustration. I learned to deal with the restricted vision by staying extremely alert and memorizing the terrain as much as possible. The truth is, I did this in every part I played because I'm nearsighted and wear glasses off the set. Even when I was Bruce Wayne, I had to pay close attention during rehearsals to make sure I'd hit my marks once the glasses came off. (Visitors to the set were always taken aback to see me in my Batsuit, sans cowl, with my glasses on. Batman from the neck down, Rip Kirby from the neck up. An odd sight indeed.)

But even these preparations didn't prevent me from occasionally stumbling when I had to step off a curb, or Burt and I from colliding frequently when we turned or ran. I developed a deep respect even for the actors with 20/20 vision who've played Zorro and, wearing masks, had to fence and jump from balconies onto chandeliers or Lone Rangers who, without peripheral vision, went leaping from horseback onto runaway stagecoaches or escaping desperadoes.

The cowl was also very abrasive on the cheeks and nose, and hotter than the fiendish Minstrel's giant barbecue. I was in and out of that cowl so much I nearly wore off the end of my nose. After just a few minutes I'd start perspiring, which meant that not only my makeup would have to be cleaned up, but my Batsuit as well. Superheroes are not supposed to sweat, and a bead of perspiration, a dark mark on the chest of my gray tunic, destroyed the carefully constructed illusion that I was an unflappable crimefighter. Consequently, as if the costume wasn't hot enough, I was quickly burdened with a loud, steamy hair dryer that hovered all around me between takes. Once again, I tried to turn the drawback into an asset, using the distraction to help me develop the powers of concentration that an actor should have anyway. Speaking of assets, I have kept several of my original cowls for all these years. I understand from collectors that they are highly valued, so I'm glad I hung on to them.

Worse than the cowl, however—in fact, worst of all—was the problem I had going to what we all took to calling (for obvious reasons) the Batroom. Whenever nature called, virtually everything had to come off: gloves, boots, utility belt, trunks, tights. On our schedule, there literally wasn't time to relieve oneself! I dealt with it by laying off coffee on days when I was in costume. Burt didn't, but, as I've said, he was better at getting in and out of those tights than I was.

The tights were not the modern Lycra they would use today, but were rougher and hotter. Burt had an ''allergy'' to Lycra and had a problem with itching that I didn't have. I felt sorry for him. They bothered him so much that between takes Burt would affect a strange, bow-legged kind of shuffling walk to communicate to the wardrobe people just how uncomfortable his tights were. Unfortunately, this was also communicated to everyone on the set and, finally, throughout the studio. Dozens of carpenters and grips and others began imitating this walk, acting as if they had terminal body lice in their jeans; Burt became the butt of some pretty stupid jokes without quite understanding why. He ended up discarding the tights in some shots, or else shaving his legs and oiling up like a Venice Beach bodybuilder. Then I ribbed him, of course.

But Burt had another problem as well. Shortly after we went on the air, the Catholic Legion of Decency decided they didn't like the way he filled his tights, so to speak. There was too much him, too much bulge. Wardrobe Master Jan Kemp tried fitting the tights with a supporter and two pairs of underwear, but neither of them worked, according to Burt. Finally, a doctor at Fox gave him pills that reduced his problem for three hours at a ''stretch,'' again, according to Burt.

Burt complained to anyone who'd listen. There followed the obligatory "Dick" Grayson and Burt "Wad" jokes, which he took with good humor, though I confess I was somewhat upset because the doctor didn't come to *me* with the pills, too. Still, I couldn't help but think back to Dozier's fears that Robin might outgrow the role. Perhaps the pills were part of a monstrous, Joker-esque plot the producer had to keep Burt from growing or his voice from dropping . . .

But the Boy Wonder's tight green shorts weren't the only aspect of the show that drew fire. More than one watchdog group got on us immediately about the possibility of Batman and Robin being gay. This wasn't exactly a new idea: back in 1953, a headline-hunting psychiatrist named Frederic Wertham got it in his thick little head that comics were bad for kids, which led to Senate subcommittee hearings and the formation of the stifling Comics Code Authority the following year. Among Wertham's many outrageous charges were that Batman and Robin were gay.

I say "outrageous" not because it wasn't conceivable. It was just *way* out of left field. We were talking about a comic book, not *The Picture of Dorian Gray*. It hadn't been on Bob Kane's mind or on Lorenzo Semple, Jr.'s mind. But now we had religious and political conservatives and even old Dr. Wertham writing about it and speaking against us.

With Nga packing to go to California

Bill Dozier, his staff, and Burt and I talked about whether or not simply to ignore it. We decided no, that the issue had to be addressed before it took on a life of its own. We all talked to the press about it, Bill telling reporters that Wertham was just a "dirty old man" and the watchdog groups were "all publicity hounds" (I really liked the thematic dog metaphor). Depending on the interviewer, I alternated between saying something like "Gays or straights, it's all the same in the ratings," or "Aunt Harriet would never allow it."

The tempest in a teapot went away quickly, but I was always dismayed by the fact that one ill-informed man with access to a printing press had all but sunk an industry back in the 1950s, and ten years later those same misguided ideas were lapping against our shores. It gave me a powerful, firsthand respect for the potency of ideas and the influence one person could have on others. And as "Batmania" spread across the nation, and Burt and I were sent on various promotional tours, I was enormously careful about what I said and did, especially with kids. Many cynics took this to be a continuation of my TV persona, but God knows, I wasn't trying to be a real-life Batman. I was just trying to show people that possibly it was the Werthams of the world who should be watched, not the rest of us.

18

I THINK IT'S significant that our most successful villains tended to be those that came from the comic books: the Joker, Penguin, Riddler, and Catwoman. It wasn't just the genius of Bob Kane, because he didn't create them all. Writer Bill Finger and artist Jerry Robinson, who worked for years on the strip, also contributed characters and designs.

But the comic book was a testing ground for villains: those that didn't cut the mustard, like Simple Simon (whose crimes were based on nursery rhymes) or the Duplicate Man (who could split into two people) didn't come back. The rest did.

The Joker is probably the most famous and well-liked Batman villain, largely because of his insane and sadistic gags and his tortured-clown countenance, which is strikingly more unusual than that of the hero. The Penguin is also a grotesque paradox, a roly-poly figure who loves birds but is also a devious criminal. The Riddler's ingenious puzzles and colorful costume were his claims to fame.

But my personal favorite has always been Selina Kyle, the Catwoman.

Bob Kane said that Catwoman was originally modeled after Jean Harlow, and that he and writer Bill Finger chose cats as a motif not just because she was a cat burglar (though that was reason enough) but because cats were as mysterious and unpredictable as women. The device made her exotic, and allowed Kane and company to accoutre her with all kinds of cat paraphernalia (cat-o'-nine-tails, her hidden catacomb, a catapult, having nine lives, etc.).

But there was obviously more to her appeal than a gimmick, more than the collection of cat symbols.

Stanley Ralph Ross was a relative newcomer to TV (he'd written songs for "My Son the Folk Singer" Allan Sherman) when he was hired to write scripts for *Batman* during the second season. Concurrently, he was also doing some *Man from U.N.C.L.E.*s, and after *Batman* left the air, he went on to write for *All in the Family* and other shows. Stanley wrote eight shows his first season, and six the third, and six of his scripts starred Catwoman.

She was also his favorite villain, and the reason, he said, was the sexual tension between Batman and Catwoman. I can tell you, that tension was real, especially with our first Catwoman, sexy Julie Newmar.

Catwoman posed a unique and wonderful dilemma for the Caped Crusader, and also for the writers. The flirtation couldn't be quite as overt back then as I would have liked it, or as it might be today on a *Hearts Afire* or *L.A. Law* (I can just see Arnie Becker representing Catwoman in a palimony suit against Batman). Thus, the relationship on the show took the form of a strong comedic flirtation between good and evil, as Catwoman constantly tried to seduce and/or eliminate Batman in any sly way she could. Meanwhile, poor Batman was torn between love/lust and resisting what he thought was an unhealthy, excessive passion. Interestingly, it was different for him in our film, when he was Bruce Wayne and Catwoman was posing as the Russian Miss Kitka. Things got pretty hot between them before they were interrupted by Catwoman's minions, but that was okay. Bruce Wayne wasn't the obsessively moral Batman.

Batman had three Catwomen (Catwomans?): Julie Newmar played the part in the first two seasons. In the third season, when she was off shooting the big screen epic *Mackenna's Gold* with Gregory Peck and Omar Sharif, Eartha Kitt took over the part. When we did the movie, former Miss America Lee Meriwether stepped in.

All three women were sleek, beautiful, and exciting, but I had a closer relationship with Julie because she was on six times compared to Eartha's two, because she was my age, and because she was unattached.

Ironically, Julie had never heard of our show or the character when she was first asked to do the part (on a Friday: they needed her for Monday). A product of the prestigious Actor's Studio, she was a dancer/actress living in New York, whom I had first seen as Stupefyin' Jones in the 1959 film *Li'l Abner*. (That was her third film. The former Julie

Newmeyer had also been a dancing girl in *Serpent of the Nile* and one of the *Seven Brides for Seven Brothers*.) Julie went from there to playing the robot Rhoda Miller on *My Living Doll* in the 1964–65 TV season, but what she really wanted to do was movies and plays. Happily, when talks broke down with Suzanne Pleshette (I don't know why) and Julie got the call to play Catwoman, her brother was visiting from college. He went wild when she told him what she was wanted for. It was his enthusiasm that got her to take the next plane west.

At rehearsals, Julie expressed some reservations about the concept of the character. It takes guts to walk into an established ensemble and voice disapproval, and Julie had guts. I was impressed. (Neil was peeved, of course, at one point muttering to Alan, "Why can't she simply do as she's told?" To which Alan replied, "She is playing a villainess, after all.")

Julie felt that Catwoman should be pure evil, teasing Batman rather than actually falling in love with him. She also felt that she should be given a little time and money to develop interesting catlike makeup, something feline for the eyebrows or lips or ears. But Bill Dozier and Stanley had their vision, and Julie went along with it. She brought everything to bear on her interpretation, including her sensual dancer's movements, inventive hissing and purring, scratch-my-belly poses, and pouting, provocative mouth. She also came up with a very clever way of wearing her belt, draping it around her hips instead of around her waist to emphasize her curves. Sheathed in a spangled, skin-tight black costume, her neon-red, curved sharp nails clawing slowly at some unseen prey, she established the character for every actress who followed—including, I'm told, Michelle Pfeiffer in *Batman Returns*. She also caused curious stirrings in my utility belt.

From the start, the flirting was as thick and ticklish as angora: a partly averted glance here, a little smile there. All very enticing, but all for the benefit of the part. She wanted the sexual tension right there on the surface when the cameras rolled. It was a fascinating rite to be a part of. I understood why male and more than a few female viewers fantasized about her.

The worldwide press hinted at an off-camera hot romance between us, and with good reason. Julie was very serious about her work and about maintaining some distance between the hero and villain of the piece, and I had somewhat the same attitude. However, men are rather simple creatures and Julie was the sexiest woman on television. As long as Julie kept at claw's length, I was able to maintain my professional cool. But she was on the set a lot and her flirting became intoxicating. She was tormenting me.

There are some actors who feel that a film experience is incomplete unless they've bedded their leading ladies. Today, for example, there's a smirking, balding hero, and a second-generation superstar, and a pair of he-men who practically have sex with the leading lady written into their contracts.

I assure you I am not one of these actors. Gorgeous costars came and went on *Batman:* among them Julie, Yvonne, Jill St. John, Lee Meriwether, Joan Collins, Leslie Gore, Deanna Lund, Grace Lee Whitney, and my old friend Annie Oakley, Nancy Kovack (who has since become the wife of esteemed conductor Zubin Mehta). If I had set my sights on them, instead of on the work at hand, it would have been exhausting and counterproductive . . . especially if we'd had problems and then had to work together, or if any of them had wanted to come back on the show and the producer hadn't wanted them. The work is what lasts, and it's too important to let your libido interfere.

Of course, Julie was very special: she was all there. And we were quite close. And she *was* the sexiest woman on TV. So it was really tough for me to remain aloof. Julie knew that. She was extremely playful. One midnight, as I entered my cottage, I tripped and looked down: even in the dark I could see a long, gray, padded plank with wires attached and a large, luminous dial with various speeds indicated on it. There was a bright red ribbon tied around the entire contraption. I switched on the light, found a red rose with a note, and read it:

> Happy birthday, Adam. This is the world's first vibrating slant board. I hope you will experience some of the relaxation and pleasure you've been missing with me.
>
> Love, Julie.

It wasn't just her looks and moves that made Julie a great Catwoman. Like the character, she was every inch the "nefarious temptress!" She was my favorite pussycat. Oh, about that hot romance the

Meeting another
caped crusader—1967

press went on about: a true crimefighter, like any other gentleman, never reveals all his secrets. Remember that *Batman* line?—"I prefer to think it's because my heart is pure, Robin." I wasn't exactly hurting for companionship in those days. I was like a kid in a comic book store, and I couldn't avoid taking a peek under every cover that looked interesting, especially when they were constantly being thrust in my face.

It's funny, though. At some point late in the first season, I got bored with those comic books and yearned for a novel. One faceless relationship is like another, none of them especially satisfying, and one weekend, while I was with Jonelle and Hunter, I got it in my head that I should try to repair my broken marriage. I realized what a fool I'd been to let Nga go, to allow my family to be broken up, and I tried to win her back with flowers, phone calls, and even a candlelit family dinner.

But it wasn't to be, though my failed efforts didn't send me to a monastery: quite the contrary. The facade of courtship I mentioned earlier was no longer a requirement, and the rest of 1966 was a time of excess that may have broken some long-standing records in that department, shattered only by what I did when the show went off. In addition to the parties and the studio secretaries, there were ladies I'd meet on airplanes, actresses from other series, and invitations from places like the Batcave topless bar in San Francisco ("We'd love to have you come and enjoy a free night of North Beach pleasures"). The work was my life. Sex was a recreation.

At one point I was spending off-hours with the secretary of a studio boss. We became an item for several months—unknown to the honcho, who coveted her himself and would have barred me from the lot had he known. After that, Lana Wood and I were also quite close. We bumped into each other by accident one weekend on Malibu beach. We remembered meeting in Hawaii, and after a while we got so friendly that we skipped the beach altogether.

I also saw Natalie on several occasions, and much to my satisfaction, she didn't need to be reminded who I was. She was divorced from Robert Wagner but not yet married to Richard Gregson, and we went out for drinks from time to time, to laugh about what a hick she thought I was the night we went out for dinner. She was right. Our paths would cross over the years, and I found her charming, and one of the most devoted Hollywood moms I've ever known. She remarried Wagner, of course, and their home on North Canon Drive in Beverly Hills was full of photos of the kids and the family. She turned down a lot of work to be at home (including Bonnie to Warren Beatty's Clyde), but she never once resented it. It was more important for her to be able to drive to Sunset Boulevard and pick up Natasha at school than for her to see her name in *Variety*. (Or appear on our show, which I'd begged her to do.)

19

ONE OF the best things about doing *Batman* was the chance to work with a variety of directors and more great guest stars than anyone this side of a hit variety show.

Because we'd come on as a mid-season replacement, most TV directors already had their work lined up for them. We had to catch whoever was free, which gave me a chance to work with more directors than I would have under ordinary circumstances. Robert Butler, Charlie Rondeau, Tom Gries, and Larry Peerce were top-notch. Tom and Larry both went on to do fine work in feature films, and Charlie brought his deft comedic touch to *F-Troop* and many other shows. Oscar Rudolph was also a favorite of mine, a man with a great sense of humor who understood that to get the best out of Burt and me he had to throw curves that weren't in the script. For one second-season episode, "Hizzoner the Penguin/Dizzoner the Penguin," he really outdid himself: for guest stars, he got us game show host Allen Ludden, newscaster Chet Huntley, rockers Paul Revere and the Raiders, belly dancer Little Egypt, Jack Benny's announcer Don Wilson, Joe Besser of the Three Stooges, and the legendary old western star Fuzzy Knight. It was an ambitious, exciting show, and a sheer delight. (Imagine the task a director would have trying to do that today—bringing the likes of Vanna White, Peter Jennings, Aerosmith, and so on, together for a prime-time show? Even if it could be done, few would be willing to attempt it.)

The only director I really didn't get along with was Don Weis, who never seemed happy to be doing television and didn't like me in particular. He'd taken offense at on offhanded comment I was said to have made to a reporter, that an orangutan could direct *Batman,* though he wasn't aware of the context of my remark: when we were searching for directors, I had said kiddingly that if we ran out of options, I'd call Hawaii and check on Peaches's availability. Never mind that Peaches is a chimp: the misquote ran in TV Guide and I was on Weis's blacklist.

When I found out that that was what was bugging Weis, I tried to explain what I'd meant; he told me to take a hike, though not in those words.

Weis complained about virtually everything I did, including how I sat in a booth as it spun round and went into a wall. I reacted with controlled surprise, as I felt Bruce Wayne should react, but Don wasn't happy with that. He also didn't like the way I picked up props to examine them as Batman—close up, so he could study them through the mask—or how Batman delivered lines. Happily, he only directed two episodes; Dozier was aware of the personality clash.

For the most part, the guest stars, like the majority of our directors, were also a delight.

Foremost among them were several of the recurring villains. I was closer to Frank and Julie than to the others, but I can't say enough about what fine people and actors Cesar Romero and Burgess Meredith were.

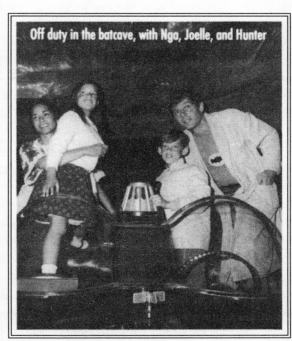

Off duty in the batcave, with Nga, Joelle, and Hunter

Cesar's Joker was so different from the way he really was that people were often amazed when they met him. He was poised, distinguished, a real old-time gentleman . . . though you could tell from the gleam in his eye and smile that beneath the surface

he had a real flair for mischief. That really came out in his performance. After years of playing leading men or smooth conmen, he was
delighted to be playing an out-and-out villain and had a great time. In
fact, this delight contributed an important element to the character.
When costumer Jan Kemp had his first meeting with Cesar and the
producers, he showed them his comic book–inspired designs for an
immaculately tailored burgundy suit with black stripes on the pants, a
green shirt, a black string tie, white face, and green hair. As he flipped
through the color drawings, Cesar started to giggle and then he started
howling. As he did, Dozier looked at FitzSimons, then at Cesar and
said, "Don't lose it!"

Cesar looked over, perplexed. "I'm sorry?"

"The laugh," Bill said. "That's the Joker's laugh."

He didn't mind the makeup, which took about an hour to put on,
though he wasn't fond of the green wig, which was hot and itchy. He
didn't complain, though. As any good actor would, he used the discomfort in his performance. That urgent madness in the Joker's manner
wasn't an act, it was Cesar literally wanting to pull his hair out.

Cesar always came ready to work, knew his lines, and was very giving
and gracious to the other actors. He also had one of the most unusual
methods of preparing for scenes I've ever seen. He would come to the
set, dressed and made up, paper towels under his chin so his whiteface
makeup wouldn't get on his clothing. Then he'd sit down in his seat
and doze off. Not just shut his eyes and rest: Cesar would go right to
sleep.

"I'm collecting my thoughts and marshaling my energy," he would
murmur through those glistening teeth if anyone asked what he was
doing.

But the moment he was called to step in front of the camera, he
was instantly vital and in character. He never missed a cue or fumbled
a line; he was *there.*

Many reviewers talked about what a stroke of genius it was, that is,
"high camp," for us to leave his mustache on under the makeup. Truth
be told, that was something we stumbled on. Originally, when Bill said
he wanted Cesar for the part, Cesar said he'd love to do it but only if
he didn't have to shave. He said that the mustache was an important

part of his debonair Latin persona, and he'd rather lose the part than his mystique. Would makeup cover it? Our veteran makeup man, Ben Nye, said he didn't think so.

As it happened, the producers wanted to do a short screen test of the makeup, to see what looked most effective on film, and Cesar agreed to be their subject. The test consisted of a close-up of Cesar turning his head this way and that, and I poked my head into the screening room to see the results. The ghostly white makeup had been applied over his face, mustache and all. As the film progressed, even without looking closely, we could see the stiff, black hairs popping through the greasepaint as though in time release. It was funny, just the kind of antic silliness we wanted to lace the show, and we decided to go with it. It wasn't something you could ever have planned.

Burgess was also a marvelous man to work with, and he found it wonderfully ironic that after having enjoyed a long and successful career, going back to 1929, he was getting more attention from playing the Penguin than from anything else he'd ever done. (Something that would happen to him again when he played Sly Stallone's mentor in the early *Rocky* films.)

I'd expected him to be disturbed by that: after all, here was an actor who'd been in *Of Mice and Men* and *Advise and Consent* among many other great films, and he was doing a comic book for TV. But he was thrilled.

"What could be better," I remember him saying, "than having women smile at you and kids shrink away from you? It's the best of both worlds."

Like Cesar, Burgess was always prepared and didn't need to be pampered. And he really loved his makeup. It transformed him from a gentle little man into this outgoing avian fiend who, even when the cameras weren't rolling, cackled and muttered to himself, going over his lines, and looked as if he were searching for a behind to pinch. Often, I'd spot him working with his cigarette holder, umbrella, or monocle: how he carried or used these props were extremely important to him, as well they should have been. In fact, one of the props was responsible for giving Burgess one of the Penguin's most memorable characteristics. The comic book character was rarely without his cigarette holder, but Burgess is not a smoker. In our first rehearsals, the smoke irritated his throat terribly and Burgess would sit there coughing. It was a nasal kind of cough, and as soon as he did it, this seasoned pro realized he was on to something: by forcing the cough a little more than necessary, he came up with the Penguin's distinctive quacking. I knew that Mickey Rooney had been strongly considered for the role of the Penguin, but negotiations broke down and the part went to Burgess: after that first rehearsal, I couldn't even imagine anyone else playing the part. Frankly, I still can't.

Costumer Jan Kemp also added his deft touches to bring the character to life. He felt that the comic book Penguin was just a bit too rotund to be believable for TV, so he came up with a slightly trimmer design, using body pads inside the costume to flesh Burgess out. The pads were somewhat restrictive, which helped Burgess to develop the famous waddling walk. The vest and gloves Jan designed were made from *faux* penguin fur, and the feathered fiend's monocle was usually glued in place using putty-like spirit gum. Otherwise, Burgess would've had a tough time holding it in place.

Burgess was also somewhat like Frank in that when he screwed up he got quite angry at himself, grumbling and squawking and stalking around. He always became particularly frustrated when there wasn't enough time to work with the trick umbrellas, which had a tendency to release a gas or liquid or sword prematurely, late, or not at all.

When it was clear that our show was "in" and a surefire career-reviver, everyone wanted to be on. Between guest villains and the many cameos, we ended up with two hundred and fifty celebrities in all, which was quite an accomplishment. Still, I'm sorry about some of the ones that got away. There was Jose Ferrer, of course, but also Robert Kennedy, who was then still the Attorney General and wanted to appear in a cameo as Attorney General. But we could never put that one together. Instead, he hung in his Washington, D.C., office a picture of me I'd inscribed, "From one crimefighter to another." Though I never got to meet him, we spoke by phone, and I discovered that he had a great sense of humor, which I don't think many people realized.

Frank Sinatra, Gregory Peck, and Liz Taylor also wanted to do cameos, but they made their desires known too late and we could never fit them in. Even with one guest spot a week, we could only accommodate twenty-six celebrities a season, tops. And those slots were committed before some of the legends came calling.

The biggest wrangling for a part was when it came time to cast King Tut. A number of big-name actors campaigned for it, including Charlton Heston and Yul Brynner (Yul was turned down because he smoked too much, and we were largely a nonsmoking set). However, Dozier was a fan of the Oscar-nominated Victor Buono (for *Whatever Happened to Baby Jane?*), and he did have both the regal, pompous bearing and wicked delivery that the character needed. He was the only villain created expressly for the show that really caught on.

The late actor was a love, very sly, erudite, sensitive . . . and extremely heavy. He weighed about four hundred pounds, and what I remember most about him is how much he cared for his home. It was built high on a hill and accessible only by a narrow dirt road, and even though Victor's great size caused his car to get stuck on the road whenever it rained, he refused to move or to stay in a hotel. He once said it was a great place from which to pour boiling oil on the people of Malibu, and since I still had my apartment there, I made it a point to stay in his good graces.

Jerry Lewis appeared as himself with the caveat that he be allowed to direct his scenes; Dozier was a big fan of his and agreed, and Jerry was very good in both departments. (I know Jerry loves directing, but I think he likes riding on the camera crane nearly as much. I've often wondered how the precocious child in him would have handled playing the Joker. Marvelously, I'll bet!)

Considering the intense jockeying that went on among actors to play villains on the show, many eyebrows were raised on the set and among Hollywood agents when the virtually unknown Malachi Throne was hired to play Falseface, a master of disguise. I'd known Malachi (pronounced *Mal*-a-chai, with a guttural "ch") from an acting group I'd been a part of with Sally Kellerman, Roy Thinnes, and Dennis Weaver, and the reason he was hired was simple: his face would never be shown, and he had one of the most distinctive voices we'd ever heard. I have to say, though, that Dozier was a bit deceptive in his negotiations with Malachi's agent. The actor was promised first-guest billing, which would have been career-making publicity. And he got it . . . sort of. Dozier was a fan of a 1963 movie called *The List of Adrian Messenger,* in which stars like Tony Curtis, Sinatra, Kirk Douglas, Burt Lancaster, and Robert Mitchum were hidden behind layers of makeup, and audiences

The batcopter getting checked out before an action scene

The batcycle — note Robin's monogrammed sidecar

were asked to play a "guess who?" game. Dozier did that with our show, putting a big "?" where Malachi's name should have gone. That had TV columnists and viewers guessing as to what famous star he might be, and brought the episode a great deal of publicity. But the experience left Malachi disappointed, and he headed east, where the story has a happy ending. Malachi made a fortune doing voice-overs.

We opened the first season with the Riddler, Penguin, and Joker, a killer lineup. Our fourth villain was Mr. Freeze, another comic book villain (though there he was known as Mr. Zero), who was played by another screen legend, the icy and elegant George Sanders. Ironically, George had made a name for himself in the 1930s and 1940s playing screen heroes like the Saint and the Falcon. George only did the show this once, at a time when his distinguished career (indeed, his life) was nearing an end. He had the same kind of bemused aloofness in person as so many of his characters, though that was the kind of man he was: never once did I get the feeling that he thought it was a comedown for him to be doing prime-time TV for $2,500 after a distinguished film career. Quite the contrary. I think the show's tone appealed very much to his own acerbic sense of humor. He also seemed amused by a bubbly extra we had on the show, future film star Teri Garr.

As was so often the case, I was sorry I had so little time to eavesdrop. Several times, I overheard him talking with fellow Englishman Alan Napier about his childhood in St. Petersburg, Russia, and how his family fled to England during the Revolution. Interestingly, though, Alan was one of the few people George would talk to. If Alan or Neil Hamilton weren't around, the actor and his male secretary would disappear into the dressing room and not come out until they were needed. There was nothing romantic about their relationship: George was just choosy about who he spent his time with. A fascinating life, ended all-too-tragically from an intentional overdose of sleeping pills six years later.

If George was there and gone too quickly, I couldn't wait to get rid of our second Mr. Freeze, Otto Preminger. George was unavailable when we brought the subzero villain back, and Otto asked for the part so he could give his grandchildren a thrill. Fair enough. But the man insisted on enhancing his reputation as one of the meanest bastards who ever walked a soundstage.

Otto was crude. Though most men have been guilty of looking on women as sex objects at some point (including yours truly), Otto was the only man I ever met who did that on his *good* days. The rest of the time, he treated them like dirt. He would swear at them, insult them, comment on their weight, the size of their nose (if it was too big) or their breasts (if they were too small), say anything that might hurt them. He would stand near men and ask someone else, in a loud voice, if that person was gay. He was as generous with his fellow actors in a scene as Ebenezer Scrooge. But he still had enough power in Hollywood that no one knocked him on his ass, and we were all quietly delighted when word spread that the Screen Actor's Guild was making him pay $11,000 in delinquent dues he owed since costarring in *Stalag 17* in 1953.

The director of his Mr. Freeze episode was George Waggner, a tough old guy himself, although Otto was oblivious to having another director on the set. He thought he, Otto, was calling the shots, and was constantly giving direction to the actors, commenting on the camera placement or lighting, meddling where he wasn't wanted. Unused to the pace and busyness of TV, he complained about the noise on the set. Finally, George told Otto that if he uttered one more word that wasn't in the script, he'd have him thrown off. And George would have done it, too.

But the threat didn't finish Otto off: he still had tricks up his silver-suited sleeve. In one scene, Mr. Freeze was—you'll pardon the expression—out cold on the floor and Batman was supposed to run in and pick him up. In most cases, an "unconscious" actor will help the person trying to pick him or her up. They'll go with that person, move the shoulders, bend the waist, do *something*. Not Otto. When I ran to pick him up, he stiffened like a sandbag and literally dug his nails into the floor. I couldn't lift the two hundred pounds of resisting weight.

I dropped him back down and we tried again. Same thing. On the next take, my foot "accidently" stepped on his hand. He yelled, but he got the message. And we were able to continue.

When it came time to bring Mr. Freeze back for a third show, and George Sanders was still unavailable, we went with the terrific Eli Wallach. It was a pleasure to give Otto the cold shoulder.

On the other hand, in our third season, I found myself consoling one of our guest stars when director Waggner turned the tables and was dishing out the bad times. Joan Collins was appearing as the Siren, who debilitates adversaries with her seven-octave voice. At the time, Joan was married to singer Anthony Newley and doing a lot of TV. There was a perception in Hollywood that her time had come and gone (little did they know . . .), and while she was quite beautiful and sexy, people were also saying that she was not a very good actress, that she was very demanding on sets, and that she was unhappy to be doing TV after having starred in films like *Island in the Sun* with James Mason and *Rally 'Round the Flag, Boys!* with Paul Newman.

Like so much of Hollywood wisdom, that turned out to be bull. From the very first day, Joan was cooperative, talented, eager to work, and grateful to have the work. But Waggner didn't see that. A man's director who was used to butting horns with the likes of Duke Wayne and Lon Chaney, Jr., Waggner bought into her reputation and leaned on her mercilessly, berating her, impugning her talent, and bringing her almost to tears on a number of occasions. I tried to console Joan between setups, and she pushed through because she's a pro. Maybe Waggner was just looking for someone to pick on or having an Otto flashback, but it was still egregiously bad form.

But of all the guest stars we had, the oddest, I think, was Liberace. I don't mean that in a bad way: he was a charming, sweet, and terminally cheerful man who was as nice to fans and total strangers as he was to friends, family, and coworkers.

No, what I mean is that he worked very, very

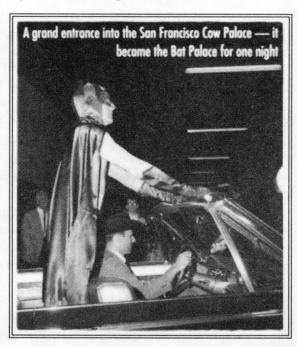

A grand entrance into the San Francisco Cow Palace — it became the Bat Palace for one night

hard to be mean, to stay in character when the cameras weren't rolling. He was starring as the benevolent pianist Harry and his villainous twin brother, Chandell, who was out to marry Aunt Harriet so he could abscond with the Wayne fortune. For the week he was on the show, Lee would walk around in his ermine robes and glittering rings, scowling like Jimmy Cagney, in character, tugging on my cape to be ornery, showing what a tough mug he could be. At least, that's how *he* perceived himself. But even when we were shooting, Lee at his most dastardly had a friendly twinkle in his eye which gave away the sweetheart inside, and we found it tough to take him seriously as a villain. Especially when he showed up for work with laryngitis and had to whisper all of his dialogue. His "real" voice was added later in postproduction.

The highlight of his appearance was when we finished shooting and he regaled us with an impromptu concert which ranged from the classics to jazz. He was delightful, a much, much better pianist than the so-called legitimate critics ever gave him credit for. (What's new? A lot of us actors feel the same way.) I saw him again in 1986, shortly before he died. I knew that he was suffering from AIDS, and the disease had clearly taken its toll on him. But his good humor and vitality were strong. His book, *The Wonderful Private World of Liberace*, had just been published, and he was busy planning a sequel, as well as a mammoth piano-themed amusement park. Lee didn't need a movie screen to be bigger than life. He was a talented and unusual human being.

So was David Wayne, who played the Mad Hatter. A distinguished Broadway actor who had starred in *Finian's Rainbow, Mister Roberts,* and as the original Sakini in *The Teahouse of the August Moon,* Wayne came up with this sneering, unctuous delivery that made the character truly memorable. He also liked the silly hats he was asked to wear, and between takes he would play with them—making sure they worked, he said, though we all knew he was just having fun. He was very warm toward all of us, and I never quite adjusted to having him try to kill me one minute, then ask how the kids were the next.

Another of my favorites among our recurring villains was Vincent Price as the bald, super-brilliant Egghead. Not only was Vincent a very good actor (another one who never got his due), but he was one of the most cultured and pleasant souls I've ever encountered. An art expert and gourmand, he was always regaling someone with tales from the museum or kitchen, which again I only caught in passing. But they must have been funny and fascinating, as everyone from Madge and Alan to the burliest technicians would listen and laugh.

Vincent was also a man who liked having fun when he was working. During one of his appearances, we had a "shoot-out" using raw eggs. The crew was behind improvised shields made of plywood and plastic, and the scene played out very well. When the director yelled "Cut," all of us stopped fighting. Except Vincent. There were still some three thousand unused eggs, and as he continued to pelt us, his minions joined in. Burt and I had no recourse but to retaliate.

But Vincent wasn't content. Still in character, he escalated the war by lobbing his little white grenades over the shields. The crew got hold of some buckets of their own and began heaving eggs at him (and us), and soon eggs were flying everywhere and at everybody. We were yelling and laughing like kids. What a mess. An ugly omelette. Pandemonium reigned for nearly ten minutes, but it was a great tension reliever; my belated apologies to the men and women who had to clean it up as we retired to our dressing rooms to get ready for the next scene.

Like Cesar, Vincent hated the hot and heavy makeup he had to wear. In his case, it was a big egg-shaped dome on top of his head. Whenever he saw a costume assistant blow-drying my perspiration spots, he'd hustle over, grab a spare, and turn it on his head. And there we'd be, Vincent with one of these heavy-duty dryers pointed to his head, a girl or guy with another dryer shoved in my armpits, Milton standing beside me shouting lines into my ear. It was a bizarre sight, ladies and gentlemen.

One of the most pleasant experiences I had with one-time guest stars was when Van Williams and Bruce Lee appeared on our show. Dozier had brought *The Green Hornet* to TV in the fall of 1966. As I've said, the show was done entirely straight and it wasn't finding quite the audience ABC had hoped. To try and generate some excitement, the Hornet and his sidekick, martial arts master Kato, were featured on our show, helping us stamp out the villainous Colonel Gumm.

Van wasn't too happy to be there, and I don't really blame him: the styles of the two shows just didn't mesh. It was difficult for us to make our scenes work, with him playing the crime as serious business and me doing it in our stylized fashion. But Van and I had fun when the cameras weren't rolling, and we're good friends today. (The episode is a cult favorite, a meeting of two legendary superheroes, so in that respect I'm glad we did it.)

The real kick, though, was watching Bruce Lee, who was a marvel. He didn't like wearing clothes, because they hindered him, and he usually stripped off his shirt as he stretched and kicked and limbered up outside the soundstage. The rest of the time, this serious young man could be found reading a book in his dressing room.

Physically, he was lean and sculpted but not overly muscular; he had the kind of grace that bodybuilders lack. With the exception of Fred Astaire, whom I met at an industry function, I've never seen anyone who imbued just the act of walking with the fluid beauty and precision of Bruce.

The twenty-five-year-old former martial arts instructor appeared on our show before he became an international star in films like *The Big Boss* and *Return of th: Dragon* (another example of someone who went overseas to return a conquering hero), though many people already knew of him by reputation. And if they didn't, they got a firsthand example. He was fond of walking up on members of the cast and crew and knocking cigarettes from their mouths with his foot, or throwing a succession of blows at their faces, never coming in contact but creating quite a breeze. You've never seen people stand as still as when Bruce was "playing" with them: they knew that if they flinched, they'd catch toes in the cheek or a fist in the mouth.

One victim of Bruce's "playfulness" was Burt. Burt and Bruce were acquaintances from before, sparring partners, but as I mentioned earlier I don't think Bruce ever took those bouts seriously. I think Burt knew it, too. On the day that we were supposed to film the close-ups of a fight between Kato and Robin (Burt's stunt double would appear in the long shots), Bruce came to the set wearing a most humorless, kick-ass expression. He didn't take his usual kicks and swings at innocent bystanders; he didn't even talk to anyone. If he blinked, I missed it. He just stalked around behind the cameras, his expression dark, his body coiled tight. He looked mean and angry.

When Burt came onto the set, we all walked through the fight choreography which had been worked out with our stunt director. When everyone was satisfied, we all sat down in our chairs for a makeup touch-up.

"That's going to play well," said a stunt man who was playing one of Gumm's thugs.

"You think so?" Burt said.

"Yeah."

The stunt man looked at Bruce, who was staring straight ahead.

Now Burt glanced over. "You okay, Bruce?"

Bruce said nothing. He just sat there rock-still, his lips taut, teeth locked, eyes narrow.

The makeup person finished. We rose.

Burt laughed nervously. "Is something bothering you, buddy?"

Bruce didn't answer. He just moved his arms, as though in slow motion, working his way through several combat positions. Van and I watched, suspecting that Bruce was putting Burt on; at least, we hoped so.

When director Oscar Rudolph arrived, he called for everyone to take positions. Bruce came forward slowly, still doing martial arts moves, communing with some private muse.

Burt was punching a fist into his open hand. He looked rather ill. His makeup seemed to have paled.

Bruce reached the set and walked toward Burt like a gunslinger at High Noon. Burt began backing away.

"Bruce," he said, "what's the matter? We're just doing a show here, you understand? This isn't real."

When he realized that everyone was watching him, Burt stood his ground and began shifting nervously from foot to foot (he said he was loosening up). He got into position, and Bruce moved in on him until they were chest to chest, and then began moving his hands in serpentine patterns around Burt's anatomy, his expression black rage.

"Is this the real Bruce?" I asked Van as we took our positions.

"First time I've ever seen it," the Hornet replied.

I wondered if Burt had insulted him in some way, and I started to get concerned. What would we do if this guy snapped? Short of running him over with the Batmobile, I couldn't think of any way to stop Bruce Lee.

Burt was smart enough not to touch him, but his arms came up in some kind of feeble defensive posture as he backed away. Bruce moved with him, still chest to chest, giving him no room to navigate. Bruce was spitting frightening martial arts sounds.

Poor Burt was convinced Bruce had snapped, had gone mad and was about to kill him or worse. Suddenly Bruce leapt back, stuck his tongue out, and cackled, "Robin's a chicken!"

He cracked up and turned away, leaving Burt just standing there. The color returned quickly to the Boy Wonder's face, whether from embarrassment or relief I'm not sure. But in a way, the encounter helped the scene: when the cameras rolled, Burt was "on" like I'd never seen him, acting every inch the hero who was fighting to protect his city from a man he thought was a villain. In truth, I think he was fighting to protect his self-respect.

I never got to meet either of the previous Batmen, Lewis Wilson or Bob Lowery. Someone had the idea to book Lowery for the show as a Wayne relative, but for whatever reason it never came to pass. In the fast-paced, high-pressure world of network TV, more terrific ideas go by the wayside than make it onto the tube. And that, frankly, was one reason I was thrilled when Dozier suggested that we use our first season hiatus to get Batman off the little screen and onto the big screen. It would give us a chance to do things we didn't have the time and money to do in the show.

Before leaving the first season, however, I want to mention what was for me the highlight of the year: the day my dad and Adele visited the set.

I'd flown them in from Walla Walla, put them up at a first-class hotel in neighboring Beverly Hills, and had a limousine pick them up in the morning. When they arrived at the studio, it was an interesting experience for the three of us.

Though they'd watched *Batman* on TV, of course, and were proud of all the attention I was getting, I think my folks were bemused to see their big boy in his Batsuit. My dad never said it, but I could discern the amazement in his stern features: "They're paying you that kind of money for this?" He could understand paying the crewmen, who were busting their backs, and he got along famously with his contemporaries Neil and Alan. In fact, when I saw Dad and Neil together, looking in

In wings as
Bruce Wayne

my direction, I had a very vivid flashback to "parents' day" at school.

But as far as Dad was concerned, the rest of us were standing around playing, and with assistants and secretaries to boot, helping us to do—what exactly? Answer mail? Wipe our sweaty brows? Hold a cold soda for us so we didn't get our gloves wet?

He was flabbergasted. However, Adele told me that he really loved every second of the month I bought them in a private club in Palm Springs, and I took a great deal of satisfaction from that. For those kinds of perks, he probably wouldn't have complained if I'd worn a dress.

20

PEOPLE WEREN'T the only asset we had on our show. We also had a lot of terrific trappings, such as the memorable exteriors of the Batcave and stately Wayne Manor.

Those were virtually the only location shots we did. The scenes of the Batmobile roaring from the Batcave were shot in Bronson Caverns in the Hollywood Hills, a movie location that's probably been dressed and redressed more times and for more years than any other location in the Free World. If you want to see the Batcave before it was located thirteen miles from Gotham City, take a look at the original *Invasion of the Body Snatchers*, *Robot Monster*, *Killers from Space*, or any of the countless science fiction films that were shot there. (If they ever had a reunion up there of everyone who filmed at Bronson Caverns, they'd empty out much of Hollywood.) The only problem the crew had out there was the fact that the cave itself was only a few inches wider than the car. Because of that, my stunt double Hubie Kerns, and Burt's double Victor Paul, could only come "tearing" from the Batcave at about twenty-five miles an hour, lest they wreck the car. Fortunately, thanks to the magic of undercranking the camera (which makes the on-screen action seem to move faster), we were able to make our exit a little more dramatic.

The exteriors of Wayne Manor were shot at a home in Pasadena. I was only there once, to shoot some exteriors for the *Batman* movie, and haven't been there since. One day several years ago, while I was in Pasadena for another film, an attractive young couple walked up to me and introduced themselves. They told me they had recently bought the estate and were conducting tours. That was very enterprising, I thought, since they knew the interiors were shot on our standing sets at the Culver City studios.

Batman might have given them a lecture about stretching honesty and integrity.

Without a doubt, however, our greatest asset was the Batmobile, our $30,000 answer to James Bond's gadget-laden Aston Martin D.B.V., which had captured the public's imagination after being introduced in *Goldfinger* in 1964.

We weren't sleek and small and European, and we didn't have machine guns behind the front parking lights (this was network TV, remember). No, our Batmobile was sleek and big, as jazzy as the characters on the show, designed to hold its own amid the colorful trappings. The work of George Barris, a well-known star-car customizer, it was a car with a checkered past.

Originally, the Batmobile was a Lincoln Futura, developed as a prototype to let the public know what kind of car was in Ford's future for the 1960s. It turned out to be the most popular show car ever for Lincoln/Mercury, and in 1959 that same Futura was shipped to MGM to be used in *It Started with a Kiss,* starring Glenn Ford and Debbie Reynolds. The car stayed at MGM because Ford (the company, not Glenn) never picked it up, and the studio sent it to George Barris's shop for storage. When they failed to pay the storage fees, he took possession of the car that was to become the most famous in the world.

It cost George about $30,000 to turn the Futura into the Batmobile for the first episode; over the next few months he built four more, though by that time there were no other Futuras available. Instead, Barris had to use smaller cars and lengthen each chassis so the Batmobiles would all look the same. The first and fifth were made of metal, the fifth being built for the feature film; in seasons two and three, it was the stunt car we used in chases and explosions. Batmobiles two and three were made of fiberglass (that made them lighter and more manageable, easier to brake and turn) though the third one had a powerful drag race engine. When it got going on the open road, you'd believe that car really was the Batmobile. The fourth car was simply an exhibition car, which toured the country on behalf of the show, and it was my least favorite Batmobile. It was covered with black flocking, like wallpaper (which, I assume, was inexpensive and easier to repair), but

Offering a souvenir batbadge

it looked cheap and touching it was like touching shark skin the wrong way. Very unpleasant. Today, Barris owns number one (which still tours) and number two. Three is in a Gatlinburg, Tennessee, museum; four was purchased by a private collector for $100,000; and five was bought by a woman for her husband's birthday for $185,000.

Nice lady.

Barris incorporated a stylized bat face into the design of the car: if you look at it from the front you can see bat ears rising up beside the headlights, a nose between them, and the grille as the mouth. Leaping into the car always made me feel like Batman, because of all the gadgets. The magic was there, though the equipment didn't work, of course: they were all dummy buttons and flashing lights. Even the fiery exhaust was fake, triggered by special effects technicians who sent an electric current to a gas cannister tucked into the rear pipe. The Batmobile was actually started with a key in a well-concealed ignition. The twin Batchutes that unfolded from the back and brought us to an abrupt halt were also operated remotely by the effects crew . . . and, truth be told, were so flimsy they'd have been ripped to shreds if we'd really been going as fast as it seemed. The cameras were always undercranked to create the illusion of speed, as they were in the scenes of us racing from the Batcave.

The car had other drawbacks as well. It bruised the heck out of my shins, since I was always running to it and banging my legs on the sharp edges of the door or the paraphernalia inside. And as it was meant to be a show car, it was not truly designed for performance. The driver's seat was like the cockpit of the old Gee Bee race plane, which was all engine and tough to fly. The suspension, brakes, and transmission were not user-friendly, making the car unreliable and sluggish, not to mention tough to turn: it took all of my race car and truck driving experience to put it through its paces.

Like some actors, the Batmobile could also be a temperamental and difficult costar. One time, we were supposed to roar into a scene but the battery wouldn't start. (The irony of Batman with a faulty *battery* . . .) Fourteen big crewmen had to get behind the car and give it a shove: viewers didn't know the difference, but to Burt and me it wasn't a pretty sight.

That spectacular car of ours got us into other trouble as well. No sooner had the "gay" controversy died down than we were hit by several local and national safety groups for not using seat belts in the Batmobile. That was true: seat belts were relatively new in cars, and no one had thought of it. I told one interviewer that the Batmobile had modern safety features that made seat belts superfluous, but that didn't do the trick. Besides, Dozier loved the idea of these two heroes taking the time to buckle up, so he had the prop people stuff fake belts in the seats, and we inserted a shot of the two of us buckling them around our waist. Over the next few weeks, all of those formerly indignant safety groups presented us with enough plaques and commendations to paper the Batcave.

We were a little less understanding with a publicity-seeking lawyers' group (I forget which one) that protested loudly about how Batman and Robin broke the law by exceeding the speed limit every time they tore from the Batcave. Dozier sent them a letter citing chapter and verse from a special permit issued by Commissioner Gordon allowing Batman and Robin to drive as fast as their duties required. We never heard from them again.

21

I N THE men's room at Laury's restaurant on La Cienaga Boulevard, my two agents, Lew Sherrell and Jerry Herdan (who was Lew's partner at the time) were standing on either side of me at two other urinals. We had left our table after a lively discussion of what my salary should be for the feature-length *Batman* film that was scheduled to start shooting during our first hiatus from the series. This was the spring of 1966, and I hadn't quite finished my first season.

I was a rookie to Fox and they were talking a number like $45,000, which was roughly equivalent to my first year's salary on the series. Fox thought that was fair. Certainly Howie Horwitz did, reminding me again that he'd done an episode almost without my participation.

Howie was kidding, I thought, and I wasn't thrilled with the number. *Batman* was the hottest thing in the country, and the studio felt a film would help to pre-sell the TV series abroad.

The studio stood to make millions of dollars in markets like England and Japan, and if they wanted the film they needed me, so I decided to take a chance. As we stood there, all in a row, I announced to my agents that I wanted them to ask for $100,000. No less, no discussion. One hundred grand, period.

I zipped up, and they turned to each other in shock, peeing on one another's shoes. They exploded at each other, cursing, until we all started laughing. The laughter wasn't just about their wet shoes, it was about the money. They weren't sure they could get it and were nervous about blowing the deal. I thought it was fair and a win-win situation.

But what was the worst that could happen? I asked. Fox could say no and it would be back to the drawing board. So Lew went for the hundred thousand and got it. That was a pretty good figure for those

At my wedding to
Marcelle, 1970

days, when studios didn't have the cushion of extra income from lucrative cable TV showings and videocassettes and laserdiscs, not to mention heftier ticket prices. We all felt optimistic, though today, in the
same situation, we could have added two zeros with no difficulty. We
got our asking price.

With just two days off between wrapping up the first season and
beginning the *Batman* movie, we were all pretty worn out. But the excitement of putting what we wanted on the big screen gave me a real
shot of adrenaline, and our tight twenty-six-day shooting schedule kept
us on our toes. The plot was fun, as the Penguin, Joker, Riddler, and
Catwoman team to kidnap key members of the United Nations. We'd
also be shooting on locations, on a lake, and staging a big fight on the
Penguin's submarine in the big tank at the studio, which would give
us and audiences some variety. And we were adding to Batman's arse-
nal, providing him with a Batboat and Batcopter and giving the audience more thrills than even our hefty TV budget allowed.

But what I was looking forward to the most was the chance to do many more scenes as Bruce Wayne: apart from the money, that was the only stipulation I made before agreeing to do the film. It would give me a chance to explore that character a bit, make discoveries which I could bring to the second season of the series. It would also, I hoped, show audiences and critics that I could play drama and light comedy. Film like that would be useful, I thought, when it finally came time to hang up my cape.

Leslie Martinson came on board to direct. He had directed my Doc Holliday pilot at Warner, as well as a Penguin episode and theatrical features (including the underrated *PT 109*). I was delighted. *Batman* required an indefinable attitude that allowed us to get on with the serious nonsense of it, to walk always on the edge; Leslie was a man on the edge. I'll never forget how, on the Holliday show, we were working after midnight on Christmas Eve, trying to finish it. We were shooting in a barn, and there happened to be a manger tucked in a corner. Afraid that we'd still be there on New Year's Eve, this good Jew dropped to his knees, turned his bright blue eyes to heaven, and in a loud, fervent, wailing prayer to Jesus, asked his permission to allow us to finish.

Les was the perfect man to direct our feature, and he helped me discover important things about myself and the characters. On the movie screen, Batman and Bruce would both be bigger characters, so I had to tone them down from the larger way I played them on the small screen. (If you watch the *Batman* film on TV, you'll see how it plays differently from the series.) I found things in the characters that surprised me, for example some steel in Bruce. He didn't have to put on the Batsuit to stand up for himself or be sexy or confident. Conversely, I realized how much he needed the Batsuit for other things. In musicals, people sing things that would be ludicrous if expressed in dialogue. The costume is like that. When he's Batman, Bruce can express anger or sadness that his social standing and emotional walls won't let him show in his day-to-day life. It proved to be a real Kabuki experience, and I was sorry I didn't have a chance to look into Japanese theater more. I think I might have found a great deal to use in my characterizations.

And how did I thank our director for helping me toward these revelations?

Most of the climactic fight on board the Penguin's submarine was shot in the big, warm studio tank (with a visibly wrinkled cyclorama of the sky behind it: you can see the creases in the finished film). The tank was located out at the Fox Ranch, and it was about three hundred fifty feet wide and four hundred feet long. Unfortu-

nately, it was less than a yard deep. Our stunt men, Hubie and Victor, did most of the falls into that tank, though not everyone was as alert as they were. In the heat of battle, one of the stunt men, a sweet guy named Acey Hudson, got carried away and decided to take a fall head-first into the tank. He cracked his head on the bottom, twisted his neck, and knocked himself out. Several of the stunt men jumped in and pulled him out before he drowned. He was rushed to the hospital and, incredibly, came out of the mishap with just a few stitches. Since time is money, the rest of the stunt crew continued with a backup man—who, incredibly, thought he was supposed to do the stunt just like Acey had. He did, and he also split *his* head open and had to be rushed to the hospital. Luckily, a third man managed to do the scene without bloodshed.

We went on location for several scenes, and only once did we have a problem. At Santa Barbara, when we were shooting on the pier, a radio station happened to mention that we were there; it was Easter vacation and about twenty-five thousand people showed up, most of them kids. They wanted to see Batman and Robin, but the producers were afraid to have Burt and I show our faces. So they had our stunt doubles, in full uniform, jump into a car and drive off, then announced that we were gone: the kids all left quickly, and we were able to get our shots.

We did some shooting on a lake the last day, to show Burt and me skipping our Batboat over the water toward the Penguin's submarine. We'd finished our last shot and were having a good time tooling around the lake while Les was standing on a buoy we were using; he was deeply preoccupied with some thought, which was typical of him. Unknown to Leslie, the crew quietly undid the buoy's hook and chain and set it adrift. When he finally realized what had happened, he started screaming, "Help! Get me off this thing!" Naturally, Burt and I just waved to him and sped off; to this day, I don't know who rescued him . . . or when.

Leslie was a good sport, and also staged what I think is one of the finest scenes we did in the film or on the show: Batman running around the wharf, holding a bomb, trying desperately to find some place to get rid of it before it explodes. He encounters a marching band, kissing lovers, nuns, a family of ducks—and finally, in exasperation, cries, "Some days, you just can't get rid of a bomb." The balance of comedy and tension was perfect. But it's not easy holding a lighted bomb over your head, sparks raining down on your cheek, as you run here and there in ninety-degree heat trying not to trip on your cape.

The movie was fun for another reason. It was great to get out of the cramped cockpit of the Batmobile and out on the open ocean, cutting loose with George Barris's latest creation. He built two Batboats: the extra wasn't for anything special; it was just there in case I totaled the first. I had my own sailboat, the *Westwind*, so being on the water was always a joy to me. I got to pilot the Batboat in several scenes, and it became my favorite show toy. Alas, I never got to drive it again: one of the boats was dismantled and the other ended up in drydock. George is presently refurbishing it.

The Batcycle was introduced in the film as well, with its detachable sidecar. Weighted down by Burt and me, it wasn't nearly as zippy as my own bike, and the winds created serious problems with my cape. I ended up having to sit on it, an unceremonious posture for a super-hero, so we tried to do as little shooting as possible from the rear. Four Batcycles were built: one is in San Diego, another at the Gatlinburg museum, a third in Chicago, and Barris has the fourth.

The Batcopter was even less enticing. I wasn't certified for helicopter flying, so I didn't get to go up in it. I climbed into the cockpit for the close-ups, then climbed out to let a pilot do the actual flying scenes. I also didn't get to do the scenes in which Batman hangs from the Batcopter on a rope ladder, fighting a tenacious shark and being dropped onto the deck of a yacht. The producers and their insurers frowned on having actors do dangerous stunts, so my good friend Hubie did those scenes for me.

I can't say enough good about Hubie. On the show and on the film, he was always enthusiastic and inventive, and a great help to me. He knew that I enjoyed doing as much of the action as I could, not out of ego but because I was very concerned about the style of movement I'd given to Batman. Hubie understood that and was very careful to duplicate it when a scene was deemed too dangerous or when I was needed elsewhere. (To save time, film and TV crews often shoot action scenes with doubles and a second-unit crew while the actors are working on dialogue scenes.)

I have nothing but praise for our costars in the film. Julie was working on another project at the time, so former Miss America Lee Meriwether was our Catwoman in the movie. She mimicked Julie's moves quite adroitly, and she was also charming and sexy in her alias as Miss Kitka, which made the romance with Bruce Wayne very easy for

In 1983, pulling our feet out of the cement — looks like a dance step we'd worked out for the occasion

Squiring Jill St. John

me. For a grown man to do the town with a brandy snifter of warm milk in his hand, and somehow create sexual electricity, was a challenge, as was going to her place for warm cookies on the couch before bedtime together. These scenes required a light touch that Lee understood well, and I can't stress enough the importance of her contribution.

Lee also meshed well with her fellow villains, played by Frank, Burgess, and Cesar. Of course, the three of them had never worked together either, and it was a pleasure seeing how these pros timed their patented giggles, squawks, and laughs, respectively, so as not to crowd one another. They all got along famously.

I was pleased with the finished product, which holds up very well indeed, particularly the Bruce Wayne scenes. The action scenes are also strong, especially Bruce's fight with Miss Kitka's thugs and the final showdown on the submarine. We did some intricate choreography during the fight, with a little Abbott and Costello slapstick—everyone getting knocked into the water—thrown in for good measure. If I have a complaint about the film, it's that our longer shooting schedule allowed us to rehearse some of the humor a little too much, and it became studied. As I mentioned before, spontaneity was an important part of the show, and we lost some of that here.

After Batman and Robin put the villains in the slammer and restored order to the United Nations, we took a short break. The movie was released in July, right before we began shooting the new season of shows; Burt and I were sent to New York to promote it.

Usually, promotional tours are pretty well planned out. You're given a list of interviews, with times and places, and a publicist is on hand to make sure transportation is in order, schedules are met, and so on.

I arrived in New York with my publicist, Paul Marsh, who took a room near mine at the Plaza. He told me that the TV and radio interviews would begin at ten A.M., and that there would be a small meeting with reporters at nine. I misunderstood: I thought he meant that he, not I, would be meeting with the reporters at nine.

I spent a particularly eventful night in my suite with some gorgeous new friends. Then, just before nine, I walked from the bedroom into the large sitting room wearing nothing but a towel. There was Paul, and with him was a large group of strangers including the press and a lady from a charity auction for whom Paul had promised to cut up tiny pieces of one of my bed sheets.

I froze, smiled, and asked if they'd seen my Batsuit. As I backed from the room, my eyes were fixed on Paul's, which were wide with horror. The reporters didn't seem to mind, though: most of them were smiling. They probably thought it was part of our "camp" act.

There was a very definite *Batman* fever in New York at the time. Our ratings were still in the stratosphere, and the movie was getting a lot of press. Burt and I were put in a bus with about twenty security people dressed up as Gotham City Police officers. We would go to a theater where the film was scheduled to play, jump from the bus dressed as Batman and Robin, and enjoy the challenge of a broken field run through the mob outside. Then we'd dash down the aisles, leap onto the stage, say a few words, feint this way and that for dramatic effect, and run back out to the bus. At one theater, we learned that if we ever stopped we were in trouble: after making our way through a thick and uncooperative crowd, I paused inside the darkened theater to catch my breath. As I leaned against a column, a teenager hit me over the head with a piece of pipe. Luckily, my plastic cowl took the brunt of the blow and I was able to stagger back to the bus. I must have looked like a drunk bat as I flopped onto one of the cots they had placed inside so we could rest.

Arriving at another theater, Burt and I were thrown from our cots by what felt like an earthquake: the crowd outside was literally trying to tip the bus over because we were late.

Ah, New York. Such friendly natives.

Actually, our security was a little unsophisticated, to put it mildly. The real police, seasoned by previous bouts of Beatlemania, would have handled things better than our Gotham force, which consisted of actors recruited from local talent agencies.

On that same day, I learned again that Batmania wasn't limited to the kids. As we returned to the Plaza and stepped out of the bus in our costumes, one gentleman who was pulling up in front of the hotel in a Cadillac convertible yelled around his big cigar, "Hey! It's Batman and Robin!" He got so excited, and was so intent on getting a closer look at us, that he slammed into the car in front of him. He was thrown forward, the cigar smashed back into his mouth, but he was unfazed. Still gripping the splintered cigar in his teeth, he jumped from the car and ran over to get our autographs.

I asked him if that was one of the Joker's exploding cigars. He laughed like I'd told the greatest joke in history. He was still laughing as the doorman and a police officer came over to talk to him about the wreck.

Actors who are struggling to get recognized don't understand the complaints of those who are. To a degree, I don't blame them. When you're well known, you can't go to Disneyland with your kids, and a stroll down Fifth Avenue is out of the question. But you never have to wait for a table at a restaurant, and you get great seats at sporting events. It's a trade-off. And it can be a very lucrative trade-off at that.

But the kind of blind, violent reaction we experienced was dangerous. *Batman* had entered popular culture in a big way, with rock-star impact, and I couldn't go anywhere without risking my life or possibly someone else's. That kind of attention makes you wonder if it's worth it. Whether it's Errol Flynn being charged with rape or John Lennon being shot in front of his own apartment building, there's a point at which the downside starts to outweigh the good, when the icon becomes more important than the person bearing it.

After just three days of constant pushing, running, and talking to interviewers, I had reached the point of never wanting to see the cape and cowl again. I had wanted to experience New York, but all I got to

Dozier showed me this cover as he said, "Remember
there've been thirteen Tarzans, kid."

experience was Batmania. I felt differently by the time I returned to Hollywood, but I never forgot this first taste of the dark side of the Batsuit.

There was also a very pleasant memory associated with promoting the film. We held the premiere in Austin, Texas, where the Batboat manufacturer had a plant, and we tied the opening in to a local charity. The only concession I asked for was a small one: that I be allowed to appear as myself and not in costume. In the movie, I was Bruce Wayne much of the time, and I felt that the audience would recognize me in or out of the mask. Besides, after New York, I was beginning to feel very strongly that I should try and distinguish myself from that icon, keep from being buried in the costume.

Burt and I and the other actors were allowed to go to Austin free of costumes, though Burgess opted to dress up. The canny old bird knew that with everyone else going plainclothes, a costumed villain would get a lot of press. And he did. His lovely young wife was a pilot, and flew him down: when he emerged from the plane, with his costume and trademark waddle, the press ate it up.

The premiere itself was a great success. The people of Austin were very gracious, and I even got to dance with the governor's wife. Oddly enough, this was the first time I really got a chance to talk with Cesar, Burgess, and Lee Meriwether.

Our *Batman* movie was a hit. Though I think some of the advertising was a little over-the-top ("Beneath that Batcape—he's all man!" and "Men die! Women sigh!"), some of it was rather clever. I especially liked the line they used on one of the posters, "See Batman in action *out* of costume! See Batman *out* of action—in costume!"

There was talk of a sequel for the following hiatus, one in which we would use an old villain along with some new villains (I remember us kicking around one concept, inspired by the jetpack scene in *Thunderball*, of an aerial villain called Disastronaut and his flying Meteorettes). We also had a horror plot in mind, though that was discarded when it started sounding too much like *Abbott and Costello Meet Frankenstein*. I believe the studio actually did some designs for a Batplane—a larger, sleeker craft than they used in the recent *Batman* film—which would have been reused in our third season of shows. But the cost of pulling it all off, especially the flying effects, intimidated the studio, and nothing came of it. Our plan, which was to do a series of films à la James Bond, died aborning.

But more than twenty-five years later, our first film continues to play in theaters and on TV, and is extremely popular in videocassette. Naturally, it continues to amaze and disappoint me that every time Burt and I ask for some kind of accounting in regard to the money owed us from the film, we're told it's still in the red. I have heard that they're telling Keaton the same thing about his films.

22

ONLY A short break separated the completion of our promotional efforts from the start of the second season. Frankly, we didn't leave ourselves enough time to hash out where we were going to go with the show in our sophomore year; as a result, it wasn't what it should have been. The villains were aimed at holding on to older demographics, the product-buying public that sponsors wanted to reach, and the plots became formulaic so we'd be able to give younger viewers familiar thrills.

Both were wrongheaded moves, I think.

We opened with one of our weakest villains, the Archer. Art Carney is a great performer, but he didn't, I think, project the kind of snarling evil that our audience had come to expect. Though ratings were strong, I'm sure viewers expected more from our big second-season return.

After a good show with Catwoman, I feel we bobbled the ball again with Van Johnson as the Minstrel, not a particularly exciting foe; that was followed by a fun but redundant bout with King Tut, then Shelley Winters came aboard as Ma Parker, followed by Walter Slezak as the Clock King. Shelley was explosive and fun to be with, but Ma Parker was unexciting; the Clock King was even worse. This was certainly not the fault of the actors involved.

At the time, Bill was preoccupied with launching *The Green Hornet,* and he felt *Batman* would more or less take care of itself. He was driven, I think, to become the first producer in history to have his shows anchoring three nights of network TV a week (*The Green Hornet* led off ABC's Friday schedule).

With Elizabeth Ashley

Whenever we were together, I quietly urged him to go to the comic books for villains, use Two-Face or the Cat-Man, very colorful criminals who were popular in the magazines at that time. But I was getting the distinct feeling by now that Bill had a real disrespect for the comic books, that he regarded them as trash and wanted to stay away from them as much as possible. He even seemed to feel that Batman was as much our creation as it was Bob Kane's. After a few weeks, I stopped pestering him about it.

Though we had many, many good episodes that year, they came later in the season, when there was already a sense on the lot and at the network that our time had passed. No one seemed to understand that when we missed the ratings top ten, it was not because the audience had abandoned us, but because we weren't giving the audience a reason to come back week after week.

Our third season was even worse, a generally very unhappy time for me.

To begin with, we were cut back to one night a week, with a cliffhanger usually coming about halfway into each half-hour episode, which always felt terribly contrived, or at the end of a show that would be continued the following week. Though that meant half as much work for cast and crew, the loss of one night took something important away from us, and it took some of the wind from my sails.

I think it affected the writers, too, because many of the scripts lacked the wit and sparkle of the first season and even the second season. Though we had some terrific actors, as always, the villains were really second-tier. We opened with the Penguin, Riddler, and King Tut, just to get viewers to tune in, then faltered with the likes of Milton Berle as Louie the Lilac, Rudy Vallee as Lord Phogg (for three interminable weeks in a row), and the talented Barbara Rush as Nora Clavicle. Zsa Zsa Gabor did what she could with the evil Minerva, but even Katharine Hepburn would have been hard-pressed to do something interesting with a villainess who ran a health spa stocked with mind-reading hair dryers.

The network was clearly losing faith in the show, and Dozier's heart was in new projects. That was understandable, in light of rising costs and falling ratings, but it was still our faces on the screen, going into tens of millions of homes, still our reputations on the line. When shows were bad, it was Burt and I who were letting the fans down.

My definition of a professional is someone who does his best when he doesn't feel like it, and for most of that season I really didn't feel like it.

As if the cutback to one night a week didn't cramp us enough, we also had a new character to accommodate. Batgirl joined the lineup, and the Dynamic Duo became what was being touted as the Tremendous Trio. Originally, ABC had considered starring her in her own series, which would have run before ours, with Robin and me helping to wrap up a case begun on her show. But visions of NBC's failed *Girl from U.N.C.L.E.* two years earlier danced in their heads, and they gave her to us instead.

Bat-Girl was introduced in the *Batman* comic book in 1961, didn't make much of an impact, and was shelved until she was reformulated by legendary editor Julius Schwartz, the wonderful comics and science fiction writer Gardner Fox, and top-notch artist Carmine Infantino and reintroduced in 1967. (The comic book called her, among other things, the Dominoed Dare-Doll, which should tell you how unfired their imaginations were by the character's return.) Batgirl was secretly prim Barbara Gordon, the librarian daughter of Commissioner Gordon. She got into the crimefighting business while heading to a costume party dressed as Batgirl and stumbling upon a crime in progress: the mugging of Bruce Wayne by the evil Killer Moth.

Dozier liked the character, but I was unenthusiastic about adding Batgirl to the cast. Ego-wise, I had no problem with the shared spotlight. Any publicity we got could only help, and if nothing else a sexy Batgirl got a lot of press. But it also seemed to me a waste of budgetary resources that could have been better used elsewhere.

We had some heated behind-the-scenes discussions about the reasons she was being introduced, and in one meeting Dozier threw out some demographic data about women controlling the dial at that hour. He maintained that Batgirl would give the ladies someone to identify with. And if she didn't, he said, there was always the skintight costume to appeal to the guys.

I resented that. Unlike during the first season, when we stumbled upon wonderful things to do, or responded to the material, not the audience, we were now calculating and titillating. Those kinds of things are always short-term solutions to problems, and I was annoyed that Bill and the network didn't see that we needed better scripts and fresh insights into Batman and Robin, not more characters.

But even as I pointed that out emphatically, I knew it was a waste of time and breath. No matter how I couched my complaints, they were interpreted as jealousy on my part. After three frustrating meetings, where the results were increasingly foregone, I shut up. Burt had wisely stayed out of this fray, though we mumbled to each other about how ridiculous the whole thing was, about how we should have had more say in the fate of our own show.

But as much as I disliked the way the show was going, I actually became very fond of the actress playing Batgirl once shooting got under way.

Originally, Mary Ann Mobley was cast, but ABC decided they wanted her for their new *Custer* series, so they went looking for another Batgirl. Producer Horwitz had worked with a number of young actresses on *77 Sunset Strip*, and he called in a few who he thought would be

A favorite appearance, on *The Merv Griffin Show*

right; one of them, a twenty-six-year-old former ballet dancer named Yvonne Craig, was perfect. I remembered her as the traitorous Russian ballet dancer Natasha from *In Like Flint*, and as soon as she walked in wearing her costume, I knew she had the part. She was only there that first day to take some publicity photographs, but she knew how to move. And when we did our first scenes together, I was impressed at how she nailed the role. She got the playful tone of the character just right, and I felt that if we had to have a Batgirl, at least they'd found a perfect one.

Off-camera, Yvonne was also great to have around, warm and witty, alert and always prepared, terrific to look at and a great sport. When she was first cast, we shot a seven-minute presentation reel to sʰ advertisers and, hopefully, generate fresh interest in the sʰ script, Batgirl was quite a flirtatious character—very ł much less straight-laced. But changes were made ʰ got from potential sponsors (women were not quite Batgirl ended up more stolid than Yvonne wanted. ʼ

talked about that privately, she respected Dozier's judgment and never complained.

Actually, she did, but just once.

When we shot the presentation reel, she found that the mask, as designed, came to a painful point on each cheek. No sooner did she mention this to Jan Kemp then the cowl went right back to the costume shop and was immediately redesigned into something rounded and more comfortable. Burt and I never had that kind of clout.

Was it a woman's charm? Not really. The mask left little dents when it came off, and they would have been extremely difficult for Barbara Gordon to explain to her father . . .

As it happens, Yvonne had a much tougher time with her costume than Burt and I had with ours. Because the Batgirl costume was tight, it was impossible for Yvonne to sit down between takes, lest she stretch the fabric and cause the knees and butt to become baggy. She also had to be careful not to tear her costume during the fight scenes, since our third season budget was tight and only one spare was made for her.

My relationship with Yvonne was strictly professional, as was Burt's.

She was actually amused by him, and I think he was a little intimidated by her: she was very poised and mature, and in many ways, he was still a kid. Burt didn't help matters by playing little frat-house tricks on her or tugging her Bat-ears as he walked by. As the newcomer, she always took these things with good-natured grace, calling him "silly boy"

and flashing him wry little grins; after a few weeks, though, it backfired on Burt and he was the one who seemed like the odd man out. He could have quoted Descartes to her, and the dynamics still would have been two adults plus one kid.

Not surprisingly, Yvonne had a slew of male admirers on the lot, many of them young and model-perfect. However, she was dating Bill Bixby at the time and she was loyal to him. Bill was between shows, *My Favorite Martian* having ended and *The Courtship of Eddie's Father* just gearing up, and he came to the set several times. He was a soft-spoken, delightful fellow, one who later joined the elite ranks of TV superheroes as one half of the Incredible Hulk. He was smart: he avoided typecasting by letting someone else get greened up for the cameras.

I confess I was glad that Bill wasn't there the day we shot the episode in which I, Yvonne, and Burt were walking down a hall, in that order. In this scene, Batman is supposed to hear something and then put his hand back, on Batgirl's shoulder, to stop the others from moving. I did that, and though I found her shoulder to be a little soft, I continued with the scene. So did Yvonne and Burt.

As I was standing there, waiting for the danger to pass, I became aware of crew members turning away, laughing. I didn't break character, but then the director, Oscar Rudolph, finally yelled, "Cut, cut!"

I stood and asked, "What's wrong?"

"Your hand, Adam. Where was your hand?"

"On her shoulder—"

"Lower!" someone shouted.

I realized then what I'd been holding, and it wasn't her shoulder. I turned to Yvonne, who pursed her lips and nodded; I apologized, though to this day I'm sure she doesn't believe it was an accident. It wasn't. I did it in an innocent manner, as a mistake, the way Batman would. It was done for a laugh, for the kind of comedy we were doing.

Yvonne was really a trooper, and looking back, I think her beauty, her (underrated) talents as an actress, and her unique style of fighting, with those high dancerlike kicks, brought class and added style to the show. She was also smart: not long after the series ended, and she found herself stuck in films like *Mars Needs Women*, she gave up acting, became a realtor, and made a fortune. She and her husband live happily and well in Santa Monica.

23

UNFORTUNATELY, THE addition of Batgirl wasn't quite the shot in the arm we needed. Dozier and the writers tried other things, like giving Dick Grayson his driver's license so Robin could drive the Batmobile, but they were all gimmicks. As the third season drew to a close, our future was in doubt.

I was still working as hard in the last days as I had in the first; we all were, even though we were all into the "What if . . . ?" phase: what were we going to do if we weren't renewed?

I was on the fence about that. Part of me had had enough of the costume, felt it was time to move on. But I knew I'd miss it if we were canceled. Besides, there were still a few things I wanted to try. I wanted to direct. I wanted to take the show on some exotic location. Our three-part show set in Londinium had been shot in Hollywood, and I thought it would be great to shoot in Paris or Rome, maybe introduce Batman's European counterparts. The Batman comic book had done that, teaming him with the Knight and the Squire in England, the Legionary in Rome, the Musketeer in France. I'd have loved to put them on the air, involve them all with new and old villains. And I think viewers would have enjoyed it, too.

But it wasn't to be, though we did come very close to getting a fourth season.

Twice.

Ratings were so-so, but we were still strong enough among the big-spending viewers that advertisers were booking spots and ABC was interested in another season. So was Fox. The studio was over-spending a million dollars a year on the show (they get a fee from the network, and only make money when there are enough episodes to syndicate), but the more episodes they had in the can, the bigger the eventual return in syndication. The studio told Dozier that if he could cut the budget, get rid of a few cast members, hold the line on salaries, and use more existing sets, we would be renewed.

I was willing to do it, provided we could get good scripts. We had a meeting where

With wife, Marcelle, and children (l. to r.) Moya, Perrin, Jill, and Nina

there was talk of eliminating Batgirl, though some executives were in favor of eliminating Robin and making Yvonne my sidekick. As fond as I'd grown of Yvonne, I thought that would be a mistake, not to mention unfair to Burt. I suggested she could guest star, perhaps even alternate with Robin.

But Bill was worried more about the look of the show. He didn't want to go out with a bare-bones, bare-looking travesty. Also, I think he was worried about his standing among his peers: he didn't want to do anything that would make him seem desperate to keep the show on. He was getting ready to do (irony of ironies!) a *Dick Tracy* pilot, and his attention was already on that. He said no to significant budget cuts; Fox and ABC hemmed and hawed, talked to the sponsors, and finally decided not to renew us.

Just like that, a cultural phenomenon came to an unseemly, unheralded end.

We had just finished shooting for the third season, and I went to my cottage, alone, to clean it out. I looked at the Batman costume hanging in the closet. There were definitely bittersweet feelings about leaving the show behind. I remember how odd I'd felt the first time I put the costume on and how I'd almost gotten used to it. I felt like the Thief of Baghdad rolling away the magic carpet that had taken me to so many interesting places, creatively as well as physically.

At the same time, though, I felt relieved and renewed, like a snake shucking its skin. I was eager to see what new skins I'd be challenged to put on.

I took the costume from the closet and folded it into a suitcase. I wanted to keep it, and I have it still: despite my own mixed feelings about the suit, cape, and cowl, I didn't want them to end up moth-eaten or dismembered in the studio wardrobe department. I hoped that someday, someone might give the costume more of a sense of importance than I felt for it at that moment.

Ironically, a few days later, NBC came calling. At the time, NBC was looking for a way to hook young adults and felt that *Batman* might help anchor a night that would include *Star Trek* and *Tarzan*, the latter of which was skewing a bit *too* young. They offered to pick up the show from ABC and go back to its first season roots: Dozier, Burt, and I were interested. However, studio space was at a premium, and unbeknownst to us, some enterprising executive had ordered the Batcave set burned and the standing sets dismantled and recycled as other sets.

NBC wasn't willing to spend the money to rebuild them, and so, for a second time, *Batman* was finished.

Lew was the one who phoned me with the news. The second person I heard from was producer Horwitz, who thanked me for a job well done and expressed the hope that we'd work together again. It was not verbal glad-handing. I know Howie was sincere.

The third person I heard from was Zsa Zsa Gabor. She was also the fourth, fifth, and sixth. She had been our last villain, and after she heard the news, she called me several times, inviting me to this party or that opening, to quiet dinners-for-two at her home. I declined. I was distracted, looking for a new direction creatively, and I needed to be alone. I have to admit, though, I understood how Zsa Zsa had managed to dazzle so many men over the years. It wasn't just her face and figure, which were impressive. When she talked to you, she had a way of making you feel like Adam, the first and only man and the one who was most important to her. I just wasn't in the mood for apples.

A month after we got our walking papers, we had a farewell party at the Sand and Sea Beach Club, where we all patted one another on the back and said our farewells. I left early, feeling depressed. I was moving on, but in four weeks the phone hadn't rung much. I was surprised by that, thinking there'd at least be interest among producers in cashing in on the goodwill I'd built among viewers. Apparently not. I'd had exactly two offers since we were canceled, both to star in single episodes of sitcoms. Not even a pilot for a series of my own.

Shortly thereafter, we all received an enormous shock. Howie Horwitz had taken his first vacation in three years. He drove to June Lake with his family, climbed onto a rock to admire the view, fell off, and was killed. It was a terrible tragedy, and really deepened my feeling of depression. Here was a man who worked hard, who was my age, who had what seemed like a bright future—and it was over. He was gone.

You feel shallow and superficial hurting for yourself under those circumstances, and my thoughts were with Howie's young family. I did what I could for them, as did Bill and everyone else, but then you back away. Everyone has to get on with their lives. I think, though, that Howie's death affected Dozier more than any of us realized. Rather than go on with new projects, he closed down his production company in 1968 and decided to devote himself to teaching. He spent many happy years away from the rat race, as a drama professor at Mount St. Mary's College; he died quietly, in his sleep, in 1991.

Over the next few weeks I vacillated between depression and the driving need to do something important, to use my celebrity to do something big and different. But Hollywood, that glorious land full of brightly colored balloons and pins to pop every one of them, made that impossible.

The rule of thumb, I found out (*now* they tell me . . .) is that after you finish a TV series, it takes a year or two for you to become employable again in something else. That, someone determined, is how long it takes the public to stop identifying you as the character you were playing. Today, actors break the mold a little faster with the help of TV movies, but those were just taking their first, halting steps back in the 1960s.

It takes longer when you've played someone who has become a part of the language or look of an era, and some actors never get another turn at bat—so to speak—witness Henry Winkler after *Happy Days*, Mickey Dolenz of *The Monkees,* or Don Adams after *Get Smart.* Ironically, Don is nothing like the Maxwell Smart character: he's a serious, erudite man and a Civil War buff. But chances are, he'd be the last person PBS would consider to narrate a show about the War Between the States. I remember him saying once, sadly and seriously, "Why don't they ask *me* to do *Kramer vs. Kramer?*"

Some actors do manage to escape typecasting, like Larry Hagman, who went from *I Dream of Jeannie* to *Dallas,* Carroll O'Connor, who went from *All in the Family* to *In the Heat of the Night,* or Robert Vaughn and Sean Connery, who went from being secret agents to playing terrific character roles. But it takes years. One outstanding success story was Guy Williams who, despite being closely identified with TV's Zorro, was able to come back as Professor Robinson on *Lost in Space.* I used to bump into him on the lot, and I asked him how he did it: he told me he was sleeping with the robot's daughter. The truth was, he'd shaved the mustache, dropped the Spanish accent . . . and waited six long, frustrating years.

Falling down the stairs again, this time in an episode of *Emergency!* Over the years, I was beaten or killed in dozens of ways.

The funny thing is, I could have avoided that trap.

Just before we'd learned that *Batman* was going to be canceled, Margaret Thatcher asked me to go to London to do a little traffic safety film for schoolchildren there. This was before Ms. Thatcher had become Prime Minister, but she was already charming, insistent, and very persuasive, and I agreed to go. Not only was it a chance to do some good, but it meant a trip to England, where I was still hoping the series could do some fourth-season location shooting. Lew came along, figuring we might be able to look into some other projects while we were there.

One of the men who entertained us was Cubby Broccoli, producer of the James Bond films. (And yes, he told me: the family name comes from the vegetable. One of his ancestors first brought the broccoli to America.) Over a lovely dinner, Cubby asked me point-blank if I'd be interested in playing 007. Sean Connery had completed *You Only Live Twice* and said he wasn't coming back, a talent search was proving unsuccessful, and it was getting close to the time when *On Her Majesty's Secret Service* was due to begin production. Lew nearly spit out his tea when a firm offer was made.

I'll have to admit I was tempted. There were three B's that really made an impact on the 1960s: Bond, Batman, and the Beatles. I had the chance to be two of them. The money would have been good, too. But the big problem, as I saw it, was that I wasn't British. Of course I could have done the accent. But the fans would have complained, and the British press would have been all over me. (As they were with Michael Keaton when *Batman* shot in London. They'd decided he was all wrong for the part and hounded him mercilessly).

In this case, though, they would have been right. In my heart, I felt that Bond should definitely be played by an Englishman, and I said so. Cubby respected my stand, and I still think I did the right thing, especially when you consider how Australian George Lazenby got roasted for his one stab at the part. He was much better than his detractors give him credit for, but anyone would have looked bad following Connery. In fact, it took Sean coming back and doing a so-so job in *Diamonds Are Forever* for my old friend Roger Moore to be able to step in with his different interpretation of Bond.

While I was in England, a former role came back to haunt me in a refreshingly positive way. I received a cable from a group of Italian film luminaries who had been granted an audience with Pope Paul in Rome. Because I'd shot *Los Quattros Implacables* there, I was invited to attend. I doubted that that was really the reason: *Batman* was going great guns in Italy, and it would help promote local filmmaking if the press could report that my last non-Batman film had been Italian. Well, it was nice to be loved, and in any case, one doesn't refuse an audience with the Pope. I fantasized that His Holiness watched our show and just wanted to meet me.

Lew and I bundled off at once to Rome, arriving on the night before our audience. With time to kill and Rome beckoning, I proceeded to show Lew to all the dives and hot spots I'd frequented while I lived there. Dawn came quickly, and we hurried back to the hotel for a few hours' sleep.

The combination of alcohol, jet lag, and too little sleep left me with the worst hangover of my life. I showered, dressed, and climbed into the car that had been sent for me. Even though I'm not a Catholic, I felt ashamed of my previous night's recklessness as I drove to Vatican City and the splendor of St. Peter's came into view. Many cities have a tangible personality, but few have the sheer charisma of the Vatican. You can't help but feel holy, humbled, and repentant.

At St. Peter's, I was ushered into a small, magnificent chamber and introduced to the other members of our group, which included the dashing Marcello Mastroianni and the stunning Sophia Loren. I confess that my throbbing headache as well as all holy thoughts evaporated as I set eyes on Sophia. I can only describe her beauty and the way she carried it this way: if you walked into the nearby Sistine Chapel and Sophia were standing there, it would be several minutes before you took a look to see what Michelangelo had done.

With some pomp and pageantry, we were shown into another small room and sat, knee to knee, in close quarters, as we awaited His Holiness. I was feeling very weak (partly because Sophia's knees were beside mine) and was barely able to concentrate as a robed aide arrived and told us that we would peel off from one side, one at a time, kneel, kiss the Pontiff's ring, and return to our seats.

Pope Paul appeared soon thereafter; there were times when Dozier had kept me waiting longer than this, which should tell you something about how Hollywood producers view their own importance. His Holiness sat, and the members of the film commission began going over in turn, the Pope saying a few quiet words to each of them.

When it was finally my turn, I rose unsteadily, my head throbbing again, and I knew at once that if I knelt I was not going to be able to get back up. Fortunately, I began to feel that it might be improper for an Episcopalian to kneel and kiss the ring of the Pope, and I convinced myself that even he'd feel awkward about it if he knew. Instead, I stopped in front of him, bowed slightly, offered my hand, and said, "How do you do, Your Excellence."

From the corner of my eye, I saw his aide tense, but to my relief and delight the Pope smiled broadly and shook my hand gently. I remember thinking how smooth his skin felt, how ethereal his touch. He was very impressive.

Then he began speaking in Italian, much too quickly for me to follow; realizing, suddenly, that I wasn't a native, he slipped into English without missing a beat.

He said, "I love your television show, Mr. West."

I was stunned.

"Thank you, Your Excellence," I said.

Wondering, then, if he'd been briefed, I had just about decided to ask him which villain was his favorite, when he said, "The costume you wear is very striking."

"Yes, Your Excellence, though not as impressive as your own."

He laughed, then said, "But your automobile is, however, more impressive than my own."

Amazing. He *had* watched our show. Popes are human, too.

I sat back down, my headache fading. If I had died then and there, my obituary would have been a classic: famous TV star praised by Pope dies in Sophia Loren's lap.

It doesn't happen any better than that. It sounded like something straight out of *Batman*.

24

MEANWHILE, BACK in Hollywood, I had the same problem Don Adams and a few others did: everything about me reminded people of the character I'd played, from my face to my voice to the way I walked.

To try and break that image, I acted on one of those two phone calls I'd had, and immediately took a five-thousand-dollar change-of-pace part as a well-to-do sleaze on one of the first episodes of *Love, American Style*, trying to convince George (Goober Pyle) Lindsey to let his virginal sister join me on a three-day golf tournament. Bruce Wayne it wasn't. And I was happy with the results. But, as I said before, the movie people in Hollywood don't much watch TV. I could have played a naked Jack the Ripper, and over breakfast at the Polo Lounge someone would have said, "Yeah, I hear Adam's back in a cape."

After that, I did little work for a year. I auditioned for a number of big films, but though the directors always gave me the obligatory "Great job!" or "Hey, thanks for coming," I heard later that they were afraid people would see me on the screen and think of Batman. I had awful visions of George Reeves, whose good work in *From Here to Eternity* and Disney's *Westward Ho the Wagons!* got pared to the bone because preview audiences yelled, "There's Superman!" No one remembered him in *Gone with the Wind* or *Samson and Delilah*. He was Superman.

And I was Batman.

Was it just two years before, in 1967, that I had been voted Most Promising New Star by the motion picture exhibitors on the strength of the *Batman* film? I considered throwing the award into the Pacific as an offering to the Gods of Hollywood. But I had this vision of them looking down and saying, "Hey, isn't that Batman?"

As Mr. Hyde

The awful thing was, I could have been working. During the run of *Batman*, I'd been approached by a big and powerful agent who wanted me to leave Lew and join him. Career-wise, it would have made sense. At the time, agents were just beginning to package projects: if a studio wanted a particular star, director, or script, the other elements came with it. I would have become part of a new package after the series ended. It would have eased the transition.

I was offered the starring role in *The Girl Who Knew Too Much,* a Cold War cheapie with Nancy Kwan as my leading lady and Communists infiltrating organized crime. I was the hero sent to stop them. The budget was low, the schedule was rushed, and Nancy and I both quickly knew we were part of film infamy. I still thought Bond should be a Brit, but as the shooting progressed on this turkey, I told myself that at least in that role I could have been wrong with class. I'm sure it was disappointing to Nancy, too, a former dancer with the British Royal Ballet and a veteran of such hits as *The World of Suzie Wong* and *Flower Drum Song.* We were both in our thirties and felt like has-beens. (Nancy has since costarred in the box office hit *Dragon: The Bruce Lee Story,* which revitalized her career. I'm happy she toughed it out until the wheel came around.)

I was so discouraged I did nothing except personal appearances for two years after that. For a while, money wasn't much of a problem. I'd managed to make some good investments, and I was also paid several hundred dollars each time a *Batman* episode was rerun. In some markets, the show was airing every afternoon, which turned out to be quite lucrative for a while.

After two years, though, I got nothing, and there still wasn't any work to speak of.

I was angry and feeling sorry for myself. I walked in the mountains with my German shepherd, and I hung out on the beach by my apartment, read book after book, and retreated from any contact with Hollywood. I refused to drive to town for meetings and auditions I knew would be unproductive, and I avoided Hollywood types. Instead, I hung out with a "wild bunch." We rode our motorcycles and did a lot of hard drinking; after a while, I didn't even bother to wait until sunset to uncork the bottle. At times I slept on the beach and chased women as if it were a hobby. I was easy.

And I did one thing more—asked myself the same question over and over: what the hell had been going through my head when I *took* that part? What happened to the man Lew called "the luckiest guy in the world"? I felt that I'd destroyed the potential others had said I had.

Oddly, though acting seemed to have given up on me, I never thought of giving up acting. I missed it. The process of the work, searching a script for nuance, subtext, working with other actors, with directors, the sense of family: that was so important to me I didn't want to turn my back on ever having it again.

But I knew that I wasn't going to have it if I didn't get back in the race and give casting directors a fair chance. The realization came to me one summer mid-morning, with the sun burning into my bloodshot eyes from the ocean outside my bedroom, and a vice tightening around my temples as punishment for my indulgence the night before. The combination of the pain and the crisp daylight and my sorry reflection in the mirror woke something up in me; several things, actually. One, the realization that if I kept up like this I was going to end up broke, alone, and probably dead. Two, the truth that even though I hid a lot, I was setting the worst kind of example for my kids and for the kids who had watched the show. That may seem corny or obvious or maybe even a little naive, but I was disgusted with myself and I needed that motivation to shed my stupid anger and self-pity. The sense that I'd let down my own children in particular, hadn't seen them much or talked with them, hit me like a mushroom cloud. I looked out at the beach, and cried.

The first call I made was to them, to tell them I loved them. The second call I made was to my agent, telling him to get me meetings and auditions, I didn't care with whom and for what. I wanted to work. More importantly, I wanted my self-respect back.

25

NOT LONG after that, I got a role with Richard Benjamin and Elizabeth Ashley in *Marriage of a Young Stockbroker,* in 1971. It was a good part but small, though I got some very good reviews. I also enjoyed some success with *Volpone* at the prestigious Mark Taper Forum at the Music Center in Los Angeles, with Sam Waterston and Avery Schreiber. Once again, the reviews were excellent. But neither project achieved what I had hoped it would: to show the people in Hollywood I could act out of a mask.

Nothing I did seemed to breach the Batman barrier, so I took what was offered to keep busy and stay in the public eye. I made another film in Europe, *Partisan,* a political adventure non-thriller; I did series work like *Alias Smith and Jones* and *Emergency,* and I did some of those TV pilots I talked about earlier. The first one was shot in 1972: *Poor Devil,* in which I played a comedic villain in support of stars Sammy Davis, Jr., as a fumbling devil and Christopher Lee as Lucifer himself. Both actors were great to be around, and I had a fun two weeks shooting with them in San Francisco. But the series failed to sell and didn't air until a year later. My next pilot was *The Eyes of Charles Sand,* in which I had a sixth-billed role as Dr. Paul Scott; I did *Nevada Smith* in 1975, costarring as Frank Hartlee with Cliff Potts as Smith and Lorne Greene as Jonas Cord. Though it was a lot of fun working with the florid and charming Mr. Greene, the show didn't sell.

I became friends with Patty Duke, whom I met at a film festival in Acapulco. She was in her middle twenties, divorced from John Astin, and having problems of her own. Casting directors had regarded her as a kid, cute Patty and Cathy Lane, so she'd done the sleazy film ver-

With wife Marcelle in 1972

sion of the even sleazier novel *Valley of the Dolls:* now casting directors regarded her as just a bad actress. Another great talent misjudged and unappreciated.

In the mid-1970s, the acting assignments dried up again. In retrospect, I realize that I should have done what Leonard Nimoy did after *Star Trek* was canceled. He took his case to the people, went out and did summer stock and regional theater, starring in *Fiddler on the Roof, Camelot, One Flew Over the Cuckoo's Nest,* and *Caligula.* He made audiences see him differently. (Of course, then he came back and did Mr. Spock again for the big screen . . . but at least he got a great deal of money each time he put on the pointy ears.)

I knew I had to get out there and work, but what I chose to do wasn't acting. It was something I'd resisted for several years: getting back into the Batsuit and making lucrative personal appearances at fairs, conventions, rodeos, car shows (with the Batmobile), and circuses. The money was better than summer stock, and took only a few intense days at a chug. The rest of the time I was free to pursue parts in Hollywood.

I often appeared with Burt. We tried to have a good time and enjoy the fans. But I felt like I was whoring it, and digging myself deeper into a hole to boot. Indeed, even in my darkest post-*Batman* days, I have never felt as low, professionally, as when one of my employers thought it would be fun for Evansville, Indiana, audiences to see Batman fly. He dangled a fat paycheck, and I allowed myself to be stuffed into a cannon and launched into a net. I have always had all the respect in the world for circus people, but this was not the life I had envisioned for myself. I felt like Mountain Rivera in *Requiem for a Heavyweight*, a once-serious fighter parading around the ring in a silly costume.

As I lay tensed in the dark cannon, the roars of the crowd echoing in my ears and fears of broken bones dancing through my head, it was more than just my wounded pride that bothered me. It was also guilt I felt for the harm I was doing to Batman. On TV or in the movie, whether Batman was being pelted with eggs or doing the Batusi or running around with a bomb, unable to throw it away because there were nuns, lovers, or ducks everywhere he tried to throw it, I could still be noble or aloof or grimly determined or deadpan. I could be entertaining within the context of the film. When you're an amateur being shot through the air like a blue-and-gray missile, arms splayed like broken wings, cape fluttering like a big flag, brain signaling for more adrenaline, it's difficult to maintain your dignity. I remember wondering, as I flew toward the distant net, what my studies with Lee Strasberg had covered that might be appropriate to this. Concentration, I suppose.

When I left the arena, I decided not to play the clown again as Batman. If for no other reason, than because I wanted to stay alive. I turned down a return engagement in Evansville and all others that I felt would be unseemly, whether they involved riding an elephant in a parade or skydiving into a mall. I would do appearances because I needed to earn a living, and because it brought joy to people. But I would be more selective about them.

I also came to terms with the part of me that resented Batman. I realized how stupid it was, like Michael Redgrave's ventriloquist character in the classic film *Dead of Night,* angry at his dummy. My anger at not getting good parts should have been directed at me or at Hollywood, not at Batman.

Ironically, one of the next things I was offered was another shot at

Batman. In 1977, Burt Ward and I were asked to do the voices for a Saturday-morning cartoon series, *The New Adventures of Batman*. At first I said no . . . but then I asked myself how I'd feel hearing someone else's voice come from Batman's mouth. I decided I wouldn't like it. In just a few weeks, I'd gone from resentment to feeling very protec-

tive about the character and my interpretation of him, and I agreed to do the series. Though the animation was stiff and disappointing, the show was done seriously, with some pretty good scripts.

Fresh from that, I won the part of a movie star in the film *Hooper* (1978), largely because Burt Reynolds and the director, Hal Needham, thought I looked enough like Burt that he could convincingly play my stunt double in the film. Burt was very complimentary about my work in the picture and in *Batman,* and I needed to hear that. Apart from that, though, I really didn't get to know him, because he usually hung out with Needham, costar Sally Field, or close friends Dom DeLuise and Jim Nabors.

I did more TV shows, playing a handicapped man on *Fantasy Island,* appearing in *Love Boat,* and hosting a game show pilot that failed to sell. Ego and top billing didn't matter, I just wanted to work, to stay visible. Then, in 1979, I hit another low point.

Burt and I played Batman and Robin yet again in a pair of prime-time specials, *Legends of the Super-Heroes,* which also featured DC's heroes Green Lantern, the Flash, Hawkman, Captain Marvel, and others, and costarred Frank Gorshin as the Riddler. My biggest hope was that if the shows were successful, we might have a chance to bring Batman and Robin into a feature film situation.

But the project was terrible, and we knew it as soon as we got on the set. There was no rehearsal time, and the scenes were shot even faster than we'd done the original *Batman* series. The budget was brutally low, the show was shot on videotape, which made it seem cheap, and the scripts couldn't have been worse. The first segment was the "Challenge" sequence, in which we battled the forces of evil, and the second one was a superhero roast. It hurts to think about it. The scriptwriters didn't understand what had made *Batman* successful, and turned the heroes into comedians, complete with slapstick routines and bad jokes. Script changes that had been promised were never delivered, and instead of helping to maintain the character's integrity, I had lent my name to this degradation. To make things worse, I didn't work for months after that.

When I finally got another film, it was the titillating *The Happy Hooker Goes Hollywood* (1980), toplining Martine Beswicke and up-and-coming Chris Lemmon, Jack's son. Phil Silvers and I had to play part of the film in drag, and to add insult to injury I never collected my full salary from the film's producers. If I took anything at all from the experience, it was respect for gorgeous Martine, a cult star who had been featured in *Thunderball* and had bared nearly all in movies like *Slave Girls* and *Prehistoric Women.* This cultured, upright, very proper and conservative young lady got naked in films simply because that was her job: you've got to love her, and I did.

The bad, low-budget films kept on coming: *Hell Riders, Young Lady Chatterly* (not even Part I, but Part II!), *Zombie Nightmare,* and *Rest in Peace,* which was financed by a group of Mormons based in Salt Lake City who gave me the impression that they wanted to fund a slate of pictures of my choosing. Both the movie and the plan were duds.

There was talk about other projects, and I hopefully and determinedly went to each and every meeting. There were inquiries from Europe, but they lasted as long as snow on Capri. Cliff Robertson, who had played the villain Shame on our show, had a good friend who was running Atari, and there was talk of my being a spokesperson for the company. Then the company fell on hard times and nothing came of it. In 1983, I cohosted a Consumer Electronics awards show in Chicago with Kreskin and Bob Shayne, who had played Inspector Henderson on the *Superman* TV show. Some of the young movers and shakers of high-tech industries were full of ideas about endorsements, but those, too, failed to pan out.

I got down so far it looked like up, and about the only thing that kept me from going back to my wicked ways during this period was my home life, which couldn't have been better. In 1972, I met a bright and witty lady named Marcelle Tagand Lear. She was divorced from a member of the Lear Jet family, and we met when she brought her two little girls, Moya and Jill, to watch us shooting one of the pilots at the Santa Monica Airport. (One of the TV pilots, I mean.) Marcelle was sweet and loving with her children and had an alluring French accent (still does). I began seeing her, and we quickly became great friends; we were married and have stayed so since. Marcelle was largely responsible for lifting me from the doldrums in which I often found myself. In this, she was ably assisted by our two precious children, Nina, born in 1976, and Perrin, born in 1979.

Strangely, in my experience, I've found that actors tend to be some of the best parents you'll ever encounter. The Joan Crawford "Mommie Dearest" stereotype is really the exception rather than the rule. Maybe it's the child in us that relates to the children around us, I don't know. But most actors who become parents love taking their kids on location and using their downtime to strengthen the family unit. Natalie and R. J. were like that. So was Burt Lancaster, when his kids were young. He would take his son, Bill, to film sets, to political rallies, and talk to him like an adult about sex or political dissidents or whatever else was happening on-screen. Cliff Robertson has always been great with his daughters, and recently took several months to go hiking through Scotland with the beautiful young Heather. The Hestons, Goldie Hawn and Kurt Russell, Roger and Luisa Moore: whatever happens to them professionally, they're there for their kids.

It's a rough-and-tumble industry. Some of us may have trouble staying married at times, but eventually that emotional maturity comes. And when it does, as obvious as this may sound, we discover that none of our roles is more important or rewarding than that of family man or woman. I'm lucky that Marcelle was there for me when I finally grew up.

26

MARCELLE WAS with me when I had one of the most unusual and ironic encounters of my post-*Batman* life. I was playing in a celebrity tennis tournament at a hotel on Maui, with the likes of Lloyd Bridges, Bill Cosby, and others. We had a gorgeous second-floor room facing the beach, and I was sitting below the terrace on a heavy iron lounge, when I cracked an eye and happened to notice something glint around the corner of the building. I looked over and saw a grubby man with a machete. I was behind some tall plants and he didn't see me: his eyes were on a young couple lying on their bellies on the golden sands nearby, about twenty feet away from me.

Good, I thought. At least he wasn't a comic book fan out to get me. But he did have the shifty, tentative manner of a man up to no good, and I watched as he walked right by me, toward the couple. I told myself I was imagining things, having a Caped Crusader flashback, that he was probably just a gardener. But that wasn't the case.

Suddenly he raised the machete and brought it down on the girl's back, breaking her skin at the shoulder blade and snapping the string top of her bikini. The girl screamed and jumped up, leaving her bikini top on the sands as she bounced off, obviously terrified and embarrassed. Her companion jumped up to cover her retreat, and the attacker slashed him laterally across the belly. Though he was bleeding, the young man grabbed the attacker's arm and held it above his head.

Meanwhile, I'd jumped up when the attacker struck, and was running over, shouting, "Drop that machete!" People farther down the beach looked over, but as I grabbed the attacker's arm I'm sure they thought, A topless girl running down the beach? Batman fighting a criminal? It's got to be *Candid Camera* or a publicity stunt.

I called for help, but no one moved, though a security man standing waist-deep in the surf had the good sense to shout, "Are you rehearsing something?"

"*No!*" I yelled, and swore loudly.

By this time, the wounded young man was weakening, while the attacker grew more frantic. Desperate now, he broke free and ran back toward the hotel, still holding the machete. While the young guy dropped to his knees, I set off in pursuit, aware that I could cut Mr. Machete off if I went back through the foliage where I'd been sitting.

Marcelle had heard the shouts and came to the balcony. As she looked down and saw me running, I yelled for her to call security. Reaching the hotel a few steps ahead of the attacker, I picked up a heavy lounge and swung it at him as he approached. The blow knocked the machete from his hand and caused him to stagger back; he recovered quickly and ran on without bothering to pick up his weapon.

Now the security man was running over, as were several other people on the beach. But I was afraid they wouldn't get there in time, so I went after the attacker, still holding the lounge and thinking to hit him with it. Good idea, in theory, but I hadn't taken more than a dozen steps when the heavy iron framework began to weigh me down. Ah, vanity: I didn't want them to see me fall or drop the lounge, so I continued running and panting, bending lower and lower but refusing to drop the lounge. Fortunately, the attacker ducked into a courtyard, and realized too late that there was no exit and he was trapped. As he turned to leave, he ran smack into me and my lounge chair, and I pushed him against the wall, pinning him there until the guard arrived to take charge. People applauded. Wonderful. They still thought we were filming. Finally, more hotel security showed up. They grabbed the guy and went to look after the poor victim on the beach. As I headed toward my wife, out of breath and arm-weary, I thought back to something Bruce Lee had once said on the set: real fights are nothing like movie fights, they're over in just a couple of seconds, depending on which guy gets the first hard lick in. Unfortunately this one seemed to go on forever and I nearly ended up having a stroke as I ran through the bushes in ninety-degree heat carrying a heavy metal chaise.

When I got back to the room, Marcelle yelled at me for having confused my real-life role of husband and father with my reel-life role as Batman, and I agreed that I'd acted rashly. But I found out that you never know how you're going to behave when you witness a crime or are mugged, not until you're in the midst of it. And by that time your mind has very little control over your actions. Probably I had read too many scripts.

Marcelle's concern for me has always been loving and encouraging. With her help, I held on to my sanity during the lean years, and things finally started to pick up for me in the middle 1980s. The old guard was passing on in Hollywood, and the new guard was happy to hire me.

I hosted shows, from A&E's *Evening at the Improv* to a cartoon series on cable's Nickelodeon. I did more pilots, most notably a comedy that I really enjoyed called *Ace Diamond, Private Eye*. Though it didn't sell, I got a close friend out of it: producer Arthur Annecharrico, who has since gone on to produce many successful series. Another project that really excited me also managed to fall through, which is too bad: it would have been a knockout.

An acquaintance of mine who worked at Universal was leaving to put together outside financing for films with the provision that they be made in Mexico. And for a time, it looked as though I'd be playing the title character in a big-screen version of the comic strip *The Phantom*. Ironically, though the money was in place, we had a problem obtaining the rights (King Features wanted a million dollars!) and the deal fell through. The story would have brought the costumed hero (a forerunner to Batman) out of the jungle and into Mexico City on a manhunt.

Rather than give up the financing, we quickly talked to Marvel Comics about bringing their superhero Daredevil to the screen, but our backers decided he wasn't sufficiently well known to risk millions of dollars on.

In 1986, writer/producer Stephen Cannell, whose track record was impeccable and included such hits as *The Rockford Files* and *The Greatest American Hero,* cast me as Captain Rick Wright in his new comedy series *The Last Precinct*. The scripts were funny, the cast was great (it included comic Rick Ducommun, Ernie Hudson, Keenan Wynn, and a terrific ensemble), but we had an awful time slot. Our show was aimed at teenagers, who weren't watching TV on Fridays from nine to ten, when we appeared, and we were gone after six weeks.

I was disappointed, of course, but I felt that the series had gone some way to breaking my typecasting stigma. It showed that I could do a different kind of comedy, and I felt that I'd now be considered for the kinds of parts Leslie Nielsen and a few others were getting. And I probably would have been, if Leslie and the others hadn't been getting them.

The Hollywood environment was making me antsy, so we moved from our home in the Pacific Palisades to a larger place in rural Idaho. It was a short flight back to Hollywood if anyone wanted to see me, and instead of going for a drive when I was depressed, I could go out back and split a log or ride a horse, even climb a mountain.

The work I did after moving was, I think, quite good, and jobs are becoming more and more plentiful. I did a picture called *Doin' Time on Planet Earth* in 1988, which got respectable reviews and proved popular on cable. It was very ably directed by Charlie Matthau, Walter's son, and we had some fun, creative times on the set. I'm proud of that little film. I played George Washington in a pilot with Ryan O'Neal, called *1775;* I did the voice of a villain called The Grey Ghost on the animated *Batman* TV series; and I have been immortalized on *The Simpsons.* I had the pleasure of appearing in one of my favorite TV shows, HBO's *Tales from the Crypt,* and starred in an NBC pilot called *Lookwell,* which is my favorite comedy of all the non-*Batman* work I've done. It was about out-of-work actor Ty Lookwell, who once played a detective on TV and fancies himself a sleuth in real life. The show was coproduced by heavyweights Bernie Brillstein and Lorne Michaels (*Saturday Night Live*), and cowritten by a guy who has since become a member of the late-night crowd: Conan O'Brien. *Lookwell* was a favorite of network head Brandon Tartikoff, but when Brandon left NBC to run Paramount Pictures, the project fell by the wayside.

Since then, I've starred in several episodes of Fox's new *Danger Theater,* costarred with the incomparable Carol Burnett in a pilot for a proposed new series, *Reel Life,* and have costarred with the magnificent Judy Davis and Peter Weller in a film written and directed by Michael Tolkin (screenwriter of *The Player*) called *The New Age.* One of the greatest compliments I've ever received was when Judy, who has done amazing work in films like *A Passage to India, Impromptu,* and Woody Allen's *Husbands and Wives,* told me that she and her son Sam always

watch *Batman* in her native Australia, and that she thought the acting
I did in the show was marvelous.

Thanks, Judy.

At present, there's also some theater work I hope to do. I'm writing
a play based on the life of Thomas Jefferson, something I've been working on for several years, and I've been talking with producers about
doing *Dracula* on the stage. I think it would be fun to play the other
leading bat of stage and screen. I recently voiced an animated Adam
West for the hit ABC show "The Critic." I starred with Betty Buckley
in the first sophisticated interactive movie, "Ride for Your Life," and
have joined Loni Anderson on the TV series, "Nurses." The talk shows
have been interesting and a nice tribute to our "Batman." There was
Letterman and Vicki and Conan and Howard Stern. Howard is a real
Batfan and he put me in his notoriously successful book. When my
energetic young agent, Fred Wostbrock, booked me on Howard's TV
show, I was a little dismayed. But Howard was terrific with me; he's a
fascinating character.

I'm delighted that I'm suddenly employable again, and I'm grateful
to be working. I was especially flattered in the summer of 1993 when
the gracious Larry Lankford asked me to come to Dallas and present
an award at the prestigious Harvey Awards for comic books (named
after pioneer Harvey Kurtzman). It was not only an honor, but it was
great having comic book writers and editors like Julie Schwartz and
Archie Goodwin come up to me and say very kind, very sincere things
about my work on *Batman*. One of the guests at the ceremony, special
effects master Ray Harryhausen, asked me if I was ever sorry I'd put on
the cowl and sent my career on the course it's taken.

I answered quickly and honestly, "No." And that's the truth.

Do I regret having left the spaghetti western trail that took Clint
Eastwood to glory?

I do not. No two careers run the same course, and I don't regret
not taking Clint's route any more than I regret not having done what
John Cassavetes did, working in pilots like *Alexander the Great* or movies
he hated like *Two Minute Warning* so he could finance small, heartfelt
films like *Faces*. Besides, Clint and I aren't alike, really, and I wouldn't
be as comfortable playing the kind of taciturn hero he plays.

Would I play Batman again if I could go back?

Whenever I confront that question, I think back to a thirteen-year-old kid who used to come home from school and climb over the wall at the studio to try and see me. He was so enterprising that when I heard about him, I told the guard to hold him the next time he came over.

He did. I went over, in costume, had the awestruck kid call home to tell his folks he'd be busy that day, then took him to the set and put him in one of the scenes as an extra. He was in heaven.

Over twenty years later, a letter from this same young man somehow found me. He wrote that he had become a successful attorney and that I was responsible for making him want to become a "crime-fighter." He added that in his spare time he worked to help underprivileged boys, and he said I was responsible for that, too, having shown him the kindness I did.

I've received many letters like that over the years, people telling me about the good influence *Batman* had on their lives, giving them a role model or simply a laugh when they needed one. Paul Newman and Clint Eastwood may have gotten meatier parts (and paychecks) over the years, but you can't put a value on fan mail like that.

The answer to the question, after a lot of thought and soul searching, is I'd do it again in a minute. I've got a good life, the love of countless fans, and the rare satisfaction of having been an important part of TV history. I don't think anyone can complain about that, nor has the right to ask for more.

Well, there is one thing . . .

Epilogue

I LOVED PLAYING Batman, giving him a grandiose verve. And, as I said before, Batman is a big enough character to be interpreted in a number of ways.

There's our way, and there's also the Tim Burton/Michael Keaton way. Since *Batman* came out in 1989, I don't think there's a question I've been asked more than, "What did you think of the new Batman?" And my stock answer has always been, "They have their vision, we had ours."

I still think that, but I'd like to elaborate.

I admired the movie from a technical standpoint, and some of the action scenes—the escape from the museum, the fight in the alley—were dazzling. But I didn't relate to the characterization of Bruce Wayne or Batman. This isn't a knock against Michael Keaton, whom I've met and even raced against in a celebrity ski tournament. He's a talented actor with extraordinary range. I just don't think they got it right, the massive box office grosses notwithstanding.

In the recent *Batman*, Bruce ranged from psychotic to addle-headed: unfocused, inattentive, shallow. I found that off-putting. And Batman shouldn't work solely for his own satisfaction, but for the good of Gothamites. In the film, he destroyed those first two hoods but did nothing for the people they'd mugged. He did more damage fleeing from the museum in his Batmobile and, later, with his crashing Bat-plane than the Joker did in the entire film.

Critics would probably have cried "camp" if Batman showed any concern for the victims or innocent bystanders. But I think audiences would have appreciated it. And it would have given the character more longevity, sequel-wise. (I didn't see the second film, but I heard it was terribly disappointing and fell way below expectations at the box office.)

In a way, the Burton film answered the question of what an emotionally scarred Batman might be like: unhappy, his rage bubbling right below the surface, behind the eyes, ready to blow. That's a valid interpretation, obviously, though it has an inherent nastiness which, for me, makes it unpleasant. I think it also dates the film in our own hostile era, something which makes it less timeless than, say, the first two Superman films.

All of this is as subjective as I care to be. I'll admit I was angry and profoundly disappointed when I was not asked to reprise the role... our Batfans expected me to come back, and I had what I thought were some exciting ideas for a new one. (Contrary to popular misconception, I wasn't asked to do a cameo as Bruce Wayne's father, Thomas. If I had been, I'd have turned it down.) Back in 1980, when producer Mike Uslan first tried to get the feature film project rolling, he told people he wanted to get away from the "camp" image, which meant using another actor.

That bothered me. I would have played the part differently, a new Batman for a new era. That's what Buster Crabbe did when he guest-starred on the *Buck Rogers* TV series as what was essentially an older Buck Rogers. He was masterful, and dominated his scenes with Gil Gerard and the rest of the cast. And, I assure you, audiences loved it.

Burt Ward and I then heard not-so-secret rumors that the producers felt we were too old. That rang hollow, too. Buster was seventy-three when he did the *Buck Rogers* show, and besides, movies can make you believe what they want you to believe about an actor's age. No, we wouldn't have been playing a teenager and twentysomething Bruce Wayne, but would that have mattered? Artist/writer Frank Miller's 1986 four-issue series *Batman: The Dark Knight* was one of the biggest comic book hits of the 1980s, and it was about a middle-aged Batman coming out of retirement. Indeed, it was the success of that comic book, its look and palette and its fresh exploration of the character, that gave impetus to the Batman movie, which had been languishing since 1980.

I'll put it another way. If William Shatner and Leonard Nimoy hadn't agreed to do a *Star Trek* film, there wouldn't have been one. Don Adams was "allowed" to bring back Maxwell Smart in a theatrical and TV movie, Robert Vaughn returned as the Man from U.N.C.L.E. in a TV film, and Connery played Bond again after a dozen years. More recently, David Carradine returned to TV as Kwai Chang Caine in *Kung Fu: The Legend Continues.*

Burt Ward and I weren't asked to return, and even more painfully, our contribution to the legend was ignored, ridiculed, and denigrated by certain of the filmmakers, though the series was aired and promoted and used in the marketing of the new films and in the merchandising.

But we certainly could have done the parts.

Granted, the pop art craze of our show would have looked dated. The BIFFs and ZAPs and BAROOOMs wouldn't have worked. The bright lights would have had to be darkened (as they were, in fact, for many scenes in our original film). The "Holy" this or that would have had to be eliminated (except possibly for one, carefully used in the heat of returning youthful exuberance, before Robin catches himself). And if Cesar Romero had returned, he might have had to shave his mustache.

But there was so much that worked, and still would. It would have worked, and it would have appealed to a wider audience, including children (the return ticket buyers).

When I saw Topol do *Fiddler on the Roof* on Broadway a few years ago, I was impressed by how age had changed what he did with the character from twenty years before. In real life, the actor had reared and married off a daughter: that's going to affect the way one plays that on stage. Same framework; different nuance and depth. I've never seen an actor return to a role without changing it to some degree, whether it was Richard Kiley to Don Quixote or Clint Eastwood to Dirty Harry.

My Batman today, in his fifties, would still be a man who believes in honor and justice. But he wouldn't be quite so idealistic and Peace Corps–eager. I suspect he'd have semi-retired from crimefighting, perhaps bitter over the losing battle he'd been fighting. He'd put the costume on only for the most compelling reasons, and spend most of his time using his fortune to help the needy, the homeless, those without hope, working full-time to battle the causes of crime. He'd probably be in nearly the same shape as before, because he'd be working out more, an older crimefighter clinging to Macho Mountain with intensity.

(Some of us older actors do this anyway, as age struggles to establish its deteriorative beachheads.)

Robin/Dick Grayson would be his own man, perhaps more conservative than Bruce, or possibly more cynical. There would certainly be more from him for Batman/Bruce to react to.

As for his old foes, those who survive or remain at large would also have grown wiser with age—and, for that reason, more dangerous. What would the Riddler be like after, say, a score of years in an institution . . . that had supposedly cured him? Or the Joker, having gone "legit" and running powerful businesses to rival Bruce's. Or the Penguin broken, perhaps homeless, found by Bruce and nursed to health. Catwoman married to a king or having become an ambassador herself or fighting for animal rights in a most affirmative way, perhaps killing poachers and creating a moral problem for Batman, who might well agree with her!

Regardless of the situation, Bruce and Dick getting the call, returning to the study, going to the Batpoles, and emerging in their costumes could well have audiences on their feet, or viewers at home smiling broadly. And it wouldn't hurt the movie franchise at all. Imagine the Classic Batman coexisting beside the New Batman. (After all, the animated Batman is all over the Fox airwaves . . . with, I might add, a voice and delivery that sound eerily like mine.) And our live-action series continues twice a day on the new FX channel.

Obviously, I'm not ambivalent about the subject, and it would be a challenge and a pleasure to drop back into the Batcave, brush away the huge cobwebs, and dust off the Batmobile. As fifty years of disappointed super-villains have painfully discovered, the classic Batman continues to dominate in a way no other hero has. However . . . who can predict whether an ultra-heinous villain may be waiting in the shadows to require our crimefighter's deadly attention.

But, sadly, Batman is not my property. Just my beloved concern.

SAME BAT-TIME...
SAME BAT-CHANNEL

AN ANNOTATED EPISODE GUIDE
TO BATMAN

"Hey Diddle Riddle"
"Smack in the Middle"

Aired: 1/12, 1/13

Guest Stars: Frank Gorshin: *The Riddler*
Jill St. John: *Molly*
Michael Fox: *Inspector Basch*
Damian O'Flynn: *Gideon Peale*
Ben Astar: *The Moldavian Prime Minister*
With: Allen Jaffe, Jack Barry, and Dick Reeves

Teleplay: Lorenzo Semple, Jr.

Director: Robert Butler

Story: The Riddler lures Batman to the Peale Art Gallery and is arrested ... then sues for false arrest. Batman realizes that the only way to prevent a trial—where he will be forced to reveal his identity—is by capturing the Riddler in the act of committing a real crime. This is made all the more difficult when the felon captures Robin and Molly takes his place!

Comment: Bill Dozier appeared as the maître d'. This was one of the few times we "cheated" on a cliffhanger: at the end of episode one, it seemed like the Riddler was going to cut up the comatose Robin. However, he was simply making a life-mask for Molly to wear.

This was my favorite episode, and we went all-out for it: we spent twenty-one days filming it, a luxury we would never have again.

Incidentally, I understand that because "our" Michael Fox came first, Screen Actors Guild rules compelled that other Michael Fox to use his middle initial "J."

"Fine Feathered Finks"
"The Penguin's a Jinx"

Aired: 1/19, 1/20

Guest Stars: Burgess Meredith: *The Penguin*
Leslie Parrish: *Dawn*

Dan Tobin: *Mr. Jay*
Walter Burke: *Sparrow*
Lewis Charles: *Hawkeye*
David Lewis: *Warden Crichton*
With: Alex D'Arcy, Johnny Jacobs, Robert Phillips

Teleplay: Lorenzo Semple, Jr.

Director: Robert Butler

Story: The Penguin commits a series of robberies without ever taking anything. In an effort to find out what his game is, Bruce goes to the fiend's umbrella factory, where he's captured and nearly roasted in a blast furnace.

Comment: We got the shooting schedule down to eighteen days for this one, but that was still too long. The awful test results of the first show came back while we were shooting this episode, which cast a pall over the set.

"The Joker Is Wild" "Batman Gets Riled"

Aired: 1/26, 1/27

Guest Stars: Cesar Romero: *The Joker*
Nancy Kovack: *Queenie*
David Lewis: *Warden Crichton*
Jerry Dunphy: *Fred*
With: Dick Curtis, Merritt Bohn, Jonathan Hole, Angelo DeMeo

Teleplay: Robert Dozier

Director: Don Weiss

Story: Furious when he isn't named in the Gotham Art Museum's Comedian's Hall, the Joker escapes from prison and robs the museum. Using a utility belt of his own design, the Joker captures Batman and Robin, whom he plans to unmask on national TV.

Comment: Nancy Kovack, best known for playing Medea in *Jason and the Argonauts*, was one of the most beautiful women I ever worked with.

"Instant Freeze"
"Rats Like Cheese"

Aired: 2/2, 2/3

Guest Stars: George Sanders: *Mr. Freeze*
Shelby Grant: *Princess Sandra*
Troy Metton: *Chill*
Guy Way: *Nippy*
With: Roy Sickner, William O'Connell, Robert Hogan, John Zaremba, Ken Del Conte, Don Hannum, Dan Terranova, John Willis, and Bill Hudson

Teleplay: Max Hodge

Director: Robert Butler

Story: Mr. Freeze can only live in sub-freezing temperatures, and is also interested in ice—the diamond kind. He has his heart set on stealing Princess Sandra's Circle of Ice diamond, and when Batman and Robin interfere he turns them into human popsicles.

Comment: A then-unknown Teri Garr had a bit part in the show. Mr. Freeze was called Mr. Zero in the comic books. We were dazzled by the work L. B. Abbott did on this show: his special effects showing Mr. Freeze's cold zones were superb. My second-favorite show, a perfect blend of humor, mystery, and menace.

"Zelda the Great"
"A Death Worse Than Fate"

Aired: 2/9, 2/10

Guest Stars: Anne Baxter: *Zelda*
Jack Kruschen: *Eivol Ekdol*
Barbara Heller: *Hillary Stonewin*
With: Jim Drum, Frankie Darro, Stephen Tompkins, Victor French, Bill Phillips, Jerry Doggett, and Douglas Dumbrille

Teleplay: Lorenzo Semple, Jr.

Director: Robert Heller

Story: Every April 1, the magician Zelda steals $100,000 from a bank in Gotham City. This time, Batman foils her scheme and Zelda moves to Plan B: she imprisons Batman and Robin in her Inescapable Doom Trap, abducts Aunt Harriet, and threatens to boil her in oil unless Bruce Wayne pays a ransom.

Comment: The Trap came from the comic books, and was a nefarious thing—a cubicle with an electrified grate through which deadly gas was pumped. Batman escaped by hitting the grate with his belt buckle, causing sparks that ignited the gas and blew open the cubicle.

Anne Baxter was forty-three and exuded sexuality. I understood, upon meeting her, why Chuck Heston and Yul Brynner fought so hard to win her in *The Ten Commandments*!

"A Riddle a Day Keeps the Riddler Away" *"When the Rat's Away the Mice Will Play"*

Aired: 2/16, 2/17

Guest Stars: Frank Gorshin: *The Riddler*
Susan Silo: *Mousey*
Tim Herbert: *Whiskers*
Reginald Denny: *King Boris*
With: Marc Cavell, Roy Jenson, William Kendis, Joy Harmon, Johnny Magnus, John Archer, John Hubbard, Marvin Miller, and Tris Coffin

Teleplay: Fred De Gorter

Director: Tom Gries

Story: After King Boris gets a bouquet of exploding roses, Batman and Robin follow the clues to the Riddler's lair. Naturally, that's just what he wanted them to do, so he can lash them to whirling generator wheels attached to a huge drive shaft.

Comment: Tom Gries was an intense young man who went on to direct a handful of films, including the wonderful *Will Penny* and the miniseries *QB VII*. He died at fifty-five. Tris Coffin had had a long and distinguished career as a heavy and hero in movie serials.

"The Thirteenth Hat"
"Batman Stands Pat"

Aired: 2/23, 2/24

Guest Stars: David Wayne: *The Mad Hatter*

Diane McBain: *Lisa*

Sandra Wells: *Babette*

Richard La Starza: *Cappy*

Gil Perkins: *Dicer*

George Conrad: *Turkey Bullwinkle*

Albert Morin: *Octave Marbot*

With: Monique Le Maire, Ralph Montgomery, Bob Legionaire, Norma Varden, and John Ward

Teleplay: Charles Hoffman

Director: Norman Foster

Story: Jervis Tetch, the Mad Hatter, kidnaps the jurors who sent him to prison, adds their hats to his collection, and sets his sights on Batman . . . and his cowl. Tetch lures Batman to his lair by asking him to pose for a plaster likeness; a fight erupts, and the Dynamic Duo end up trapped in quick-setting plaster.

Comment: Diane McBain was a beautiful young actress who I'd met when she was costarring in *Surfside Six* in the early 1960s. Unfortunately, parts became scarce for her later in the decade, and she gave up acting to become a secretary. She returned briefly to TV as Foxy Humdinger on *Days of Our Lives* about ten years ago.

"The Joker Goes to School"
"He Meets His Match, the Grisly Ghoul"

Aired: 3/2, 3/3

Guest Stars: Cesar Romero: *The Joker*

Donna Loren: *Susie*

Sydney Smith: *Vandergilt*
With: Kip King, Bryan O'Byrne, Tim O'Kelly, Cheri Foster, Linda Harrison, Donna Di Martino, Joan Parker, Breeland Rice

Teleplay: Lorenzo Semple, Jr.

Director: Murray Golden

Story: The Joker goes to Gotham City High to build a gang comprised of dropouts. When Batman and Robin get on his case, he captures them and straps them to electric chairs connected to a slot machine. When the correct sequence appears, the heroes will fry.

Comment: Linda Harrison, who played a cheerleader, married Dick Zanuck, son of the studio head, and had a brief film career, most notably starring as Nova in *Planet of the Apes.*

"True or Falseface"
"Super Rat Race"

Aired: 3/9, 3/10

Guest Stars: Malachi Throne: *Falseface*
Myrna Fahey: *Blaze*
S. John Launer: *George W. Ladd*
Larry Owens: *Bevans*
With: Billy Curtis, Joe Brooks, Patrick Whyte, Gary Owens, Michael Fox, Brenda Howard, and Mike Ragan

Teleplay: Stephen Kandel

Director: William A. Graham

Story: The ultimate master of disguise—in just seconds, he can look and sound like anyone, male or female—Falseface steals a precious crown and ends up with Batman on his trail. The Dynamic Duo captures a member of Falseface's gang, who reveals the location of the boss's hideout ... except it's a trap, one which leads to Batman and Robin being lashed to a train track with Alfred as their only salvation ...

Comment: Gary Owens went on to star as the announcer on *Rowan and Martin's Laugh-In,* and it was particularly nice to work with Billy Curtis, one of the busiest little actors in Hollywood history. The show was unique in that, for the final chase, the camera was mounted inside the Batmobile for some memorable point-of-view shots.

"The Purr-fect Crime"
"Better Luck Next Time"

Aired: 3/17, 3/18

Guest Stars: Julie Newmar: *Catwoman*
Jock Mahoney: *Leo*
Ralph Manza: *Felix*
Harry Holcomb: *Mark Andrews*
With: Pat Zurica and Alex Sharp

Teleplay: Stanley Ralph Ross and Lee Orgel

Director: James Sheldon

Story: Searching for the fabled Captain Manx treasure, Catwoman snatches one of two gold cat statues which hold a clue to its whereabouts. When she goes after the second statue, Batman and Robin tail her to her fur factory headquarters. But the joke's on Batman: while he's occupied, Robin finds himself in a pit with a floor that's vanishing slowly into a wall to reveal a trio of hungry tigers below.

Comment: Jock Mahoney—actually, O'Mahoney—was one of the later movie Tarzans, and Sally Field's stepfather. He was a tough, fun fellow, and appeared again in our third season.

Burt wasn't happy about doing the tiger scene. The animals were fairly inert until the crew dangled meat over their heads . . . right in front of Burt's face. After that, they were *very* active. Though Burt was ten feet above them, the tigers came perilously close to taking a bite out of him.

"The Penguin Goes Straight"
"Not Yet, He Ain't"

Aired: 3/23, 3/24

Guest Stars: Burgess Meredith: *The Penguin*
Kathleen Crowley: *Sophia Starr*
Harvey Lembeck: *Eagle Eye*
Al Checco: *Dove*
William Beckley: *Reggie Rich*
Hope Sansberry: *Mrs. Van Climber*
Douglas Bank: *Lt. Coppie*
With: Jim Drum, Bill Welch, and Ed McCready

Teleplay: Lorenzo Semple, Jr.

Director: Les Martinson

Story: Pretending to have turned over a new leaf and become a crime-fighter, the Penguin frames Batman to make it appear that he and Robin have become lawbreakers. While looking for the Penguin at an amusement park, the Dynamic Duo are captured, bound, and left behind a shooting gallery...where Commissioner Gordon and Chief O'Hara are about to test their marksmanship!

Comment: This was the first episode directed by Les Martinson, who would direct our film. A resourceful director and wonderful man.

"The Ring of Wax"
"Give 'Em the Axe"

Aired: 3/30, 3/31

Guest Stars: Frank Gorshin: *The Riddler*
Elizabeth Harrower: *Miss Prentice*
Linda Scott: *Moth*
Michael Greene: *Matches*
Joey Tata: *Tallow*
Ann Myers: *Mme. Soleil.*
With: Al McGranary

Teleplay: Jack Paritz and Bob Rodgers

Director: James B. Clarke

Story: Tracking the Riddler to the library, where he's stealing a book on an ancient Inca treasure, Batman and Robin are nabbed, tied up, and doomed to be turned into human candles as they're lowered toward a vat of boiling wax.

"The Joker Trumps an Ace"
"Batman Sets the Pace"

Aired: 4/6, 4/7

Guest Stars: Cesar Romero: *The Joker*
Dan Seymour: *The Maharajah*
Jane Wald: *Jill*
Tol Avery: *Prescott Belmont*
With: Angela Greene, Jacques Roux, Norm Alden, and Bebe Louie

Teleplay: Francis and Marion Cockrell

Director: Richard C. Sarafian

Story: The Joker's after a set of gold golf clubs belonging to a visiting maharajah. The visiting prince is abducted and the Caped Crusaders pursue . . . only to wind up captured and shoved into a chimney that's filling with toxic gas.

Comment: This show marked the first of many appearances of Byron Keith as Mayor Linseed . . . spoofing, of course, then-Mayor of New York, John Lindsay.

"The Curse of Tut"
"The Pharaoh's in a Rut"

Aired: 4/13, 4/14

Guest Stars: Victor Buono: *King Tut*
Ziva Rodann: *Queen Nefertiti*

Donald "Red" Barry: *Vizier*

Frank Christi: *Scrivener*

With: Olan Soule, Emanuel Thomas, Bill Quinn, and Bill Boyett

Teleplay: Robert C. Dennis and Earl Barret

Director: Charles R. Rondeau

Story: After being hit on the head, a college professor begins to believe that he's the reincarnation of King Tut. And what's a king without a kingdom? He plots to rule Gotham City and transform it into a modern-day Thebes. He begins by constructing a towering sphinx in Gotham Central Park, from which he issues his commands. To gain a bargaining edge, Tut has his Tutlings abduct Bruce Wayne. While Bruce is being transported by ambulance up a mountain road, his gurney slides out the back door and heads for a cliff.

"The Bookworm Turns"
"While Gotham City Burns"

Aired: 4/20, 4/21

Guest Stars: Roddy McDowall: *The Bookworm*

Francine York: *Lydia Limpet*

John Crawford: *Printer's Devil*

With: Jan Peters, Tony Aiello, and Jim O'Hara

Teleplay: Rik Vollaerts

Director: Larry Peerce

Story: With crimes inspired by book plots, the Bookworm draws Batman out by pretending to assassinate Commissioner Gordon while he dedicates a bridge. A cat-and-mouse chase ensues, ending with Robin captured and strapped to a giant bell, about to have his neck wrung.

Comment: Roddy was a very congenial man, everybody's pal, but he clearly saved his real feelings and friendship for the close circle of Hollywood friends he'd grown up with, like Elizabeth Taylor. In the two weeks we worked together, I came to envy him that: whatever the ups and downs he experienced professionally, there was always that core of people he knew he could count on.

"Death in Slow Motion"
"The Riddler's False Notion"

Aired: 4/27, 4/28

Guest Stars: Frank Gorshin: *The Riddler*
Francis X. Bushman: *Van Jones*
Sherry Jackson: *Pauline*
Theo Marcuse: *Von Bloheim*
Richard Bakalyan: *C. B.*

Teleplay: Dick Carr

Director: Charles R. Rondeau

Story: Disguised as Charlie Chaplin and the Keystone Kops, the Riddler and his crew steal the box office take at a silent film festival—and it's the Dynamic Duo once more in pursuit. As befits the theme of the show, Robin is abducted and tied to a giant buzz saw while Batman is on the Riddler's trail.

Comment: This episode was, I believe, the last acting job of silent film star Francis X. Bushman; he died later that year. The star of the original *Ben Hur* and other classics was eighty-three at the time, alert, and happy to be working. (The vast fortune he earned in the silents had been wiped out by the stock market crash in 1929.) I was sorry (again!!) I didn't have much time to talk with him.

"Fine Finny Fiends"
"Batman Makes the Scene"

Aired: 5/4, 5/5

Guest Stars: Burgess Meredith: *The Penguin*
Julie Gregg: *Finella*
Victor Lundin: *Octopus*
Dal Jenkins: *Shark*
Louie Elias: *Swordfish*

With: Howard Wendell, Bill Williams, Lisa Mitchell, Frank Wilcox, Anne Reece, and Charles La Torre

Teleplay: Sheldon Stewart

Director: Tom Gries

Story: Alfred is abducted by the Penguin, brainwashed, and sent to help rob the Multimillionaire's Annual Award Dinner. Fortunately, Bruce and Dick notice that their butler is not quite himself and, with his help, are able to trace the Penguin to his seaside hideout. *Unfortunately*, the villain is able to nab them and place them into a vacuum tank from which all the air is slowly removed.

SECOND SEASON: 1966–67

"Shoot a Crooked Arrow"
"Walk in the Straight and Narrow"

Aired: 9/7, 9/8

Guest Stars: Art Carney: *The Archer*
Sam Jaffe: *Albert A. Aardvark*
Barbara Nichols: *Maid Marilyn*
Robert Cornthwaite: *Alan A. Dale*
Doodles Weaver: *Crier Tuck*
Loren Wing: *Big John*
With: Arch Moore, Steve Pendleton, Lee Delano, James O'Hara, and Myron Dell

Teleplay: Stanley Ralph Ross

Director: Sherman Marks

Story: After robbing from the rich—namely, Bruce Wayne—the Archer is put in jail. But he's been giving bundles of money to the people of Gotham City, and they bail him out . . . part of a devious plan to win the public trust? Tracking him to his hideout, Batman and Robin are caught in a net, lashed to poles, and are about to be run through with lances. (Thank heavens for rockets in your boots!)

Comment: Because we'd shot the movie between seasons, we had new equipment (and stock footage) to jazz up the adventures. Dick Clark appeared as himself in the episode. This episode boasted what may have been our strongest cast overall: though I don't think that Art was really right or comfortable with the Robin Hood–type part, Sam and Doodles were really into it, as was Robert Cornthwaite, whom I'd admired since he played the singleminded scientist in *The Thing*.

"Hot Off the Griddle"
"The Cat and the Fiddle"

Aired: 9/14, 9/15

Guest Stars: Julie Newmar: *Catwoman*
Jack Kelly: *Jack O'Shea*
James Brolin: *Ralph Staphylococcus*
David Fresco: *Zubin Zucchini*
With: Buck Kartalian, George Barrows, Charles Horvath, George Neise, and Edy Williams

Teleplay: Stanley Ralph Ross

Director: Don Weis

Story: Catwoman establishes a school for cat burglars, her goal being to obtain a pair of priceless violins. When Batman and Robin chase her down, they're gassed and bound to huge aluminum sheets, under the rising heat of giant magnifying glasses.

Comment: The late Jack Kelly was a fellow Warner alumnus who had played Bart Maverick in *Maverick*. James Brolin was young, up-and-coming, and dated Dozier's secretary Jane. They later married.

"The Minstrel's Shakedown"
"Barbequed Batman"

Aired: 9/21, 9/22

Guest Stars: Van Johnson: *The Minstrel*
Leslie Perkins: *Amanda*
John Gallaudet: *Courtland*

Norm Grabowski: *Treble*

Remo Pisani: *Bass*

With: James O'Hara, Del Moore, Eddie Garrett, Herbert Moss, Stu Wilson, Tom Anthony, Vince Dedrick, and Army Archerd

Teleplay: Francis and Marion Cockrell

Director: Murray Golden

Story: Threatening to cause a stock market crash unless members of the exchange pay him vast sums of money, the singing Minstrel is hunted down by the Dynamic Duo. Alas, he traps them and places them on a giant electric spit, intending to roast them.

Comment: Van impressed me a great deal. He was a very young fifty— vital and oozing star quality. Despite his many years in film, he seemed to thrive on our hectic pace.

Phyllis Diller put in an appearance as a scrubwoman.

"The Spell of Tut" "Tut's Case is Shut"

Aired: 9/28, 9/29

Guest Stars: Victor Buono: *King Tut*

Mariana Hill: *Cleo Patrick*

Michael Pataki: *Amenophis Twefik*

Peter Mamakos: *Royal Lapidary*

Sid Haig: *Royal Apothecary*

With: Boyd Santell, Bea Bradley, and Rene Paul

Teleplay: R. C. Dennis and Earl Bennet

Director: Larry Peerce

Story: Another conk on the head, and another attempt to rule Gotham City, beginning with the robbery of amber jewelry and the infiltration of Commissioner Gordon's staff by Cleo. Attempting to track Tut to his lair, Robin is captured and placed in a pit filled with alligators.

Comment: The Green Hornet and Kato poked their heads from the window as Batman and Robin were climbing the wall.

"The Greatest Mother of Them All"
"Ma Parker"

Aired: 10/5, 10/6

Guest Stars: Shelley Winters: *Ma Parker*
Tisha Sterling: *Legs*
Mike Vandever: *Mad Dog*
Robert Biheller: *Pretty Boy*
Peter Brooks: *Machine Gun*
James Griffith: *Tiger*
With: David Lewis, Fran Ryan, and Budd Perkins

Teleplay: Henry Slesar

Director: Oscar Rudolph

Story: Robbing the good women at the Ladies Auxiliary's Mother of the Year Award festivities, Ma Parker and her brood are pursued by the Caped Crusaders. Though they're caught and sent to jail, Ma's own plants are working the prison. It's an unsuspecting Batman and Robin that ride off, their Batmobile rigged with a bomb that will explode when the car hits sixty. The heroes also get to sample the institution's electric chair.

Comment: Early in the shoot, Shelley slipped on water that hadn't been cleaned up and fell flat on her back. She lost her dignity and then her temper, though I could see her using that anger throughout the shoot.

Henry Slesar, our writer, had written a number of terrific science fiction and mystery tales, as well as scripts for *The Man from U.N.C.L.E.*

"The Clock King's Crazy Crimes"
"The Clock King Gets Crowned"

Aired: 10/12, 10/13

Guest Stars: Walter Slezak: *The Clock King*
Eileen O'Neil: *Millie Second*

Herb Anderson: *Harry Hummert*

With: Ivan Triesault, Linda Lorimer, Jerry Doggett, Roger Bacon, and Sandra Lynn

Teleplay: Bill Finger and Charles Sinclair

Director: James Neilson

Story: Clock King and his Second Hands become prey for Batman and Robin when they rob a jewelry store. Though the heroes intercept them on a second job, the villain escapes by using giant clock main-springs to slow the heroes down. Pursuing the criminals to a factory, Batman and Robin are locked inside a giant hourglass, their time running out as the sands of time pour in.

Comment: Guest villain Slezak usually played villains in the movies. The idea of casting a European-born actor as the Clock King was an attempt to bolster syndication value overseas.

Coauthor Bill Finger was, of course, one of the earliest and best writers of the Batman comic books, a largely unheralded force in the creation of the character and his milieu.

Sammy Davis, Jr., put in a cameo appearance on this episode.

"An Egg Grows in Gotham"
"The Yegg Foes in Gotham"

Aired: 10/19, 10/20

Guest Stars: Vincent Price: *Egghead*

Gail Hire: *Miss Bacon*

Edward Everett Horton: *Chief Screaming Eagle*

Steve Dunne: *Tim Tyler*

Ben Weldon: *Foo Long*

With: Albert Carrier, Gene Dymarski, Ben Alexander, Grant Woods, Burt Mustin, Anthony Brand, Jonathan Hole, and George McCoy

Teleplay: Stanley Ralph Ross

Director: George Waggner

Story: The dome-headed Egghead plots to make it impossible for the metropolis to make payments due on its lands by stealing the charter; when that happens, he plans to foreclose and take over. To make matters worse, he's concluded that one of the city's millionaires must be Batman and, after abducting them, decides that Bruce Wayne is his man.

Comment: Egghead was suggested to us by Dick Zanuck, head of studio boss Darryl.

It was Dozier's idea to cast Edward Everett Horton, who was eighty years old and was best known as Fred Astaire's sidekick in several films and the narrator of TV's "Fractured Fairytales." Horton was so good, so funny, that he had me falling down in hysterics in his few scenes.

That episode also featured 1930s film star Mae Clark, announcer George Fenneman, and Bill Dana appearing as Jose Jimenez.

"The Devil's Fingers"
"Dead Ringers"

Aired: 10/26, 10/27

Guest Stars: Liberace: *Chandell*
Marilyn Hanold: *Doe*
Edy Williams: *Rae*
Sivi Aberg: *Mimi*
With: James Millhollin, Diane Farrell, and Jack Perkins

Teleplay: Lorenzo Semple, Jr.

Director: Larry Peerce

Story: While Bruce and Dick are on vacation, the mad pianist Chandell courts Aunt Harriet, intending to wed her and claim the Wayne fortune. The men return—just in time for Batman and Robin to tackle Doe, Rae, and Mimi as they attempt to commit a robbery. But it's a trap, and the Dynamic Duo are lashed to a perforation machine that's going to turn them into player piano rolls.

"Hizzoner the Penguin"
"Dizzoner the Penguin"

Aired: 11/2, 11/3

Guest Stars: Burgess Meredith: *The Penguin*
George Furth: *Gallus*
Cindy Malone: *Lulu*
Don Wilson: *Walter Klondike*
With: Woodrow Parfrey, Murray Roman, Pat Tidy, Peg Shirley, James O'Hara, John Indrisano

Teleplay: Stanford Sherman

Director: Oscar Rudolph

Story: The Penguin runs for mayor of Gotham City and, to ensure his defeat, Batman runs against him. But the Penguin doesn't intend to lose. Kidnapping the Dynamic Duo, he prepares to cast his "vat" by immersing them in sulphuric acid.

Comment: We had a larger-than-usual guest cast on this show, including game show host Allen Ludden, newscaster Chet Huntley, Joe Besser (one of the latter-day Three Stooges), old-time Western sidekick Fuzzy Knight, belly dancer Little Egypt, and hot rock-and-rollers Paul Revere and the Raiders.

I'm not sure that this "cast of thousands" was a good thing: though the parade of faces provided a moment of fun, and even a touch of verisimilitude, it was becoming gimmicky and detracted from the stories and main characters. Moreover, it became hellish for the writers: they were contractually obligated to make these speaking parts, which often resulted in contrived, show-slowing exchanges. My feeling by this point was becoming forget the gimmicks: let's just tell a fun, exciting story. But Dozier enjoyed the guests and the process of coming up with parts for them, so we kept doing it.

"Green Ice"
"Deep Freeze"

Aired: 11/9, 11/10

Guest Stars: Otto Preminger: *Mr. Freeze*
Nicky Blair: *Shivers*
Kem Dibbs: *Chill*
Marie Windsor: *Nellie*
Dee Hartford: *Miss Iceland*
With: James O'Hara, Charles O'Donnell, Robert Wiensko, Mike Durkin, and Joan Twelve

Teleplay: Max Hodge

Director: George Waggner

Story: After escaping from jail in an ice-cream truck, Mr. Freeze abducts Miss Iceland from the Miss Galaxy contest, intending to make her his wife. Tracking the villain to his cold storage warehouse, Batman and Robin are stopped with a blast from the Freeze Gun and put into "cones" to be turned into giant frozen desserts.

Comment: It was a delight to have Marie Windsor on the show. The 1940s and '50s screen star was full of spunk and fun. She was a welcome oasis from the despicable Otto.

"The Impractical Joker"
"The Joker's Provokers"

Aired: 11/16, 11/17

Guest Stars: Cesar Romero: *The Joker*
Kathy Kersh: *Cornelia*
Christopher Cary: *Angus Ferguson*
Louis Quinn: *Latch*
Larry Anthony: *Bolt*
With: Nalerie Szabo, Larry Burrell, and Clyde Howdy

Teleplay: Jay Thompson

Director: James B. Clark

Story: The Joker has been using a bizarre black box to help him commit robberies, one which seems to stop time. When Batman and Robin get their hands on the device, they find it's simply a device which hypnotizes people into thinking no time has passed. But while they get the box, the Joker gets them: Robin placed in a spray-wax machine, Batman tied to a huge key-duplicator.

Comment: Howard Duff was working nearby on his show *The Felony Squad*, and popped over to guest on this episode (and once again in season three).

"Marsha, Queen of Diamonds"
"Marsha's Scheme of Diamonds"

Aired: 11/23, 11/24

Guest Stars: Carolyn Jones: *Marsha*
            Estelle Winwood: *Aunt Hilda*
            Woody Strode: *Grand Mogul*
            With: James O'Hara, H. Douglas, Joyce Nizarri, Ben Gage, and Charles Stewart

Teleplay: Stanford Sherman

Director: James B. Clark

Story: Putting both Commissioner Gordon and Chief O'Hara under her spell—and stealing a choice diamond while she's at it—Marsha uses the Commissioner to lead Batman to her and hits him with a love dart. Though he manages to beat the potion, Marsha abducts Robin and informs Batman that unless he agrees to marry her, the Boy Wonder will die!

Comment: What a cast! Woody Strode was one of the most imposing figures I've ever met. The veteran of such films as *The Ten Commandments*, *Spartacus* (he was the gladiator pitted against Kirk Douglas), and *The Professionals*, I feel he has never gotten his due as an actor.

Carolyn Jones told me she was of Dutch/Chinese heritage, which gave her the most alluring saucerlike eyes. She had a great sense of humor, and while she's best known as Morticia on *The Addams Family*, she was also an Oscar-nominated actress (for *The Bachelor Party*). My own personal favorite among Carolyn's performances, however, was as a victim in the 3-D classic *The House of Wax*.

"Come Back Shame"
"It's the Way You Play the Game"

Aired: 11/30, 12/1

Guest Stars: Cliff Robertson: *Shame*
Jack Carter: *Hot Rod Harry*
Joan Staley: *Okie Annie*
Timothy Scott: *Messy James*
John Mitchum: *Rip Snorting*
Milton Frome: *Laughing Leo*
With: Eric Shea, Kathryn Minner, and James McHale

Teleplay: Stanley Ralph Ross

Director: Oscar Rudolph

Story: Based in an amusement park, the crooked, car-rustling cowboy Shame snatches a race car as part of his plan to build a vehicle that can outrace the Batmobile. To trap him, Bruce lets it be known that he's installing super-modern parts in the Wayne limousine . . . which he allows Shame to steal. In a fight at Shame's hideout, the Dynamic Duo are knocked unconscious and staked to the ground in front of a cattle stampede.

Comment: Cliff became a good friend of mine. He loved the show and, a superb writer himself, he relished the clever dialogue. I remember him standing by, cracking up as I played the torero, using my cape to defend Robin and myself from a stampede. Two years later, Cliff won the Oscar for *Charly*. It's also a little-known fact that he was one of Steven Spielberg's mentors. Some day, hopefully, Cliff will write his own story for publication!

Werner Klemperer put in a brief appearance as his *Hogan's Heroes* character, Colonel Klink.

"The Penguin's Nest"
"The Bird's Last Jest"

Aired: 12/7, 12/8
Guest Stars: Burgess Meredith: *The Penguin*
Grace Gaynor: *Chickadee*
Voltaire Perkins: *Judge Moot*
Lane Bradford: *Cordy Blue*
With: Vito Scotti, James O'Hara, David Lewis, Marvin Brody, and Violet Carlson
Teleplay: Lorenzo Semple, Jr.
Director: Murray Golden
Story: This time around, the Penguin's scheme is to open a restaurant, collect handwriting specimens of his wealthy patrons, and have a forger fake checks in their hand. Unfortunately for the fowl fiend, his forger is in prison and, once he has the samples, the Penguin is unable to get himself arrested. Solution? Kidnap Chief O'Hara, which gets Batman and Robin into the act . . . although they can't do much as the Penguin pins them down with machine gun fire.
Comment: Writer Stanley Ralph Ross appeared as the character Ballpoint Baxter, and Ted Cassidy had a cameo as Lurch from *The Addams Family*.

Lane Bradford was a serial star who had appeared in films like *Don Daredevil Rides Again* and *Zombies of the Stratosphere* (in which a very young Leonard Nimoy played his first alien!). After one take in which Robin and I had our heads handed to us by the Penguin's goons, Lane helped me to my feet and said, "Y'know, Adam, I remember when the good guys used to *win* these things."

"The Cat's Meow"
"The Bat's Kow Tow"

Aired: 12/14, 12/15
Guest Stars: Julie Newmar: *Catwoman*
Joe Flynn: *Benton Belgoody*

Sharya Wynters: *Eenie*

Tom Castronova: *Meanie*

Chuck Henderson: *Miney*

Ric Roman: *Moe*

Jay Sebring: *Mr. Oceanbring*

Peter Leeds: *Harry Upps*

Maurice Dallimore: *Sterling Habits*

With: Judy Stragis, Anthony Eustrez, Calvin Brown, and James O'Hara

Teleplay: Stanley Ralph Ross

Director: James B. Clark

Story: The Catwoman has a voice-stealing machine, which she uses, for starters, against a pair of hot rock stars. After she snatches Commissioner Gordon's voice, Batman and Robin give chase . . . only to be knocked out by the feline felon's drug-tipped claws and placed inside an echo chamber, where Catwoman plans to drive them batty with a leaky faucet.

Comment: Joe Flynn was best known as Captain Binghamton on *McHale's Navy*. Like most comic actors I know, he was serious, even brooding between takes. Come to think of it, most of the so-called sexpots I've known were prudes. I guess that's why it's called "acting."

In addition to Steve Allen, who appeared as Allen Stevens, the show featured rockers Chad and Jeremy and Hawaiian singer Don Ho.

"The Puzzles Are Coming"
"The Duo is Slumming"

Aired: 12/21, 12/22

Guest Stars: Maurice Evans: *The Puzzler*

Barbara Stuart: *Rocket O'Rourke*

Paul Smith: *Artemus Knab*

With: Robert Miller Driscoll, Alan Emerson, and Jay Della

Teleplay: Fred De Gorter

Director: Jeff Hayden

Story: When the Puzzler hints to Batman that super-rich Artemus Knab is in danger, the Caped Crusaders hie to his rescue . . . only to be gassed by the evil tipster. Following another clue, they find the Puzzler's lair, only to be captured and placed in a hot-air balloon—and the gondola is set to fall off at twenty thousand feet.

Comment: Maurice Evans was a distinguished Shakespearean actor who absolutely reveled in parts like the Puzzler; with the exception of Cliff Robertson, I never saw an actor have so much fun on our show. Although the character was essentially a Riddler knockoff, Evans's name had clout in Europe. He went on to star in two other pop-culture smashes: *Planet of the Apes* and *Rosemary's Baby*.

"The Sandman Cometh"
"The Catwoman Goeth" (syndicated as
"A Stitch in Time")

Aired: 12/28, 12/29

Guest Stars: Michael Rennie: *The Sandman*
Julie Newmar: *Catwoman*
Spring Byington: *J. Pauline Spaghetti*
With: Richard Peel, Tony Ballen, Pat Becker, Jeanie Moore, Lindsey Workman, Ray Montgomery, and Valerie Kairys

Teleplay: Ellis St. Joseph and Charles Hoffman

Director: George Waggner

Story: Millionairess J. Pauline Spaghetti has insomnia, and the European villain Sandman teams with Catwoman to help her . . . while helping themselves to copies of her financial records. Batman and Robin arrive on the scene, Sandman gets away, and the Dynamic Duo follow—though the sleep-inducing malefactor gets his hands on Robin, puts him into a trance, and orders him to kill the Caped Crusader.

Comment: Michael Rennie was a friend of Dozier's. Rennie very much needed the work and was doing a lot of TV at the time, shows such as *Lost in Space* and *The Invaders*. I found him to be somewhat aloof, not unlike the alien Klaatu he played in *The Day the Earth Stood Still*.

Then-unknown James Brolin made his second appearance on the show as Officer Reggie Hogan. In addition to a great featured cast, we were fortunate to have the legendary Gypsy Rose Lee as a newscaster.

"The Contaminated Cowl"
"Mad Hatter Runs Afoul"

Aired: 1/4, 1/5

Guest Stars: David Wayne: *The Mad Hatter*
Barbara Morrison: *Hattie Hatfield*
Jean Hale: *Polly*
Richard Collier: *Otto Puffendorfer*
Leonid Kinskey: *Professor Overbeck*
Jesslyn Fax: *Bonbon*
With: Lennie Breman, Victor Ames, Paul Bryar, Gil Stewart, Margaret Teele, and Ivy Bethune

Teleplay: Charles Hoffman

Director: Oscar Rudolph

Story: Convinced that the Mad Hatter will certainly attempt to steal a rare jewel on display in the Top Hat Room, Batman and Robin are there to welcome him. However, the criminal is ready for them, and sprays Batman's cowl with a radioactive spray that turns it pink. Though Batman is forced to go back to the Batcave for another cowl, he and Robin pick up the Hatter's trail . . . only to be captured and placed inside a large fluoroscopic cabinet.

"The Zodiac Crimes"
"The Joker's Hard Times"
"The Penguin Declines"

Aired: 1/11, 1/12, 1/18

Guest Stars: Burgess Meredith: *The Penguin*
Cesar Romero: *The Joker*
Terry Moore: *Venus*
Charles Fredericks: *Leo Crustash*
Howard Wendell: *Basil Bowman*
With: Hal Baylor, Dick Crockett, Joe Di Reda, Charles Picerni, Eddie Saenz, Louis Cordova, and Vincent Barbi

Teleplay: Stanford Sherman and Steve Kandal

Director: Oscar Rudolph

Story: The Joker and Penguin team up to execute the former's zodiac crimes, each of which is inspired by a sign of the zodiac. Though they are able to nab the Penguin, the Dynamic Duo is captured by the Joker at the Gotham City Museum, where they are left, helpless, beneath a giant meteorite that is about to drop on them.

Comment: This was the first of our trio of three-parters. The intention was to edit the episodes together and release them abroad as feature films. The show marked a rare TV appearance of Howard Hughes's onetime protégée (she says wife), Terry Moore. Then-unknown Rob Reiner—Burt Ward's old pal and son of Carl—appeared as a delivery boy.

"That Darn Catwoman" "Scat, Darn Catwoman"

Aired: 1/19, 1/20

Guest Stars: Julie Newmar: *Catwoman*
Leslie Gore: *Pussycat*
J. Pat O'Mally: *Pat Pending*
David Renard: *Prince Ibn Kereb*
With: Jock Gaynor, George Sawaya, Allen Jenkins, Tony Epper, Steve Franken, and Rolla Altman

Teleplay: Stanley Ralph Ross

Director: Oscar Rudolph

Story: Thanks to a mind control drug, Catwoman makes Robin a member of her gang, and he helps her rob a fortune from a safe at Wayne Manor. Though they're pursued by the Caped Crusader, Catwoman captures Batman and has him strapped to a huge mousetrap, which Robin prepares to spring . . .

Comment: Pop singer Leslie Gore was really cute, and Burt was crazy about her. But she was very proper and, as far as I know, he only lusted for her in his heart.

"Penguin Is a Girl's Best Friend"
"Penguin Sets a Trend"
"Penguin's Disastrous End"

Aired: 1/26, 2/1, 2/2

Guest Stars: Burgess Meredith: *The Penguin*
Carolyn Jones: *Marsha*
Estelle Winwood: *Aunt Hilda*
Alan Reed, Jr.: *General MacGruder*
Bob Hastings: *Beasley*
With: Kimberly Allen, Frank Baron, Frank Conte, Milton Stark, Ted Fish, and Brad Logan

Teleplay: Stanford Sherman

Director: James B. Clark

Story: Suckered! That's what Batman and Robin are when they try to prevent Penguin from committing a crime and discover that he's shooting a movie. Rather than face false-arrest charges, Batman agrees to appear in the film . . . kissing Marsha, Queen of Diamonds. Later, Batman and Robin track Penguin to what they're sure is a real crime, only to be trapped in an oversized catapult—about to be flung to their deaths.

Comment: Estelle Winwood was eighty-four years young, a Hollywood veteran of films like *The Misfits*, *Camelot*, and a fine little fantasy film called *The Magic Sword*. She was as eccentric and delightfully dotty as many of the characters she played; sort of like a fun-house Madge Blake.

Bob Hastings was Lt. Carpenter on *McHale's Navy*.

"Batman's Anniversary"
"A Riddling Controversy"

Aired: 2/8, 2/9

Guest Stars: John Astin: *The Riddler*
Deanna Lund: *Anna Gram*

Martin Kosleck: *Professor Charm*
Ken Scott: *Down*
Jim Lefebvre: *Across*
With: Bryon Keith, Eddie Quillan, Tom Kelly, and Bud Furillo

Teleplay: W. P. D'Angelo

Director: James B. Clark

Story: After putting in a surprise appearance at a dinner honoring the Dynamic Duo, the Riddler escapes—with a gift intended to go to charity. After the Riddler eludes Batman a second time, the Caped Crusader and the Boy Wonder pose for a marshmallow sculpture atop a giant cake . . . only to learn that the Riddler has decorated the cake with quicksand frosting!

Comment: John Astin and I had met in Italy right after I'd finished *The Relentless Four*. He was funny, as friendly as could be, and he gave the Riddler his own twist.

Deanna Lund was a gorgeous young actress who went on to star in *Land of the Giants* the following season.

"The Joker's Last Laugh"
"The Joker's Epitaph"

Aired: 2/15, 2/16

Guest Stars: Cesar Romero: *The Joker*
Phyllis Douglas: *Josephine Miller*
Lawrence Montaigne: *Mr. Glee*
J. Edward McKinley: *Mr. Flamm*
Hollie Haze: *Miranda Fleece*
With: Clint Ritchi, Ed Deemer, and Oscar Beregi

Teleplay: Lorenzo Semple, Jr.

Director: Oscar Rudolph

Story: Behind the facade of Penthouse Comic Book Publishers, The Joker turns to counterfeiting. When Bruce comes calling to try and smoke him out, the Joker spots the Boy Wonder and has him tied to a printing machine—and Bruce is made to throw the switch!

Comment: This was the last script Lorenzo did for the show. In one of those life-imitating-art ironies, National Periodical Publications would one day vacate their offices at 909 Third Avenue in New York . . . and *Penthouse* magazine would move in! I remember going up there one day, unannounced, only to find that the big picture of *Batman* in the reception area had been replaced by a big picture of *Caligula*.

"Catwoman Goes to College" "Batman Displays His Knowledge"

Aired: 2/22, 2/23

Guest Stars: Julie Newmar: *Catwoman*
Paul Mantee: *Cornell*
Jacques Bergerac: *Freddy the Fence*
Whitney Blake: *Amber Forever*
Jan Burrell: *Alma Mater*
With: Sheldon Allmann, Paul Picerni, and David Lewis

Teleplay: Stanley Ralph Ross

Director: Robert Sparr

Story: Catwoman goes to school, studies criminology, and figures out how to outwit Batman: she disguises one of her underlings as the Caped Crusader, sends him out to rob a supermarket, and the real Batman is arrested for the crime. Escaping from prison to prove his innocence, Batman is joined by Robin and the two end up in a giant coffee cup beneath an acid-filled percolator.

Comment: Paul had starred in *Robinson Crusoe on Mars*, and as soon as I read the script I suggested him for the part. It was good seeing him again. Art Linkletter had a cameo in the show.

"A Piece of the Action" "Batman's Satisfaction"

Aired: 3/1, 3/2

Guest Stars: Van Williams: *The Green Hornet*
Bruce Lee: *Kato*

Roger C. Carmel: *Colonel Gumm*
Diane McBain: *Pinky Pinkerston*
Alex Rocco: *Block*
Seymour Cassel: *Cancelled*
Harry Frazier: *Mr. Stample*
With: Angelique Pettyjohn, James O'Hara, Jan Watson, and
Dusty Cadis

Teleplay: Charles Hoffman

Director: Oscar Rudolph

Story: The Green Hornet and Kato come to Gotham City in pursuit of the notorious Colonel Gumm: when they arrive, Batman and Robin aren't sure whether they've two extra friends or foes. They form an uneasy truce until the Hornet and Kato are trapped in a perforation machine and turned into giant postage stamps.

Comment: Our classiest cameo appeared on this show: Edward G. Robinson.

Diane McBain was spoofing Dorothy Provine's flapper character Pinky Pinkham from *The Roaring Twenties*.

"King Tut's Coup"
"Batman's Waterloo"

Aired: 3/8, 3/9

Guest Stars: Victor Buono: *King Tut*
Grace Lee Whitney: *Neila*
Lee Meriwether: *Lisa*
Nelson Olmsted: *John E. Carson*
Tommy Noonan: *Jolly Jackson*
Richard Bakalyan: *Fouad Sphinx*
With: Lloyd Haynes, Tol Avery, Suzy Knickerbocker, Tim
O'Kelly, Walter Reed, Terri Messina, and Barry Den-
nen

Teleplay: Stanley Ralph Ross

Director: James B. Clark

Story: Convinced that the daughter of a socialite—a dead-ringer for Cleopatra—will make a suitable queen, King Tut kidnaps her. Batman is able to locate her but, unluckily, is caught by the king's Tutlings, placed in a sarcophagus, and lowered into a pool of bubbling oil.

Comment: Grace Lee Whitney had a busy year: she also starred as Yeoman Janice Rand on the first season of *Star Trek*. Lee, of course, was our *Batman* movie Catwoman.

"Black Widow Strikes Again"
"Caught in the Spider's Den"

Aired: 3/15, 3/16

Guest Stars: Tallulah Bankhead: *Mrs. Max Black*
Donald "Red" Barry: *Tarantula*
Mike Lane: *Daddy Long Leggs*
Al Ferrara: *Trap Door*
Grady Sutton: *Irving Cash*
Milton Stark: *Irving Bracken*
Pitt Herbert: *Irving Leghorn*
Don Briggs: *Irving Irving*
With: George Chandler, Walker Edmiston, and Richard Krisher

Teleplay: Robert Mintz

Director: Oscar Rudolph

Story: Robbing banks with the help of her brain short-circuiting device, the Black Widow meets her match in Batman and his AntiShort-Circuiting Bat Electrodes. Though the Widow is able to escape using her paralytic spider venom, Batman and Robin follow her to her den, only to be trapped in a giant web occupied by a pair of huge black widows. Is joining the gang the only way out?

Comment: Tallulah was quite ill when she did our show, and died the following year. Respiratory problems did not stop her from chain-smoking off in a corner, by herself, with most of the cast and crew intimidated by her regal air. I found myself drawn to her courage and early in the shoot I walked over to ask her if everything was to her liking.

"No!" she snapped. "Why the hell do you need a teleprompter? Why can't you learn your lines?"

I slunk away with my cape between my legs, leaving her, like Hera, enveloped in a tester of cloudlike smoke.

George Raft also cameoed on this episode. After my encounter with Miss Bankhead, I decided to steer clear of Mr. Raft. His characters were known to let a tommy gun do their talking!

"Pop Goes the Joker"
"Flop Goes the Joker"

Aired: 3/22, 3/23

Guest Stars: Cesar Romero: *The Joker*
Diana Ivarson: *Baby Jane Towser*
Fritz Feld: *Oliver Muzzy*
Reginald Gardiner: *Bernie Parks*
With: Ian Arvan, Jerry Catron, Jack Perkins, Jody Gilbert, Owen McGiveney, and Gail Ommerle

Teleplay: Stanford Sherman

Director: George Waggner

Story: The Joker sets about destroying great works of art (sound familiar?), but his defacements are hailed as great *new* works of art. The Clown Prince of Crime opens an art school for the wealthy, and Bruce joins. Not surprisingly, the Joker holds the class for ransom. But the Boy Wonder is on the case and, with Bruce's help, he tackles the thugs. Not that it does much good: the two are beaten, and Robin is set to be sculpted by a set of rotating knives.

Comment: This was one of our best-written shows, a savvy send-up of the world of pop art.

Guest star Fritz Feld was a frequent Abbott and Costello costar and was one of my favorite people. He was down-to-earth, nothing like his eccentric screen persona, and he had amazing physical and facial dexterity. You learn from actors like Fritz, who never really get their due. I'd love to see the Academy of Motion Picture Arts and Sciences start handing out life achievement awards to some of these great but unheralded actors.

My dialogue coach Milton Stark got to do a small part in this episode.

"Ice Spy"
"The Duo Defy"

Aired: 3/29, 3/30

Guest Stars: Eli Wallach: *Mr. Freeze*
Leslie Parish: *Glacia Glaze*
Elisha Cook, Jr.: *Professor Isaacson*
H. M. Wyant: *Frosty*
With: Anthony Aiello, John Archer, Alfred Daniels, Ron Riley, and Eddie Nesh

Teleplay: Charles Hoffman

Director: Oscar Rudolph

Story: Headquartered inside an iceberg, Mr. Freeze boards the *Gotham Queen* and abducts a scientist (from Iceland, of course) who has developed a process for creating instant ice. Moving to another base, beneath an ice skating rink, Freeze is found by Batman and Robin, who end up in a Sub-Zero Temperature Vaporizing Cabinet for their efforts.

Comment: Wallach was amazing. He is one of those rare actors who moves from medium to medium with equal skill, adapting immediately to the unique demands of each. He was a great Mr. Freeze, though nothing will ever top his evil but strangely sympathetic Calvera in *The Magnificent Seven*.

THIRD SEASON: 1967–68

"Enter Batgirl, Exit Penguin"

Aired: 9/14

Guest Stars: Burgess Meredith: *The Penguin*
Elizabeth Harrower: *Drusilla*
Jonathan Troy: *Reverend Hazlitt*
With: Jon Walter

Teleplay: Stanford Sherman

Director: Oscar Rudolph

Story: In an effort to keep the police at bay, the Penguin abducts Commissioner Gordon's daughter, Barbara, intending to make her his bride . . . and unaware that she is secretly Batgirl.

Comment: This was the show that introduced Batgirl and the start of a season I didn't much enjoy.

"Ring Around the Riddler"

Aired: 9/21

Guest Stars: Frank Gorshin: *The Riddler*
Joan Collins: *The Siren*
Peggy Ann Garner: *Betsy Boldface*
James Brolin: *Kid Gulliver*
With: Jerry Quarry, Paul Rojas, Armando Ramos, Nicholas
Georgiade, Peggy Olson, and Gil Perkins

Teleplay: Charles Hoffman

Director: Sam Strangis

Story: The Riddler attempts to take over the boxing game in Gotham City with the help of Lorelei Circe, a.k.a. the Siren. While Batgirl tackles the woman with the seven-octave range, the Riddler and Batman face off in the ring.

Comment: Heavyweight Jerry Quarry had lost a heartbreaker to Eddie Machen the year before, and we all contributed to a kitty for anyone brave enough to "bell-the-cat" and ask him about the fight. The money went unclaimed.

"The Wail of the Siren"

Aired: 9/28

Guest Stars: Joan Collins: *The Siren*
Mike Mazurki: *Allegro*
Cliff Osmond: *Andante*

Teleplay: Stanley Ralph Ross

Director: George Waggner

Story: The Siren is still at large, and uses her high-pitched voice to make Commissioner Gordon her slave. His assignment: learn the true identity of Batman.

Comment: Mazurki was a former wrestler, a giant of a man who always played thugs and Neanderthals. He was, in fact, an extremely bright and articulate man, well-read and quite gentle.

"The Sport of Penguins"
"A Horse of Another Color"

Aired: 10/5, 10/12

Guest Stars: Burgess Meredith: *The Penguin*
Ethel Merman: *Lola Lasagne*
Horace McMahon: *Glu Gluten*
With: Lewis Charles, Herbert Anderson, Joe Brooks, Constance Davis, and Allen Emerson

Teleplay: Charles Hoffman

Director: Sam Strangis

Story: The Penguin and the equally insidious Lola enter a horse in the prestigious Bruce Wayne Handicap, doing everything they can to make sure they win . . . and that the proceeds do not go to charity.

Comment: It was *really* exciting to have Ethel Merman on the show. What a career, and what a voice! I was surprised at how soft-spoken and charming she was, though she had a sharp sense of humor and was fun to be around. She was one of the few guest stars I made it a point to be around when there was any down-time.

"The Unkindest Tut of All"

Aired: 10/19

Guest Stars: Victor Buono: *King Tut*
Patti Gilbert: *Shirley*
James Gammon: *Osiris*
With: Cathleen Cordell and James Ramsey

Teleplay: Stanley Ralph Ross

Director: Sam Strangis

Story: After hiding a bug in the Batmobile, Tut traces it to a spot below Wayne Manor . . . and puts two and two together, daring Batman and Bruce Wayne to appear at the same time.

"Louie the Lilac"

Aired: 10/26

Guest Stars: Milton Berle: *Louie the Lilac*
Lisa Seagram: *Lila*
Dick Bakayan: *Arbutus*
With: Karl Lukas, Schuyler Aubrey, and Jimmy Boyd

Teleplay: Dwight Taylor

Director: Sam Strangis

Story: After Louie begins putting Gotham City's flower children under his spell, Batman tracks him to his flower shop headquarters, where he and Robin are to be fed to giant carnivorous lilacs.

Comment: Milton and I got off to a terrible start. He was Mr. Television, of course, a great comic force, and he arrived on day one like Travis at the Alamo, ready to whip me and everyone else into shape. He told me I was doing Batman all wrong, that I should play him like a buffoon, like a Keystone Kop. I was irate, and suggested that, given his history of cross-dressing, perhaps he'd like to give Yvonne some pointers as well. Our initial antagonism made for some good scenes in an otherwise weak episode, and by the end of the shoot we had developed a great deal of respect for each other. So much so, in fact, that he asked me to do a *Hollywood Palace* he was hosting, and I was glad to oblige. At his request, I did the show in costume, one of the rare times I ever did Batman on TV away from our show.

"The Ogg and I"
"How to Hatch a Dinosaur"

Aired: 11/2, 11/9

Guest Stars: Vincent Price: *Egghead*
Anne Baxter: *Olga, Queen of the Cossacks*
Alfred Dennis: *Omar Orloff*
Mary Benoit: *Petula*
Jon Lormer: *Professor Dactyl*
With: Violet Carlson, James O'Hara, James Lanphier, Par Becher, and Donald Elson

Teleplay: Stanford Sherman

Director: Oscar Rudolph

Story: Two fronts for Batman: Egghead kidnaps Commissioner Gordon, while Olga and her Cossacks plot a major theft. The end result: the duo are plotting to hatch a dinosaur egg and release the monster on helpless Gotham City.

Comment: Perennial Errol Flynn sidekick and *Gilligan's Island* star Alan Hale, Jr., appeared as a character named Gilligan. He was a merry soul, and I saw why he and Flynn clicked. We had lunch together, and his stories about Old Hollywood were gems.

"Surf's Up! Joker's Under"

Aired: 11/16
Guest Stars: Cesar Romero: *The Joker*
Sivi Aberg: *Undine*
Skip Ward: *Riptide*
Ron Burke: *Wipeout*
With: Ronnie Knox, John Mitchum, Johnny Green, and Joyce Lederer
Teleplay: Charles Hoffman
Director: Oscar Rudolph
Story: In order to control lucrative Gotham Beach, the Joker abducts a championship surfer and has his skills electronically transferred to himself. The only way Batman can prevent him from becoming the muscle beach hero is by beating him in a surfing match.
Comment: Surfing in the Batsuit was a low point for me. We crossed the line between parody and stupidity in this show, I fear.

"The Londinium Larcenies"
"The Foggiest Notion"
"The Bloody Tower"

Aired: 11/23, 11/30, 12/7
Guest Stars: Rudy Vallee: *Lord Phogg*
Glynis Johns: *Lady Penelope Peasoup*
Lyn Peters: *Prudence*
Larry Anthony: *Digby*
Lynley Lawrence: *Kit*
Stacey Maxwell: *Rosamond*
With: Maurice Dallimore, Monty Landis, Harvey Jason, Nanette Turner, and Gil Stuart
Teleplay: Elkan Allan and Charles Hoffman

Director: Oscar Rudolph

Story: The Dynamic Duo head overseas to Londinium to help prevent the theft of the Crown Jewels by the nefarious Phogg and Peasoup. However, their stay threatens to be a brief one, as a bomb is hidden in the Batmobile, slated to go off when they reach their European Batcave.

Comment: It would have been more effective if we'd gone to Europe to shoot this episode, but by then our budgets weren't what they had been.

Still, I was happy to work with Glynis who, early in her career, had been billed as "The Girl With the Upside-Down Eyes." She did have unusual eyes, and I used that in the show, relating to her in this quizzical, "Who is she?" manner.

Rudy Vallee, of course, was a former superstar who had an ego the size of the Batcave and took himself very, very seriously. Not long after he did our show, he tried to have the L.A. street he lived on renamed Rue de Vallee. Between shots, he used to play reel-to-reel tapes of his greatest hits and lip-synch them for the cast and crew. It was a trifle embarrassing . . . but he'd been such a star at one time that you had to allow him his self-indulgence.

"Catwoman's Dressed to Kill"

Aired: 12/14

Guest Stars: Eartha Kitt: *Catwoman*
James Griffith: *Manx*
Dirk Evans: *Angora*
Karen Huston: *Queen Bess*
With: Jeanie Moore and Gerald Peters

Teleplay: Stanley Ralph Ross

Director: Sam Strangis

Story: Though Batman, Robin, and Batgirl are able to prevent the Catwoman from making off with some expensive clothes, Batgirl is captured and placed on a pattern cutting machine: if the heroes try to stop Catwoman's next crime, Batgirl will be made into batclothes!

Comment: Eartha was sexy, charismatic . . . and very outspoken. She was a very early activist/feminist and seemed to have a chip on her shoulder. She had courage, though. The following year, at a luncheon at the White House, she told Lady Bird Johnson exactly what she thought of the war in Vietnam. The F.B.I. hounded her for years after that.

Trendy fashion designer Rudy Gernreich costarred as himself on the show.

"The Ogg Couple"

Aired: 12/21

Guest Stars: Vincent Price: *Egghead*
Anne Baxter: *Olga, Queen of the Cossacks*
With: Billy Corcoran, Donald Elson, Violet Carlson, Ed Ling, and Penelope Gillette

Teleplay: Stanford Sherman

Director: Oscar Rudolph

Story: The evil duo team up again to plunder Gotham City's museums and banks . . . and to attempt to drown Batgirl in a huge vat of caviar.

Comment: As I recall, the caviar was actually diced Jell-O.
I'm not sure which would have been worse.

"Funny Feline Felonies"
"The Joke's on Catwoman"

Aired: 12/28, 1/4

Guest Stars: Cesar Romero: *The Joker*
Eartha Kitt: *Catwoman*
Ronald Long: *Karnaby Katz*
Sandy Kevin: *Giggler*
Bobby Hall: *Laughter*
With: David Lewis, Rusty Lane, Dick Kallman, Louis Quinn, and Christine Nelson

Teleplay: Stanley Ralph Ross

Director: Oscar Rudolph

Story: Joker and Catwoman team up to raid the Gotham City branch of the Federal depository. Batgirl gets wind of the plot and tracks them down . . . only to be caught and bound with fast-contracting Cat Whiskers.

Comment: Former JFK press secretary Pierre Salinger appeared as Lucky Pierre on the show and comedian Joe E. Ross played a talent agent.

"Louie's Lethal Lilac Time"

Aired: 1/11

Guest Stars: Milton Berle: *Louie the Lilac*
Nobu McCarthy: *Lotus*
Ronald Knight: *Sassafras*
John Dennis: *Saffron*
With: Percy Helton

Teleplay: Stanford Sherman

Director: Oscar Rudolph

Story: When Bruce and Dick are abducted by Louie the Lilac, Commissioner Gordon calls the Dynamic Duo to rescue them. When he can't get a hold of them, Alfred contacts Batgirl and asks for her help in rescuing his employer. Though she manages to locate Louie's lair, she ends up in a vat that is filling with scalding oil . . .

"Nora Clavicle and Her Ladies' Crime Club"

Aired: 1/18

Guest Stars: Barbara Rush: *Nora Clavicle*
June Wilkinson: *Evilina*
Inga Neilson: *Angelina*
With: Byron Keith, Jean Byron, Larry Gelman, and Judy Parker; and, as policewomen: Ginny Gan, Elizabeth Baur, Rhea Andrece, and Alyce Andrece

Teleplay: Stanford Sherman

Director: Oscar Rudolph

Story: Mayor Linseed's wife, Millie, compels her husband to dismiss Commissioner Gordon and replace him with feminist Nora Clavicle and her policewomen. But Nora's new job is just an effective cover for criminal activities . . . as Batman, Robin, and Batgirl learn when they're tied into a human knot, the slightest move designed to strangle them.

Comment: Barbara and I had costarred in *The Young Philadelphians*, and she was a charming lady. She was married to Jeffrey Hunter in the early 1950s and made a number of fine films including *Robin and the Seven Hoods* and *Hombre*.

"Penguin's Clean Sweep"

Aired: 1/25

Guest Stars: Burgess Meredith: *The Penguin*
Monique Van Vooren: *Miss Clean*
Charles Dierkop: *Dustbag*
Newell Oestreich: *Pushbroom*
With: John Vivyan, John Beradino, William Phillips, Richard
Jury, Len Felber, and Pam McMyler

Teleplay: Stanford Sherman

Director: Oscar Rudolph

Story: Shades of Auric Goldfinger: while visiting Gotham City's mint, Penguin contaminates all the money with disease germs. Rushing to the hospital where an antidote is kept, Batman and Robin discover that not only has the Penguin beaten them to it and vaccinated himself, but he's left behind infected flies to finish off the Caped Crusaders.

Comment: John Vivyan was TV's celebrated *Mr. Lucky*. Here, he played a bank manager. You do what you have to, gentle readers.

Monique Van Vooren was a Belgian nightclub star who had made a number of B-films in the 1950s. Our show helped to relaunch her career as she went on to star as a hedonistic baroness in *Andy Warhol's Frankenstein*, among other cult favorites.

"The Great Escape"
"The Great Train Robbery"

Aired: 2/2, 2/8

Guest Stars: Cliff Robertson: *Shame*
Dina Merrill: *Calamity Jan*
Hermione Baddeley: *Frontier Fanny*
Dorothy Kirnstein: *Leonora Sotto Voce*
Brian Sullivan: *Fortissimo Fra Diavolo*
Victor Lundin: *Chief Standing Pat*
With: Barry Dennen

Teleplay: Stanford Sherman

Director: Oscar Rudolph

Story: Shame and his gang hit the Gotham City Opera House, where they're met by Batman, Robin, and Batgirl. However, a dose of gas turns the Dynamic Duo into cowards, and Shame makes off with Batgirl.

Comment: Cliff returned, this time with his new bride, Dina.

Cameoing in this episode were Jerry Mathers (*Leave It to Beaver*) as a doorman, and Arnold Stang as a gun shop proprietor.

"I'll Be a Mummy's Uncle"

Aired: 2/22

Guest Stars: Victor Buono: *King Tut*
Angela Dorian: *Florence of Arabia*
Kathleen Freeman: *Rosetta Stone*
Joey Tata: *Suleiman the Great*
With: Jock Mahoney and Tony Epper

Teleplay: Stanley Ralph Ross

Director: Sam Strangis

Story: Discovering that a lode of Nilanium, the world's strongest metal, is located beneath Wayne Manor, King Tut buys property nearby and aims to dig for it . . . stumbling, instead, on the Batcave and Batman's true identity.

Comment: Henny Youngman appeared as Manny the Mesopotamian.

"The Joker's Flying Saucer"

Aired: 2/29

Guest Stars: Cesar Romero: *The Joker*
Corinne Calvert: *Emerald*
Richard Bakalyan: *Verdigris*
Jeff Burton: *Shamrock*
Tony Gardner: *Chartreuse*
Fritz Feld: *Professor Greenleaf*
With: Byron Keith and Ellen Corby

Teleplay: Charles Hoffman

Director: Sam Strangis

Story: A two-pronged attack from the Joker: not only does he plan to construct a flying saucer and terrorize Gotham City, but he's planted a bomb in the Batmobile which is set to go off at midnight.

"The Entrancing Dr. Cassandra"

Aired: 3/7

Guest Stars: Ida Lupino: *Dr. Cassandra*
Howard Duff: *Cabala*
With: David Lewis, G. David Schine, and Bill Zuckert

Teleplay: Stanley Ralph Ross

Director: Sam Strangis

Story: Bad enough that invisible thugs have struck the Gotham City Bank: when Batman, Robin, and Batgirl catch the brilliant alchemist Dr. Cassandra robbing a jewelry store, she fires her Alvino Ray gun at them, reducing them to two-dimensional figures and sliding them under Commissioner Gordon's door . . .

Comment: Ida Lupino, who considered herself a poor man's Bette Davis, was anything but. Bette was a complainer; Ida was not. She had dignity and strength, and reminded me a lot of Barbara Stanwyck. She was married to costar Howard Duff.

"Minerva, Mayhem and Millionaires"

Aired: 3/14

Guest Stars: Zsa Zsa Gabor: *Minerva*
Jacques Bergerac: *Freddie the Fence*
Bill Smith: *Adonis*
Al Ferrara: *Atlas*
Mark Bailey: *Apollo*
Yvonne Arnett: *Aphrodite*
William Dozier: *Adonis*
With: Boyd Santell, George Neise, and Howie Horwitz

Teleplay: Charles Hoffman

Director: Sam Strangis

Story: Minerva's Mineral Health Spa isn't quite as innocent as it seems. Minerva literally picks her wealthy clients' brains via mind-reading hairdryers (get your hair *and* your brain washed!), then uses the information to steal from them. When Bruce Wayne comes calling, Minerva gets the combination to the Wayne Foundation safe, and Bruce realizes that something corrupt is afoot. When he and Robin seek to foil the villainess, they're overcome and placed in a giant pressure cooker.

Comment: Dozier was our executive producer, of course, and Howie was our producer.

This was it: the end of the line. One of our weaker shows, and a sad way to go-go.

Also available from Titan Books

DON'T PANIC
DOUGLAS ADAMS & THE HITCH HIKER'S GUIDE TO THE GALAXY

by Neil Gaiman

This is the story of an ape-descended human called Douglas Adams who, in a field in Innsbruck, in 1971, had an idea.

It is also the story of a book called, at a very high level of improbability, *The Hitch Hiker's Guide to the Galaxy*; of the radio series that started it all; the five book trilogy it comprises; and the computer game, towel and television series that it, in its turn, has spawned.

Also available from Titan Books

BATMAN THE COLLECTED ADVENTURES: VOLUME 2

by Kelley Puckett and Mike Parobeck and Rick Burchett

Based on ITV's award-winning *Batman: The Animated Series*.

This second volume in Titan's *Batman The Collected Adventures* series, based on the immensely popular cartoon series, combines high quality graphic artwork with exciting new stories featuring Batman back in his traditional crime-fighting role.

This volume contains six action-packed stories, in which Batman, Robin and Batgirl battle a variety of artful and cunning villains, including the Riddler, Man-Bat, Clayface and Harley Quinn. Each story is presented in the same, refreshingly unique style of the TV series.

Also available from Titan Books

THE AVENGERS DEADLINE

by Patrick Macnee

An original novel, featuring the characters John Steed and Emma Peel from the cult sixties TV series.

Someone is tampering with speeches reported in the continental editions of British newspapers: antagonising other nations and causing anti-British riots abroad. John Steed and Emma Peel are called in to go undercover at *The Courier* newspaper in Fleet Street. Their mission: to identify and track down the Brotherhood, a band of neo-fascist ruthless criminals who will stop at nothing - not even murder - to bring down the Government and seize power.

Also available from Titan Books

COLUMBO
THE GRASSY KNOLL

by William Harrington

An all-new mystery based on the Universal TV series.

Lt Columbo, everyone's favourite rumpled TV detective, must unravel the mystery that has held the world's attention for thirty years: who killed President John F. Kennedy?

Controversial talk-show host Paul Drury is silent - murdered in his hillside mansion. Discounting burglary as a motive, Columbo soon finds out how many people had reason to kill the arrogant celebrity: Alice Drury, his beautiful ex-wife; Bobby Angele, top country singer; Jessica O'Neill, famous movie star.

But Columbo's next discovery is more startling still. Someone sabotaged the broadcast of Drury's final show, which promised to expose JFK's real assassin. Now, the computer files of that show are gone - perhaps destroyed by the killer of Paul Drury?

Before Columbo solves this mystery, he has to deal with another: thirty years ago in Dallas, who shot JFK?

Newly revised and updated from Titan Books

THE STAR TREK COMPENDIUM

by Allan Asherman

The Star Trek Compendium is your official guidebook to the *Star Trek* universe. Relive the voyages of the *Starship Enterprise* with a complete show-by-show guide to the series (as well as the Emmy Award winning animated shows and the *Star Trek* movies), including plot summaries, fascinating behind-the-scenes production information and credits for each. Follow the creation of Gene Roddenberry's series step-by-step - and *Star Trek*'s road to the big screen. Illustrated with over 125 specially selected photographs - including at least one from each episode - and fully indexed, this is the indispensable reference work to one of the most memorable television shows of all time - *Star Trek*.

This newly revised edition includes new material from *Star Trek VI: The Undiscovered Country*.

Also available from Titan Books

THE ART OF STAR WARS
A NEW HOPE

Edited by Carol Titelman

A New Hope was part of the original title of the movie that became *Star Wars*, the ultimate film entertainment experience of the 1970s that is now one of the most-loved movies of all time. *The Art of Star Wars: A New Hope* contains the first film's complete script by George Lucas and is beautifully illustrated with the movie's fantastic works of art. In this unique compilation of all the imagination and beauty that went into the first of the film trilogy, the magic of *Star Wars* lives on.

This volume includes:

- Photographs
- Costume sketches
- Finished production paintings
- A selection of cartoons and spin-off art
- Many of the spectacular *Star Wars* posters
- The first rough concepts and preliminary drawings
- Storyboards of action sequences detailing the evolution of the story and characters
- Some of the creative art by the young fans who have always sustained the *Star Wars* legend.

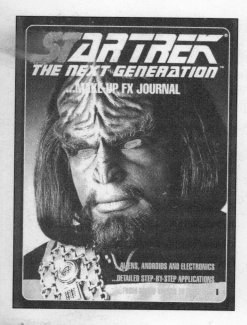

For a complete list of all Titan's publications, please send a large stamped SAE to Titan Books Mail Order, 42-44 Dolben Street, London SE1 OUP. Please quote reference BC on both envelopes.